A Play of Bodies

A Play of Bodies

How We Perceive Videogames

Brendan Keogh

The MIT Press
Cambridge, Massachusetts
London, England

This book was set in ITC Stone Sans Std and ITC Stone Serif Std by Toppan Best-set Premedia Limited. Printed and bound in the United States of America.

Library of Congress Cataloging-in-Publication Data

Names: Keogh, Brendan, author.
Title: A play of bodies : how we perceive videogames / Brendan Keogh.
Description: Cambridge, MA : MIT Press, [2018] | Includes bibliographical
    references and index.
Identifiers: LCCN 2017031162 | ISBN 9780262037631 (hardcover : alk. paper)
Subjects: LCSH: Video games--Psychological aspects. | Video games--Design. |
    Video games--Philosophy.
Classification: LCC GV1469.34.P79 K46 2018 | DDC 794.8--dc23 LC record
    available at https://lccn.loc.gov/2017031162

10 9 8 7 6 5 4 3 2 1

The operation of expression, when successful, does not simply leave to the reader or the writer [themselves] a reminder; it makes the signification exist as a thing at the very heart of the text, it brings it to life in an organism of words, it installs this insignification in the writer or the reader like a new sense organ, and it opens a new field or a new dimension to our experience.

—Maurice Merleau-Ponty, *Phenomenology of Perception* (2012)

When I looked into [a videogame arcade,] I could see in the physical intensity of their postures how rapt these kids were. It was like one of those closed systems out of a Pynchon novel: you had this feedback loop, with photons coming off the screen into the kids' eyes, the neurons moving through their bodies, electrons moving through the computer. And these kids clearly believed in the space these games projected. Everyone who works with computers seems to develop an intuitive faith that there's some kind of actual space behind the screen.

—William Gibson, interview (Greenland 1986)

Push buttons and analog sticks and watch for patterns in response until you have a sense of the relationship between the two.

—Cardboard Computer, *Kentucky Route Zero README.txt* (2013)

Contents

Acknowledgments

This book owes its existence to the support, guidance, feedback, and inspiration offered by a range of colleagues, videogame designers and critics, and friends. I wish to thank in particular Larissa Hjorth, Christian McCrea, Daniel Golding, Thomas Apperley, Julie Berents, Darshana Jayemanne, Benjamin Abraham, Leena van Deventer, Benjamin Nicoll, Cameron Kunzelman, Emily van der Nagel, Michael McMaster, James Meese, Heidi Hoffman-White, April Tyack, Doug Wilson, Claire Hosking, Marcus Carter, Fraser Allison, Zoya Street, Robbie Fordyce, Luke van Ryn, Sam Crisp, Zolani Stewart, Seth Giddings, Ingrid Richardson, Marigold Bartlett, Terry Burdak, Jason Wilson, and James Manning. I also owe endless gratitude to my partner, Helen Berents, for her love, support, and stoic efforts to read more rough drafts and overwrought sentences than anyone should ever have to deal with in a single lifetime.

Parts of this book draw from and extend on arguments I have made in previous publications. An earlier version of the theoretical foundations of chapter 1 is found in "Across Worlds and Bodies: Criticism in the Age of Videogames," *Journal of Game Criticism* 1 (2014): 1–26. The analysis of *Angry Birds* in chapter 2 extends on my essay "Paying Attention to *Angry Birds*: Rearticulating Hybrid Worlds and Embodied Play through Casual iPhone Games," in *The Routledge Companion to Mobile Media*, ed. Gerard Goggin and Larissa Hjorth, 267–276 (New York: Routledge, 2014). Parts of chapter 5 draw from my previous writing about videogame time and memory in my essays "'You Really Are You, Right?': Cybernetic Memory and the Constitution of the Posthuman Self in Videogame Play," in *Design, Mediation, and the Posthuman*, ed. Dennis M. Weiss, Amy D. Propen, and Colbey Emmerson Reid, 233–248 (London: Lexington Books), 2014), and "When Game Over Means Game Over: Using Permanent Death to Craft Living Stories in *Minecraft*," paper presented at the Ninth Australasian Conference on Interactive

Entertainment, Melbourne, 2013. The brief discussion of *Binary Domain* in chapter 6 draws from a longer analysis in my article "Hackers and Cyborgs: *Binary Domain* and Two Formative Videogame Technicities," *Transactions of the Digital Games Research Association* 2 (3) (2016): 195–220. My thanks go out to all the reviewers and editors of these previous publications as well as of this current book for constantly challenging and strengthening my work.

Introduction

At night you can see the lights sometimes from a passing tanker or trawler. From up on the cliffs they are mundane, but down here they fugue into ambiguity. For instance, I cannot readily tell if they belong above or below the waves. The distinction now seems mundane; why not everything all at once!
—Narrator, *Dear Esther* (The Chinese Room 2012)

MediaMolecule's videogame *Tearaway* (2013) begins with an ultimatum from its two narrators: "This is not your world."

In *Tearaway*, I navigate a humanoid creature with an envelope head named Iota through a papercraft world. I walk past cardboard trees and through confetti blizzards. Fern trees uncurl in streamers; houses stand as creased cardboard. The ground I walk over moves under Iota's slight weight, like a piece of paper gently pressed by a finger. In this conventional platforming videogame, I move around the world to solve simple puzzles and fight off enemy "scraps"; I pick up items and throw them around.

Except "I" do not do these actions. "I" do not jump while playing *Tearaway*, nor do "I" fight. "I" hold a PlayStation Vita videogame device in my hands, and "I" look at its screen, and "I" listen to the sounds it produces as "I" move my thumbs over its buttons and thumbsticks (miniature joysticks that can be moved with a single thumb). It is Iota who jumps and moves and attacks and throws in response to the movement of my body against a piece of hardware. The continuous movement of my thumb through space is detected by the Vita so that when my flesh pushes against the X button, a digital switch is flicked from 0 to 1 to tell the videogame that Iota should be animated in such a way as to jump. But even Iota isn't really jumping. Iota doesn't exist. Iota is just a variety of pixels on a flat screen turning on and off in quick succession according to principles of animation and perspective that allow me to perceive a three-dimensional (3D) creature jumping through a 3D space in response to my thumb pushing down the X button.

But it would be wrong to say I feel distinct from the actions that Iota, my playable character, is shown to be performing at my behest. I feel a sense of presence through and as Iota, a sense of participation. If you were to ask me what I was doing while I played *Tearaway*, I would say simply, "I am jumping," not "I am pressing the X button."

But Iota is not all I am able to control in *Tearaway*'s world. *Tearaway* is peppered with moments that harness the diverse input systems and affordances of the PlayStation Vita hardware. As I rub my left and right thumbs against the device's small thumbsticks, paper mushrooms along Iota's path spin and dance in different directions; I push my finger against the glass of the Vita's touchscreen where the videogame presents grubby fingerprints, and I drag objects around the world, remove obstacles, and extend origami ledges for Iota to walk across. Some parts of the world are patches of translucent white paper with a pattern of Xs, squares, triangles, and circles that mimic the pattern of the Vita's *rear* touchpad. Here, if I push against the back of the Vita with fingers that are already supporting the heft of the device, "my" fingers rip into the world, tearing the thin veneer of paper that seals off the virtual world in a reverse trompe l'oeil, where the actual world is made to look as if it is part of the virtual. As I play, the Vita's front-facing camera is constantly looking at and capturing my face, presenting it back to me on the screen as a hole in the papercraft world's sun so that in a looping reflexivity I become part of the world I am looking down at in my hands—I have some presence in this world but am looking down at it from the outside at the same time.

I am not the only one confused by just who "I" am in this system of flesh and hardware and lights and sounds. Near the start of the game, I walk Iota toward a doorway where *Tearaway*'s second narrator appears. "Ah, it's Iota, our messenger!" he says to my character before immediately addressing "me" the player: "And I see you're still with us! Up there, peering in, poking around!" Then back to Iota: "We call them the Yous. They live outside our world, and that's the You you're trying to deliver the message to. You both want the same thing. So work together!" For the videogame, as for me, just who I am in this collection seems to flicker between bodies and between worlds. I am both Iota and myself; I am both here and there.

This virtual world is not my world. It is not, truly, a world at all. Yet I perceive it *as if* it were a world, and I engage with and feel some sense of presence in this world *as if* I somehow enter it. But I don't enter it. I peer in; I poke around. This videogame is not the holodeck that Janet Murray dreamed of stepping into with her entire body in tow, a medium that we would "look through" rather than "at" (1997, 271). Nor is this the

Figure 0.1
Pushing my fingers into the world of *Tearaway* (MediaMolecule 2013).

disembodied cyberspace that Case desired to jack into, leaving behind "all of the meat and all that it wants" in William Gibson's novel *Neuromancer* (1984, 9). How we come to feel embodied in videogame play is much more complicated than simply stepping out of one world and skin and into others. David Sudnow had it right in 1983 when he called the spaces depicted by videogames "microworlds": small worlds under glass that we don't inhabit in any straightforward manner but that we engage with from a distance, our actions reflected back to us, translated by lights and color and sound. I do not "enter" *Tearaway*'s world in any unambiguous fashion. I peer down at it and poke around it from the outside, and in doing so I feel some sense of presence under the glass. But this presence is not simply "me"; it is an augmented me. It is me-and-Iota; it is "you" and "You," as the narrator distinguishes us while also drawing us together.[1] Any clear distinction between the actual and virtual is destroyed by the perforations my grubby fingers inflict on *Tearaway*'s flimsy world. I tear holes through the videogame's diegesis to look at it, listen to it, touch it, play with it, but never to fully enter it. Videogame play requires a multitude of worlds and a multitude of bodies.

Tearaway exemplifies the complex and fascinating ways our bodies engage with videogames: we look at, hear, and touch them with technologically augmented senses and limbs to implement some change, to feel some liminal and flickering sense of presence through the screen. But this corporeal engagement goes two ways: as we touch the videogame, it touches us back. In *Tearaway*, a camera looks up at me from the Vita device, peering at my face and rendering it before me on the screen; characters react to my shouts through the Vita's microphone; small springs under the Vita's buttons are constantly pushing back against my thumbs; the very fabric of the world feels my fingers pushing against the glass that both depicts and contains it. We intermingle with videogames. We poke them, and they in turn poke us back.

In 2003, Torban Grodal compellingly called videogames "stories for eye, ear, and muscles." Through an entanglement of eyes-at-screens, ears-at-speakers, and muscles-against-interfaces, we perceive videogames as virtual spaces consisting of objects and actors with texture and weight. With our senses, we reach through the perforations of these flimsy, paper microuniverses that are never fully sealed off from us but also in which we are never fully present, and in that reaching we both constitute these worlds and become incorporated into them—a merging of actual and virtual bodies and worlds. It is this entanglement that this book is centrally concerned with when it asks: How does our embodied sense of perception constitute— and become constituted by—the phenomenon of videogame play? In short, how do we perceive videogames?

The very visible and explicit ways players *use* videogames with their bodies has always mattered to the study of videogames: the way players must press buttons without focusing on the buttons they press (Kirkpatrick 2009); the social spectacle of players' bodies flailing in front of motion sensors or with plastic guitar controllers in hand (Simon 2009; Juul 2010); the rigid training and machinelike finger movements of professional videogame players (McCrea 2009; Taylor 2012; Harper 2013); touchscreens smeared with fingerprints by mobile-videogame players on their morning commute (Richardson 2009); the ways particular videogame communities become demarcated as being for bodies of a particular gender (Kennedy 2007); the ways in which different bodily configurations are commodified by corporate and military agents (Dyer-Witheford and de Peuter 2009; Ash 2015; Parisi 2015). Each of these aspects make themselves known throughout this book's chapters, but my immediate interest is in the more banal and everyday ways that players and videogames *always* incorporate each other in the reflexive cycles that *Tearaway* highlights—or, rather, how that bodily incorporation *is* the experience of videogame play. I want to understand how it is I come to feel some sense of embodied presence in the projected worlds of videogames, even as I am always aware that I remain present in this world alongside the videogame. How is it my sense of embodiment can become distributed across both sides of the glass? How is it exactly that *Tearaway*'s characters and world can "feel" like paper? How is it exactly that the lights and sounds and plastic that are *Tearaway* can be perceived as characters embedded within a world at all?

I arrived at these questions through an altogether different initial inquiry. I wanted to better understand how videogames "mean," how they matter as both popular culture and art. Growing up in the 1990s, when the videogame console sat next to the VHS player and each was an entirely *normal* domestic screen medium, I find myself unconvinced by claims that the "interactivity" of this "new" medium is unprecedented and radically different from all the other ways human bodies have engaged with and experienced creative works in different media over the previous centuries and millennia. I feel that the invaluable research into how the systems and mechanics of videogames "as games" produce procedural and immersive meanings—led by theorists such as Janet Murray, Ian Bogost, Espen Aarseth, Brenda Laurel, Marie-Laure Ryan, Alexander Galloway, and many others—accounts for only half of the story. These theorists thoroughly detail how the mechanical and procedural aspects of videogames that differ from other screen media produce meaning, but less how these systemic skeletons fundamentally relate to the audiovisual and haptic flesh in which they are wrapped. Videogames *are* different from movies, literature, theater, painting, music, and architecture, but they also structurally relate to each of these media in some way. The similarities are no less important than the differences. I settled on the middle road: videogames require particular configurations of an embodied audience with a material creative work—as do all media. I became interested in the embodied phenomenon of *playing* a videogame insofar as that embodied phenomenon is a fundamental aspect of understanding, of reading, of *perceiving* that videogame.

I took to heart N. Katherine Hayles's notion (explored in chapter 1 in greater detail) that a "text" is "the rich connections between [a work's] physical properties and the processes that constitute it as something to be read" (2004, 72). My initial interest in what players do "in" videogames found itself shifting to questions of how it is we come to convince ourselves we are "in" a videogame at all. I set as my goal the prediction made by Jon Dovey and Helen Kennedy that the textual and performative tensions inherent to the videogame form "point the way towards a development of a *phenomenology* of [video]games that takes account of both their textual and experiential properties" (2006, 93, emphasis added). How videogames mean and how bodies engage with videogames are not, it seems, unrelated questions at all or even just related questions—they are the same question.

In this book, I work toward *a phenomenology of videogame experience* that is concerned primarily not with what players do to videogames but with how the lived bodily experience of players is augmented by and part of videogame play. I am motivated conceptually by *The Address of the Eye: A Phenomenology of Film Experience* (1992), in which Vivan Sobchack "mistrust[s] what has become the certain ground, the *premises*, of contemporary film theory" (xvi, original emphasis). Likewise, I intend to present a phenomenology of videogame experience that mistrusts what has become the certain ground of videogame theory: an effortless transferal of agency into a virtual world to take on a virtual body, an ultimate transcendence historically marketed by publishers and broadly desired by players that leaves the carnal meat behind. Although my interest remains focused on how we perceive the *virtual*—a term that has come under valid scrutiny as digital technologies become all pervasive in everyday life—it is an interest in how this virtual is constituted as part of the actual, not discrete from it. I focus on what is actually happening in the embodied engagement between the playing body and the videogame that is typically seen as the background of meaningful videogame play, not meaningful videogame play itself. I focus on where the videogame is touched, seen, heard, and ultimately understood through a perceiving, located, and augmented body—a body the player often works hard to forget in order to feel that sense of "immersion" within the virtual.

Like Sobchack, I find phenomenology a fruitful method through which to interrogate the media we intimately live as perceptual existence. Phenomenology asks us to turn our attention to what is commonly experienced as the perceptual background or horizon of conscious thought by first dispelling the assumption that we possess bodies; rather, we *are* bodies. I find a phenomenological method grounded in the analysis of a diverse range of videogame texts as they are encountered and incorporated by players useful to "*reanimate* the taken-for-granted and the institutionally sedimented" (Sobchack 1992, 28, original emphasis), to interrogate the experiences we preconsciously live. Such an interrogation is urgently required as newly visible demographics of videogame creators push videogames in directions that our current conceptualizations struggle to comprehend. As the videogames discussed throughout this book highlight, we can no longer take for granted that videogames have goals, provide challenges, offer choices, or offer pleasures that are solely "interactive" in nature. Nothing is certain anymore. We must naively go back to the embodied experience of video-game play and see what is there.

Maurice Merleau-Ponty's work on perception and the embodied experience of being-in-the-world provides my conceptual foundations. As chapter 1 explores in more detail, Merleau-Ponty's work *Phenomenology of Perception* (2012, originally published in French in 1945) demonstrates how we live in a "lifeworld" constituted by the sensorial perception we take for granted as the background of all knowledge production. However, we live in a time when it is impossible to ignore the role of nonhuman processes in constituting our sensorial perception. We and our lifeworlds are dynamically co-constituted. This is vividly evident in the experience of videogames, where wires and screens and sounds and feedback and global corporate actors are caught up in a medium directly concerned with augmenting sensorial experience. As such, the phenomenology of this book, too, must be augmented. Interested as I am in videogame play's doubled instability of worlds and bodies, I find myself indebted to those poststructuralist, science and technology studies, and feminist theorists of the late twentieth and early twenty-first century who have provided more nuanced ways of decentering the human to understand the embodied self as *emergent* from an amalgam of heterogeneous materialities. I bring this embodiment literature to game studies and media studies alongside the close analysis of specific videogame *texts* and devices to interrogate particular aspects of the player's embodied experience of videogame play—to render the very normal act of videogame play strange again.

I am far from the first scholar to apply phenomenological principles to the study of videogames. Timothy Crick, James Ash, Helen Kennedy, Ingrid Richardson, Peter Bayliss, Rune Klevjer, and others have at different times forwarded different phenomenologies of videogames. Crick critiques Sobchack's own reductive understanding of the "electronic presence" of digital media (including videogames) as somehow less embodied than the cinematic to argue instead that videogames are "a holistic experience, and it is precisely our capacity as sensual embodied beings in the world that allows us to engage with a game's artificial world in a way that would engage those senses in real life" (2011, 266). Ingrid Richardson (2005, 2007, 2009, 2011, 2012), across a number of publications, explores the postphenomenological aspects of videogames on mobile devices. James Ash (2013) draws from Heidegger in his study of how players become "attuned" to videogames. Rune Klevjer (2012) considers the "prosthetic telepresence" allowed by the "proxy embodiment" of videogame avatar play. The common thread across all these works: videogames distribute embodiment across actual/virtual worlds in complex and irreducible ways.

Others would argue that such a method has been tried, tested, and found wanting. In 2008 at the Philosophy of Computer Games conference, Ian Bogost presented a talk titled "The Phenomenology of Videogames" that called for an "alien phenomenology" that "seeks to understand how the myriad objects that constitute videogames relate to one another" (2008, 32). Bogost rightly noted that the study of videogames historically has unfairly privileged the agency of the autonomous player, who freely chooses how to act "within" the virtual world, and he instead argued for a move beyond what he perceives as a player-centric phenomenology and toward an object-oriented or speculative-realist approach to understanding how videogames fit into a world in which humans are just one aspect. As part of a broader "material turn" of game studies (Apperley and Jayemanne 2012), Nick Montfort and Bogost's platform studies book series, starting with *Racing the Beam* (2009), and Bogost's object-orientated ontology study *Alien Phenomenology* (2012) are ventures into this direction of understanding aspects of the videogame beyond the player's human experience of them. James Ash echoes this project in his book *The Interface Envelope* (2015) as he considers how matter, objects, and technology work to shape human capacities for the explicit purpose of creating capital.

My desires for this current book, however, are more carnal. To be sure, the player must be decentered from the full technologically augmented experience because no videogame player truly chooses how to act separate from the tangible affordances and constraints of the system across which they find themselves distributed. It is not sufficient to comprehend how I play "as" Iota in *Tearaway*; we must comprehend how my embodiment as me-and-Iota is constituted across bodies and worlds. As Seth Giddings and Helen Kennedy rightly note in their own study of the nonhuman agencies active in videogame play, to truly understand the experience of videogame play is to "attend to both the operations of nonhuman agency and the human pleasures of lack of agency, of being controlled, of being *acted upon*" (2008, 30, original emphasis). Whereas Bogost, Montfort, Ash, and others find worth in the object-orientated approach that situates the videogame squarely within the material world, a more traditional phenomenological approach—albeit one augmented by poststructuralist and feminist scholars—better serves my present interest in understanding how we both constitute and are constituted by a lived experience of the videogame as at once an actual activity and a virtual presence. Chapter 1 lays the theoretical groundwork for this approach, but I can summarize here by saying that this book is squarely interested in the corporeal capacity of perceiving through senses that are themselves augmented by the technologies and feedback that we perceive.

Naive as my analysis aims to be, it is one of description rather than prescription. The videogames in which I anchor my analysis are deliberately eclectic, from blockbuster to obscure titles, from mainstream to niche titles, from corporate to hobbyist titles. It is entirely likely that the reader will not be familiar with each and every videogame I mention, but this should not prevent an engagement with the observations that have emerged from my playing of those games. Rather, my hope is that such an eclectic mix will instill an appreciation for both the consistencies and the sheer diversities of videogame experience that exist and, most importantly, will force me to commit to an analysis "from below" that focuses on how particular embodied assemblages of player-and-videogame are constituted. My intent here is to forward a phenomenology of videogame experience that can account for *any* videogame work in its particular configuration of player-and-videogame, not a single configuration of player-and-videogame that is the same for *all* videogame works.

Videogames as a Play of Bodies

A film, says Sobchack, "is given to us and taken up by us as perception turned literally inside out and toward us as expression" (1992, 12). Before a film is interpreted, it is engaged with as perceived form: looked at, listened to, felt. Film's "address of the eye" "implicates both *embodied, situated* existence and a *material* world; for to see and be seen, the viewing subject must be a body and be materially in the world" (23, original emphasis). The film's viewed images and heard sounds are only ever imperfectly incorporated into this embodied, situated viewer's lived experience. Indeed, the "play of images" that is film, Sobchack argues, depends on this mutual resilience: "There are always two embodied acts of vision at work in the theater, two embodied views constituting the intelligibility and significance of film experience" (24). The film is looked at, and the film looks.

Videogames are not films. Yet the parallels between the doubly embodied and situated experience of film and the complex presence across worlds and bodies felt by players in the experience of videogames are striking. Videogames also demand a primarily perceptual engagement with a screen and the space depicted "beyond" it. Videogames demand an embodied, situated audience that *looks* and *listens*, but to this demand they also add the requirement for this audience to physically *touch* and *move*. To consider videogame experience as it is perceived is to account for the particular material engagements that videogames not only demand with both physical interfaces and audiovisuals but also to which they respond. The videogame is played, and the videogame plays.

This view requires us to push back against a conceptualization of videogames as primarily a subset of a broader, materially agnostic "game" category. As videogames became a serious topic of scholarly study in the late 1990s and early 2000s, an ancestry was mapped from the digital play of videogames back to preexisting forms of nondigital games and play. This connection was both commonsensical and strategic. Videogames are games; it says it right there in the name. So surely they share core formal traits with other games, such as rules, mechanics, systems, and goals. Further, at a time when videogame theorists were concerned about the encroaching interests of media, film, and literature departments regarding videogames, drawing a fundamental link between videogames and traditional games became a claim of legitimacy. As Jesper Juul claims explicitly, "If we think of video games as *games*, they are not successors of cinema, print, literature, or new media, but continuations of a history of games that predate these [media] by millennia" (2005, 3–4, original emphasis). Thinking of videogames as games is also an act of validation that works to transition them across the high/low-brow cultural divide that is itself a distillation of a Cartesian mind/body dualism. Those creative works that engage the mind (literature, classic music, painting) are considered more worthy and meaningful than those "lowly" forms that evoke the body (pulp films, pop music, romance novels, pornography). Considering videogames "as games" that are intellectualized as complex systems of mechanics and procedures is a claim to validity that reacts against the idea of videogames as "mindless," "addictive," and, broadly, merely carnally and sensuously satisfying.

An overlap between digital and nondigital play undeniably exists, and exploring this overlap provoked many of the insights gleaned in the first decades of game studies. For the purpose of this book, however, I am not interested in a validation of videogames that leaves the playing body and its pleasures behind. Videogames very much *are* successors of cinema, print, literature, and new media *as well as* a continuation of a millennia-long history of games. To consider videogames as exclusively a formal subset of "games," though, is insufficient if we are to account for the complex, material entanglement between the playing body and the audiovisual components that produce the videogame's virtual world.

This stance is not purely ideological, but pragmatic. Aspects of videogame experience are incompatible with traditional notions of how games are experienced. This incompatibility has long challenged game and media scholars alike, who have tried to reconcile what particular videogames *are* with how "games" formally are understood to function: Alexander Galloway's notion that "no gameplay is actually happening" when the player stands the character still on a street corner in *Shenmue* (Sega AM2 1999) to watch a virtual sunset (2006, 10); Espen Aarseth's rallying against the representational aspects of an audiovisual medium when he says that it does not matter what *Tomb Raider*'s Lara Croft looks like, only that the avatar allows player action (2004, 48); Graeme Kirkpatrick's dubious claim that "if [*Journey* (Thatgamecompany 2012)] only offered a smooth simulation with pleasurable forms derived from steering your avatar up and into the clouds of red flags, it would cease to be a game and perhaps become a work of art" (2013, 179), despite that being an accurate description of the core experience of many experiential videogames. These examples are selective, but they highlight the broader conceptual tensions between what we consider games to be and what videogames already are.

The burgeoning visibility of alternative, artistic, and hobbyist videogames in recent years has made the distinction even more jarring as traditional conceptualizations of videogames "as games" struggle to account for the more abstract, experimental, and confident avant-garde videogames of the past decade. Videogames such as Anna Anthropy's *Dys4ia* (2012) and merritt k's *Lim* (2012) are short, linear experiences that offer very little challenge to the player but are powerfully expressive. Stephen Lavelle's *Slave of God* (2012) and Fernando Ramallo and David Kanaga's *Panoramical* (2015) let the player "do" very little other than navigate abstract and overwhelming audiovisual environments. Meanwhile, the "noninteractive" videogame cutscene, once projected to be eventually abandoned when technology afforded other modes of interactive storytelling, has remained central to the videogame form for more than twenty-five years. Queer and transgender artists and writers have taken up the interactive-fiction platform Twine to move videogames in radically new directions (see kopas 2015). A videogame formalism that focuses centrally on the official elements of nondigital games, such as rules, mechanics, goals, and player agency can well account for those videogames most aligned with traditional understandings of games, but it struggles to account for the broader ecology of creative works that are removed from that history—those videogames that can *only* be videogames.

Thus, when James Newman claims that "the pleasures of videogame *play* are not principally visual, but rather are kinaesthetic" (2002, no page, original emphasis), he is not necessarily wrong, but nor is he entirely correct.

His statement is true in the strictest sense—and understandable in the context of the early 2000s, when videogame scholars had to differentiate their object of study from those of film and literature studies. However, what such a statement elides is the fundamental significance *of* the visual (and indeed the aural) in *producing* the digitally kinaesthetic. I am made anxious by the trend I see in videogame evaluations—both scholarly and journalistic—that work to distinguish a core "gameness" from an audiovisual skin, such as when Kirkpatrick claims that "the test of gameness is subtraction: strip away the other features and you still have a game" (2013, 42). Replace the exquisite woodcrafted play pieces with rocks in the mud, and you can still play some version of chess, as Aarseth argues (2004, 48). Replace the goalposts with safety cones, and you can still play a game of soccer, of sorts. But what would it mean to strip away the "other features" of a videogame? If one were to remove the carefully crafted animations and sounds that present *Tearaway*'s papercraft world, then *Tearaway* would simply no longer be *Tearaway*. What would *Super Mario Bros* (Nintendo 1985) be without Super Mario? How might one discuss the mechanics or rules of *Space Invaders* (Taito 1978) without discussing the aliens, shields, lasers, and spaceships that *are Space Invaders*? Videogames are not a core game wrapped in an interchangeable audiovisual skin; videogames are materially constituted *by* their audiovisuality.[2]

Mechanistic analyses of videogame play—presuming a central "gameness" of systems and rules as well as a superfluity of the audiovisual design that manifests those systems and rules—take the sensorial engagement with the videogame for granted. On the contrary, to adequately account for the embodied experience of videogame play we must start with the embodied and sensorial engagement *with* the videogame as an audiovisual medium that mechanistic analyses take for granted. This means that a phenomenology of videogame experience cannot start with the commonly accepted grounds that videogames are a type of game, as this obscures rather than reveals how videogames are sensorially perceived. To start with the senses is instead to ask how videogames engage the body as a form of *audiovisual-haptic* media.

Videogames are experienced perceptually. David Sudnow identified this factor in his groundbreaking but largely overlooked book *Pilgrim in the Microworld* (1983). When Sudnow first became entangled with *Missile Command* (Atari 1980), he was fascinated by the synergy of his hand's movements at the joystick and the screen's visuals before his eyes: "as you watch the cursor move, your look appreciates the sight with thumbs in mind, and the joystick-button box feels like a genuine implement of action" (21–22).

Both Sudnow and this book argue that videogames are looked at, listened to, and physically touched in order for players to perceive an imperfect and partial sense of presence "in" the videogame even as they play "at" the videogame.

As I look down on the world of *Tearaway* from the hole in the virtual sun, I also partially embody Iota and control his bodily movements within the limits of his abilities. But I do not "become" Iota in any simple sense. I am also aware that I can see him on the screen; I engage with a virtual world *through* his body, but I also look *at* his body as an object in that world. I can also control the virtual "camera" to see things that he cannot. When Iota missteps and "dies," I reload the videogame and rewind his life and use the memories of that failure to ensure I do not repeat the mistake. I embody Iota, but I do so partially. My embodiment straddles worlds where I am partially Iota and partially "me." If film experience is, as Sobchack says, a "play of images" that flickers between incorporated and resisted, looked at and looking, then videogame experience is *a play of bodies* that flickers between present and absent, corporeal and incorporeal, immanent and transcendent, actual and virtual, "me" and "not me." It is from this fundamental understanding of how videogames are corporeally perceived that this project begins.

Organization of the Book

Chapter 1 begins by theorizing the dynamic circuit of player-and-video-game literalized by *Tearaway* as reflexive, irreducible, and meaningful. I start with Maurice Merleau-Ponty's phenomenology but swiftly move on to the challenges to embodiment theory posed by feminist theorists of the late twentieth and early twenty-first centuries, such as Donna Haraway, Iris Marion Young, Gail Weiss, and Judy Wajcman. Where the notion of a discrete human player distinct from and in control of the videogame is an echo of an Enlightenment era liberal rational subject distinct from "his" world, the theorists introduced in this chapter are invaluable for understanding the pluralist, partial, and situated ways bodies have always been constituted by and as part of the world. This chapter concludes by building on N. Katherine Hayles's work on the materiality of texts to demonstrate what this dynamic embodiment means for comprehending the corporeal experience of videogames as inherently meaningful.

A key aspect of understanding videogames as an embodied experience is identifying how the player feels a sense of presence "in" the virtual world of the videogame while remaining aware that they are situated in the actual world. It is a liminal, distributed presence across worlds and across bodies that is never resolved and that is fundamental to how videogames are experienced. Chapter 2 turns to the contemporary case of smartphone videogames to ask how this sense of virtual presence is constructed through the player's perception and attention. Existing outside of the dominant videogame design paradigm, smartphone videogames—in particular those "casual" videogames designed for a more populist audience—provide a fruitful case to challenge traditional understandings of how players engage with videogames. By contrasting the wildly successful videogame *Angry Birds* (Rovio 2009) with the niche videogame *Ziggurat* (Action Button 2012), both produced for Apple's iPhone series, this chapter forwards the notion of *co-attentiveness* to understand how the player might feel a sense of immersion in a virtual world without ever really forgetting that they exist in the actual world, in front of a screen, engaging with sights and sounds and input.

The next two chapters turn squarely to the somatic basis of videogame play: what is done with and to the player's hands, eyes, and ears. Although much literature has focused on the very visible ways in which players engage with videogames by waving limbs or swiping touchscreens or moving around actual spaces by means of devices equipped with a geographical positioning system (GPS), chapter 3 very deliberately looks at what the playing body does at the most banal and seemingly sedate mode of videogame play: sitting on the couch while holding a "gamepad" controller. My intent here is to challenge the easy assumption that some forms of videogame play are somehow "more embodied" than others due to the amount of visible physical exertion they require. On the contrary, *all* videogames require a body; some just ask that the player's conscious attention be turned away from that body's actions. I build on Henri Lefebvre's notion of "dressage" to explore what I call the *embodied literacy* of gamepad play (following Hayles's "embodied textuality" explored in chapter 1). Such a "literacy" is political and normative, both influenced by and sustaining dominant modes of engaging with videogame design and privileging particular bodily configurations at the videogame. Rather than assume that more "natural" input devices are inherently better because they are easier to learn, I take a close look at the gamepad to highlight the literacies, habits, and tastes that the learned player internalizes.

Chapter 4 turns to the other half of this equation: what the eyes and ears are doing while the hands dance across an input device. Whereas explorations of the embodied pleasures of videogame play can risk sidelining visual and audible pleasures to focus instead on the player's configurative actions, here I argue that looking and listening are embodied activities in their own right and are vital components of videogame play. To act in a videogame is in part to *look* and *listen*; the movements of fingers against an input device are meaningful only in union with how the audiovisual feedback is engaged with. As suggested earlier, such a claim decentralizes the common assumption that "mechanics" or "rules" are more formally central to videogames than their audiovisual veneer. I look at two music-centric videogames to work through what a conception of videogames as fundamentally audiovisual might look like. Dylan Fitterer's *Audiosurf* (2008), a rhythm videogame that produces spaces and play styles *from* music, shows how the sensorial experience of videogame play is irreducible, where sounds and sights and touched devices all act as sensorial lenses onto the somatic experience of playing a videogame. Stephen Lavelle's overwhelming and dizzying videogame *Slave of God* (2012) takes this argument a step further, making a case for the audiovisual engagement as not just complementary to the player's actions but engaged with in their own right, not unlike the embodied experiences of film or music. The point this chapter makes cannot be overstressed: videogames are looked at, listened to, and touched, and no one of these perceptual facets onto the videogame experience comes before or is distinguishable from the others.

In chapter 5, I look to the embodied constitution of temporality in this circuit of worlds and bodies that the player finds themself caught up in. In particular, I focus on the entirely common phenomena of character death, failure, and repetition. Players often consciously perceive videogames as an authentic central timeline with a series of inauthentic branches where they failed this or that challenge, but the actual experience of playing the videogame embraces all the failures—all the deaths, all the restarts, and all the Game Overs. In a performance akin to Bill Murray's character in the film *Groundhog Day* (Ramis 1993), when a character performs a superhuman feat in a first-person shooter such as *Call of Duty 4: Modern Warfare* (Infinity Ward 2007), it is typically only after many deaths and retries teach the player what is required of them. This chapter contrasts this entirely ordinary experience of digital time travel with those few videogames that work to represent character death as something more "permanent" in order to understand how videogame temporality is constituted and perceived across worlds as the embodied experience of repetition and failure.

Just as those theorists who have done the most work for advancing embodiment theory have been feminist, race, and queer studies scholars concerned primarily with accounting for a more representative spectrum of embodied experiences, it is those videogame creators that have traditionally been excluded from the homogenous and hegemonic "videogame industry" who provide the most fruitful challenges to traditional and normalized understandings of what videogames are and how they are experienced. As the tools of videogame development and distribution have become more accessible, the past decade has seen a great widening of both who makes videogames and the sorts of videogames they make. Small and experimental videogames made by nonmale, queer, transgender, and nonwhite creators have directly contested many of the traditional tenets of "good" videogame design and taste: they are expressive videogames with no fail states, with short personal stories, or with audiovisual aesthetics completely at odds with the commercial videogame industry's fetishizing of new technologies. Chapter 6 thus concludes this book with two metaphoric characters that function conceptually to show the dominant and marginal ways that the embodiment of videogame experience functions culturally. The "hacker" represents the configurative and transcendent desires of the hegemonic, masculine "gamer" who values very specific styles of videogames and who, a historical study shows, still largely determines how videogames are broadly evaluated. In contrast to the hacker is the "cyborg," a creature of technological embodiment concerned less with transcendental control and more with partial and immanent incorporation *with* the machine. Considering videogame play as a form of cyborg-play rather than a form of hacker-play, this final chapter argues, allows us to account for the vast range of videogames whose pleasures fall beyond the traditional ones of control and configuration. Here, my ultimate desire for this project is laid bare: I wish to advance a phenomenology of videogame experience that affords an appreciation of this wider spectrum of videogames that are incompatible with the traditional ways videogames have long been understood.

It is important to note that my focus throughout this book is primarily on the player-and-videogame circuit of single-player videogames. In taking this focus, I do not mean to trivialize the many social engagements of the multiplayer videogame form or the vast body of literature on these experiences (see Taylor 2006, 2012; Surman 2007; D. Wilson 2011; Carter, Gibbs, and Wadley 2013; Harper 2013; Stein 2013). Rather, I want to highlight that in most cases, single player or multiplayer, there is a preconscious engagement between player body and videogame hardware and software, with hands wrapped around input devices, eyes on screens, and ears directed at speakers. Although there are always exceptions and edge cases (such as *Johann Sebastian Joust* [Die Gute Fabrik 2013], which has players face each other, rather than a screen), it is the intimate coupling of player and videogame that I am most squarely interested in, which exists just as centrally in multiplayer videogames.

I hope this book lays the groundwork for a phenomenological appreciation of videogame experience that does not easily separate player from character, actual from virtual, real from fictional, story from game, embodied from textual, active from passive, acting from interpreting but that, to follow Donna Haraway (1991c), is located in the *splice*, in the hybrid *all-at-once*. This is an approach that appreciates what videogames are, not what games are meant to be. I feel a presence in *Tearaway*'s microworld in my hands, and I also poke at it and peer into it from the actual world where my playing body resides. It all matters. It is all the matter of videogame play. It is all what I do—what I *am*—when I play a videogame. It is this flickering play of bodies that is the meaningful, sensorial, situated experience of videogame play.

1 Across Worlds and Bodies

Boundaries of texts are like boundaries of bodies, and both stand in for the confusing and invisible boundary of the self.
—Shelley Jackson, "Stitch Bitch: The Patchwork Girl" (1998)

Something felt tangibly different about *Grand Theft Auto IV* (Rockstar North 2008). The previous title in the series and its own spin-offs—*Grand Theft Auto III* (DMA Design 2001), *Grand Theft Auto: Vice City* (Rockstar North 2002), and *Grand Theft Auto: San Andreas* (Rockstar North 2004)—presented me with large, open, urban sprawls and invited me to treat them as my playground. I would direct my playable character to run around, steal cars, terrorize cartoon pedestrians, cause traffic jams with a rocket launcher. All these crimes sound horrific, but each videogame presented them as juvenile frivolities. This was the violence of Bugs Bunny more than the violence of Scarface. These videogames were lighthearted and irreverent. But *Grand Theft Auto IV* felt different. In terms of the videogame's rules and what actions it required of me, *Grand Theft Auto IV* was largely indistinguishable from its predecessors. I still used my left thumb to push against the PlayStation gamepad's thumbstick to navigate my character around the 3D space. I still pressed "Triangle" with my thumb on the PlayStation gamepad to steal a car. I still squeezed the right-hand trigger with my index finger to accelerate. I could still shoot people indiscriminately and attract the cops' attention. But all of it felt different.

Nico Bellic, the character I moved through the streets of *Grand Theft Auto IV*, moved more slowly than the protagonists of the previous games. When I stretched out my left thumb to push up on the left thumbstick while playing *Grand Theft Auto III*, my nameless character would break into an easy jog, Uzi held high as he bounced down the street without a care in the world. Nico, however, would stroll at a slow pace, his shoulders hunched as I watched him from the camera positioned behind him. The videogame's introductory cinematic sequence presented him as an illegal immigrant with a dark past, and that past seemed to be weighing heavily on him in a very tangible sense. Cars, too, felt heavier yet slipperier than the floaty toy things of the previous games. It took a long time for me to get used to this change, and at first my muscle memory would send my stolen vehicles sliding and smashing into oncoming traffic as I tried to adjust to this change in virtual friction and gravity. Once I adapted, my few car crashes felt less bombastic but somewhat more serious: not the fast, *Blues Brothers* beat-ups of the previous games, but solid *crunch*es as one solid metal object collided with another.

One day, not long after *Grand Theft Auto IV*'s release, my brother came to visit. As teenagers, we had spent countless hours together causing mischief in *Grand Theft Auto III*, one of us playing as the other spectated. He was excited to try this new title in the series. He loaded my saved game and immediately pulled out a shotgun and shot at a passing car's windscreen. In previous iterations, the car door would automatically open and the cartoon body of the driver would flop out. But in *Grand Theft Auto IV* the windscreen visibly fractured and splattered with blood from the inside. A single, monotone note droned endlessly as the car's driver fell forward onto the horn. My brother looked aghast and immediately handed the gamepad back to me. "That was horrible!" he exclaimed, disgusted not at his actions so much as at how the videogame had presented them—at how his actions *felt*.

Grand Theft Auto IV felt different. The possible actions were the same, but they were no longer presented as juvenile frivolities; now they were cynical and down-beat violence. The tone, the atmosphere, the *meaning* of playing *Grand Theft Auto IV* shifted with this altered texture of my actions. UK game industry magazine *Edge* identified this shift in its review of the game: cars "feel really weighty"; combat has "real heft" (*Edge* 2008, 83). The virtual world and its objects have a real sense of physicality. The virtual people of *Grand Theft Auto IV*'s world dynamically respond to the objects they connect with (cars, sidewalks, bullets) and crumple as though there is real weight behind these audiovisual representations. Crucially, the *Edge* review identified this weight not just as a physical heaviness present in *Grand Theft Auto IV* but as a thematic one. Through the story of Nico Bellic, this sequel has darker themes than its predecessors, which "may seem a bit *heavy* for a [*Grand Theft Auto*] game" (*Edge* 2008, 83, emphasis added). A symbiosis connects *Grand Theft Auto IV*'s tonal gravitas and its physical gravity, a weight that is at once metaphorical and literal. Where its predecessors expressed cartoonish playfulness and *light*heartedness in their violence, *Grand Theft Auto IV* evokes a subdued grimness and an oppressive heaviness.

How does *Grand Theft Auto IV* feel this way? What does it mean to say *Grand Theft Auto IV* feels heavy? Or that first-person shooter *Halo* (Bungie 2001) feels meaty? Or that hyperviolent top-down shooter *Hotline Miami* (Dennaton 2012) feels rhythmic? Or that the minimalist experience of *Flower* (Thatgamecompany 2009) feels relaxing? How does a videogame "feel" like anything at all?

Through the material object I physically hold and touch and the audiovisuals I look at and listen to, *Grand Theft Auto IV* is able to depict a particular world for me to imperfectly embody through my joint control of Nico Bellic's virtual body and the virtual camera that frames him. If *Grand Theft Auto IV* can be perceived as being about the downfall of American Empire as observed through the eyes of an immigrant, it is not merely the narrative content that communicates such meanings. Its heaviness, its grimness, its sluggishness are felt through my physical embodiment and incorporation of the videogame's form: grasping the controller in my hands, looking at the moving images on the screen, listening to the music and sound from the speakers. *Grand Theft Auto IV* is a work that incorporates the player's embodied experience *as* a significant aspect of its textuality. Before I even have a chance to interpret *Grand Theft Auto IV*'s themes or narrative as heavy, the videogame *feels* heavy through my body wrapped up with the videogame's input device and audiovisual elements.

This chapter asks what it means to consider videogame experience as an *embodied textuality* where the synthesized embodied experience of audiovisual design, videogame hardware, and the player's physical body constitute the site of meaningful engagement with the videogame. It argues that videogames can be studied as texts, but only if our notion of what a text is takes into account the material instantiation through which that text is embodied. The concept of embodied textuality stems from N. Katherine Hayles's call for a mode of textual analysis that accounts for how the text is materially embedded in the world (2005, 102). Hayles is concerned primarily with how print-centric notions of textuality influence appraisals of hypertext literature, and she notes that the new textual forms offered by digital media demand that we "explore the possibilities of texts that thrive on the entwining of physicality with information structure" (102). Videogames are such texts. They blend narratives and fictions with virtual bodies and objects that are physically *felt* through hands wrapped around plastic controllers or tapping away at keyboards or smearing touchscreens. The player's embodied engagement with the material form of the videogame precedes any interpretative engagement with the videogame's virtual "content," even—especially—when that material engagement is not given the player's conscious attention. My brother was not consciously paying attention to the specific materiality of the gamepad in his hand or the audiovisuals that make *Grand Theft Auto IV*'s violence feel so ghastly; he was paying attention *through* this materiality to his character on a city street holding a shotgun. But he *felt* this virtual world through its actual materiality all the same. This embodied textuality is the foundation of videogame experience; it is how videogames are meaningful.

This hybridity of player with videogame, however, must not begin with the assumption that the player's body that fuses with the videogame exists in any predetermined, essentialized sense. The body-at-the-videogame is a particular, augmented version of the player's body: limbs are wrapped around controllers and extended through the screen; senses become heightened or muted; identities, abilities, literacies, and perspectives are taken up and put aside; flesh integrates with plastic and code in what Martin Lister and his colleagues highlight as a "literally cyborgian" phenomenon ([2003] 2009, 306). To account for embodied textuality, then, is to be *reflexive*; it is to account not only for how the player instantiates videogame play but also for how the player is incorporated into, becomes part of, and is ultimately made by the system of videogame play they instantiate. This accounting ultimately points toward locating the videogame experience as a *coming-together* of the player and the videogame not as preexisting, separate, distinct subjects or objects but as a cybernetic assemblage of human body and nonhuman body across actual and virtual worlds. Neither player nor videogame come first, but both are made in the relationship with each other, and it is through this amalgam that I am embodied in and as the videogame text, as both "Nico Bellic" the character controlled in the world of *Grand Theft Auto IV* and "me" the player of *Grand Theft Auto IV*.

Players become incorporated into an assemblage that is the *player-and-videogame*. But as the theorists discussed in the first section of this chapter demonstrate, embodiment is always a dynamic and ongoing process. The player-and-videogame shapes the player as much as it is shaped by the player. The first section starts with Maurice Merleau-Ponty and his foundational work in *Phenomenology of Perception* (2012) before moving on to those more contemporary theorists who account for the *intercorporeality* of embodiment and critique the liberal, rationalist underpinnings of an embodiment that starts with an essential, preexisting, normative notion of *the* body to show instead how the world and the body constitute each other in ongoing processes.

If the world and the body constitute each other in ongoing processes, and if we perceive the audiovisual-haptic feedback loop of videogame play as constituting virtual spaces beneath the glass, then what happens to the play of bodies across actual and virtual worlds? How does the actual/virtual player produce the virtual/actual world they partially inhabit? This chapter turns to these questions in the next section, highlighting the central role of perception in the way the player transforms a flat screen of lights and sounds into a space beyond the glass to inhabit (only ever partially).

The final section, then, takes these freshly explored notions of embodiment through videogame play to return to Hayles's idea of an embodied textuality and the much older debates of form and content that such a notion echoes, laying the groundwork for an understanding of the pleasures and meanings of videogame play as not easily separating player and character, actual and virtual, real and fictional, story and game, embodied and textual but as existing in the hybrid *all-at-once* splice where the player is present across the perforation of worlds and bodies torn apart and folded over each other.

To Be a Partial Body

Marking a clear distinction between an objective consciousness that possesses autonomy over its world and a subjective body constrained by its situated flesh obscures the ways in which experience is produced through our embodied being-in-the-world. There is no consciousness for us to be—there exists no world for us as embodied beings—without the foundational experience of our senses. To understand how players are embodied in videogame play is first to appreciate embodiment as always partial and mediated. To understand how elements such as a videogame's visual art, music, input device, and interface are perceived by (and ultimately make) the player's embodied experience of that videogame is first to understand how our perceptual experience of our world is always-already influencing and altering (and ultimately making) our lived experience of our selves.

Toward a Decentered Self

Phenomenology of Perception provides one place to start thinking about how perception produces knowledge, looking extensively at how embodiment constitutes (and is constituted by) its world spatially, temporally, and sensorially. As Merleau-Ponty claims in his preface, "The world is not what I think, but what I live" (2012, lxxx). Advancing the phenomenological notion of being-in-the-world as a "pre-objective perspective" (81) and arguing against a Cartesian splitting of mind from body, he demonstrates the fallacies of an ideal, objective "view from nowhere" through the simple example of a cube that can never be seen in its entirety from any one perspective (211). To perceive a cube is to see some facets of it while others remain hidden from view, yet those hidden faces are present in our perception of the cube *as* a cube. That the cube can be perceived as such without ever being seen in its entirety depends on a knowledge that we as embodied subjects can perceive *from* various positions successively. In contrast to an objective view that sees "from nowhere," our embodied experience of the world through particularly configured and presented bodies always perceives from *somewhere*—our perceiving (and knowing) is always partial and situated. Before conscious thought comprehends the cube as a unified whole, we first perceive it from a particular perspective, understanding that the edges shifting away from us and the surfaces obscured to us could, if we were to move, be perceived from different perspectives, and all these situated angles combined would present to us, objectively, the cube. The cube as an object with six equal faces is the "limit-idea" through which I express "the carnal presence of the cube that is there before my eyes and beneath my hands in its perceptual evidentness" (Merleau-Ponty 2012, 211). Objective view is only ever emergent from continuous, subjective, and situated perception. Mind and body, objectivity and subjectivity are ultimately inseparable; one informs and constitutes the other.

We experience the world through our body, but we experience our own body itself more as a frontier where our "natural ignorance of ourselves" (Merleau-Ponty 2012, 117) constantly moves the body through which we perceive to the background of those perceptions. The body acquires its own *ways of moving* through the world—that is, the body cultivates habits. As ways of moving are habitualized by the body, they retreat to the background of our perception and are perceived *through*. Merleau-Ponty notes that such habitual knowledges of the body are not restricted to "the body" as a sealed-off, organic construct; rather, the body incorporates the world into its habits:

Without any explicit calculation, a woman maintains a safe distance between the feather in her hat and objects that might damage it; she senses where the feather is, just as we sense where our hand is. If I possess the habit of driving a car, then I enter into a lane and see that "I can pass" without comparing the width of the lane to that of the fender, just as I go through a door without comparing the width of the door to that of my body. The hat and the automobile have ceased to be objects whose size and volume would be determined through a comparison with other objects. They have become voluminous powers and the necessity of a certain free space. Correlatively, the subway door and the road have become restrictive powers and immediately appear as passable or impassable for my body and its appendages. (144)

Continuing with further analogies of a blind man's walking stick, Merleau-Ponty argues that to get used to such instruments is "to take up residence in them ... to make them participate with the voluminosity of one's own body" (145). Habit expresses how we appropriate instruments into our embodiment to dilate our being-in-the-world. Speaking specifically of the typist at the typewriter, reaching for keys without needing to consciously remember in what order the keys are positioned, Merleau-Ponty claims that this habit is "*a knowledge in our hands*, which is only given through a bodily effort and cannot be translated by an objective designation. The subject knows where the letters are on the keyboard just as we know where one of our limbs is—a knowledge of familiarity that does not provide a position in objective space" (2012, 145, emphasis added). Our preconscious perception of our world through a body is always already altered by the objects and instruments we incorporate into our embodied experience of the world and by the habits we develop through reaching for and adapting to these objects. As I have habitualized a motor knowledge of typing on a QWERTY keyboard, I do not have to "think" about how my hands are producing this sentence, but the moment a finger slips and presses the wrong key, I know that I have made an error. It just feels wrong in my hands.

Although Merleau-Ponty offers significant insights into how objects and instruments are incorporated into the body, his focus remains centrally on *the* body. The body might be altered by the "appendages" that it takes up, but it is still *the* body—stable and persistent. Merleau-Ponty makes significant interventions into a Cartesian mind/body dualism by accounting for the role of embodiment in shaping perception, but the body he refers to exists before the fact, essential and unchanged in the face of the social world. What if, rather than an essential human body and peripheral appendages, the perceiving, subjective "self" were understood as produced *by* this amalgam body-and-world?

Discursively decentering the human body to situate human subjectivity and the construction of the "self" as constituted *between* human and nonhuman actors has been (and continues to be) the response to phenomenology across a range of disciplines. As anthropologist Gregory Bateson stresses, the thinking system of body-and-instruments-and-worlds is much broader than what is commonly conceived of as "the self": "the total self-corrective unit which possesses information, or, as I say, 'thinks' and 'acts' and 'decides,' is a system whose boundaries do not at all coincide with the boundaries either of the body or of what is popularly called the 'self' or 'consciousness'" (1972, 317). Like Merleau-Ponty, Bateson uses the metaphor of the blind man with a stick. But whereas Merleau-Ponty sees the stick incorporated into the blind man's preexisting body, Bateson argues that stick and man can be considered only as a single system with no clear boundaries between the two: "Where does the blind man's self begin? At the tip of the stick? At the handle of the stick? Or at some point halfway up the stick? These questions are nonsense, because the stick is a pathway along which differences are transmitted under transformation, so that to draw a delimiting line across this pathway is to cut off a part of the systemic circuit which determines the blind man's locomotion" (1972, 318). The stick is incorporated into the blind man's self (that is, his sense of being-in-the-world), *and* the blind man is incorporated into the stick. To understand our embodiment of the world, then, is to understand our bodies not as stable and essential but as essentially unstable, as an *intercorporeal* affair continuously mediated by our ongoing interactions with other human and nonhuman bodies.

Scholars in the emerging schools of new materialism and speculative realism, following the likes of Bruno Latour and Graham Harman, have also worked to dislodge the notion that agency resides in the intentional, rational subject at the center of their own world (see Bennett 2009, 30). However, with respect to this book's interest in the co-constituted sensorial experience of player-and-videogame, feminist theorists of embodiment have most constructively critiqued and advanced Merleau-Ponty's work on the construction of subjectivity through perception by accounting for the ways the social world and its constructions of gender, ethnicity, class, and sexuality, no less than the "natural" world of objects, influence our being-in-the-world. Iris Marion Young (1980, 2005b), Judith Butler (1988), Elizabeth Grosz (1994), Gail Weiss (1999), and Sara Ahmed (2006) critique, challenge, and strengthen Merleau-Ponty's work by connecting the lived body more explicitly than Merleau-Ponty does to "how the body lives out its positions in social structures of the division of labor, hierarchies of power, and norms of sexuality" (Young 2005a, 26). Merleau-Ponty's claim that "man" is "an historical idea, not a natural species" (2012, 174) produced through its corporeal habitualizations allows Butler to "examine in what ways gender is constructed through specific corporeal acts" (1988, 521) and Young to identify femininity as "a set of structures and conditions that delimit the typical *situation* of being a woman in a particular society, as well as the typical way in which this situation is lived by the women themselves" (2005b, 32, original emphasis). In a sustained feminist critique of Merleau-Ponty's work, Weiss confronts Merleau-Ponty's implication that there exists "*the* body" to instead argue for *an essential instability* of bodies; rather than "a cohesive and coherent phenomenon that operates in a fairly uniform way in our everyday existence," there is "a multiplicity of body images, body images that are copresent in any given individual, and which are themselves constructed through a series of corporeal exchanges that take place both within and outside of specific bodies" (1999, 1–2). Young similarly contests Merleau-Ponty's configuration of the lived body as, in her words, "a transcendence that moves out from the body in its immanence in an open and unbroken directedness upon the world of action" and argues instead that feminine bodily existence "remains in immanence or, better, is *overlaid*, with immanence, even as it moves out toward the world" (2005b, 36, original emphasis). To accurately account for the dynamism and socially embedded nature of embodied experience is not to start with a pregiven, essential "human" body and move beyond it but to account for how embodiment *emerges from* phenomena both natural and social in an ongoing coming together of multiple corporealities—how we are made by our world that we make in ongoing processes.

Rather than our bodies existing before the incorporation of objects such as feathers or cars or sticks or typewriters (or, indeed, videogames), it is the intercorporeal assemblage of feathers-and-bodies, cars-and-bodies, sticks-and-bodies, typewriters-and-bodies (and, indeed, videogames-and-bodies) that modulates our being-in-the-world. The move is semantic, but it decenters *the* human body as the stable locus that the universe orbits to make way for a diversity of human and nonhuman bodies that are constantly made and remade in their relations with other human and nonhuman bodies.

If we are to understand how bodies produce meaning in videogame play, then, we cannot start with an essential player body and peripheral tools. We have instead a cybernetic amalgam of material and virtual artifacts across which the player's perception and consciousness are distributed and transformed and from which the player's embodied experience of playing a particular videogame emerges. The conceptual shift here that feminist theorists afford is important: the player cannot be considered before or distinct from the videogame but instead reflexively as producing the videogame experience that in turn produces the player. Images, sounds, input devices, the affordances and restrictions of the playable character's body, the social context of play, cultivated tastes, and the player's competency with videogames influence and alter the incorporation of the videogame into the player's embodied experience no less so than the player's embodied experience alters the videogame with each moment of play. A phenomenology of videogame experience must not start with the experience of the player's body; rather, it must start with the experience through which the player's amalgam embodiment in and as part of the videogame performance emerges.

Cyborgs, Posthumanism, and Postphenomenology

Others have challenged traditional conceptions of the self as stable and persistent by examining the body as it confronts active digital technologies. The personal computer (PC) or the smartphone is not necessarily "more" incorporated into our being than the walking stick or the hat feather. Yet the fact that computers seem, as Donna Haraway puts it, "disturbingly lively" while we ourselves become "frighteningly inert" (1991b, 152) provides a particularly vivid demonstration of how our embodiment of the world has always been caught up and entwined with nonhuman bodies. Considering how bodies are caught up with technologies provides a significant precursor to thinking about how bodies become entangled with the microworlds of videogames.

In the essay "Manifesto for Cyborgs," originally published in 1985, Haraway conceptualizes the ways bodies engage with digital computers as cyborgian: "a cybernetic organism, a hybrid of machine and organism" (1991b, 149).[1] Haraway uses the metaphor of the cyborg and its transgressions of the ingrained borders between the human and the machine to expose a much wider array of dualisms reinforcing patriarchal dominance in Western society: "self/other, mind/body, culture/nature, truth/illusion, total/partiality, God/man" (1991b, 177).[2] To expose the constructedness of such dualisms, she argues in several works for a necessary *partiality* of such actors, always spliced with other actors. Our identities are always "contradictory, partial, and strategic" (1991a, 55). As our identities are always situated and partial, so are the knowledges we produce. For Haraway, this is not a problem to resolve (a move that only ever confers impartial status to one partial perspective) but a reality to account for: "the knowing self is partial in all its guises, never finished, whole, simply there and original; it is always constructed and stitched together imperfectly, and *therefore* able to join with another, to see together without claiming to be another" (1988, 586, original emphasis). To see an object is always to have some aspects of that object obscured from view; to be viewing from somewhere is to be incorporated into and as part of a world.

For Merleau-Ponty, objective consciousness emerges from the knowledge that as embodied subjects we can view an object from successive perspectives, but for Haraway we never transcend a subjective, situated, and partial perspective. The metaphoric identity of the cyborg embraces this corporeal partiality as more accurate of the human experience than a god's eye view from nowhere. Or, as Haraway more notoriously concludes in her manifesto, "I would rather be a cyborg than a goddess" (1991b, 181). In chapter 6, I revisit the figure of the cyborg as an identity to take up in its tensions against the "hacker" in technoculture.

For Hayles (1999), too, increasingly lively, active, and pervasive technologies challenge the rational liberal subject as the dominant means through which to understand what it means to be human. Rearticulating the body and the self as caught up with machines and technologies flies in the face of classic Enlightenment understandings of the human subject as free, autonomous, and rational and as possessing agency over both their own body and the natural world. The rational liberal subject possessed a body but was not usually represented as *being* a body (Hayles 1999, 4). Hayles configures human identity with technology as *post*human in a way similar to how Haraway configures it as cyborgian: "in the posthuman, there are no essential differences or absolute demarcations between bodily existence and computer simulation, cybernetic mechanism and biological organism, robot teleology and human goals" (1999, 3). In *How We Became Posthuman*, Hayles maps how through the nineteenth and twentieth centuries and into the twenty-first century information lost its body as it became caught up in liberal and positivist models that downplay the centrality of embodiment to all knowledge production (1999, 4). In response to this loss, Hayles's use of the term *posthuman* signals not a desired transcendence beyond humanity but the end of a particularly narrow and hegemonic conception of the human *as* transcendent. Or, to invert Haraway's desire to speak for the "embodied others ... [w]ho are not allowed *not* to have a body" (1988, 575), the conceptions of "human" that Hayles's posthuman reacts against only ever served those privileged few who *were* allowed to not have a body.

Posthumanism is not a futurist progression away from being human afforded solely by digital media but a rearticulation of how human knowledge and information have always been caught up with and mediated by the world in which they are situated. Merleau-Ponty's woman with a feather in her hat does not simply incorporate the feather into her being; rather, her being is actively made in part by the feather. Human *being* is a process; the will, autonomy, agency, and ultimately the "self" of the human subject is always already mediated by the active existence of other objects and instruments and spaces. The flesh is no longer the center but rather only one material component in a cybernetic amalgam of bodies by which we constitute the world through which we ourselves are constituted.[3]

What the cyborg, the posthuman, and feminist embodiment theorists point toward is a construction of the self between bodies and worlds that constitute each other, with embodiment always emergent from its context. The self is constructed through the human's incorporation of the non-human, such that a clear distinction between "human" bodies and a "non-human" world/technology becomes impossible. Confronting the same tensions, Don Ihde proposes *post*phenomenology as a "modified, hybrid phenomenology" (2009, 23) that is explicitly indebted to the feminist theorists, who "have rediscovered the need to see embodiment as an important aspect of all knowledge gaining and constructing activities" (1993, 7). What phenomenology is to the rational liberal subject with "his" free will and normative essence, postphenomenology is to Hayles's posthuman and Haraway's cyborg, whose bodies are always already inscribed by gender, race, class, and an appreciation that technology transforms our perceptions of the world and thus the very fabric of our being-in-the-world.

Ihde connects technologically and socially mediated forms of embodiment back into the traditional concerns of phenomenology by contrasting the embodied perspectives of different textual forms. Whereas both reading and writing privilege "an elevated and overhead position" that reflects the god's-eye view from nowhere of objective consciousness, more contemporary moving-image media, "while still *viewed* from a usually *fixed* position, now begin to vary the 'text' with that which 'moves' and which develops a virtual 'movement' of bodily positionality (as in television, cinema, etc.)" (1993, 86, original emphasis). A similar insight sparked Merleau-Ponty's fascination with film as a medium that directly addresses the senses: "a movie is not thought; it is perceived" (1964, 58). The unfixedness and motility of the textual frame, Ihde points out, situate us as subjects in a "doubled world" where we are both overhead readers and embodied viewers: "To both 'see' in an embodied position, and to 'read' in an apparent position, and to be able to easily 'hermeneutically' transpose between the two positions is part of what it means to perceive in the now *postmodern* lifeworld. Our perspectives are multiple, refracted, and compound" (1993, 87, original emphasis). What we are left with, then, is a reflexive and hybrid notion of what it means to be a body not only where sensorial perception precedes conscious thought but also where that perception is always already caught up with and distributed across a heterogeneous assemblage of materials and properties that constitute our posthuman embodiments: walking sticks, glasses, hats, smartphones, footpaths, monitors, genders, cars, coffee mugs, QR codes, GPS satellites.

Just as the human does not precede their world, the videogame player does not precede the *worlds* they bring together in their perception of videogame play. If the self is constructed by and distributed across the web of body-and-world, then this can only be compounded when physical body-and-worlds are spliced with the perceptually virtual body-and-worlds in vivid instantiations of Haraway's cyborg.

Actual Bodies at Virtual Worlds

David Sudnow's book *Pilgrim in the Microworld* (1983) presents beautiful vignettes that articulate how this splicing of player and videogame is acted out. One of the earliest serious considerations of videogame experience, *Pilgrim in the Microworld* details Sudnow's increased competency and appreciation of the videogame *Breakout* (Atari 1976). Similar to *Pong* (Atari 1972), *Breakout* has the player turn a small, handheld dial clockwise and counterclockwise to slide an on-screen paddle horizontally across the bottom of the screen. The goal is to keep a small ball bouncing between the paddle and the colored bricks in rows at the top of the screen until it has destroyed all the bricks. Much like Merleau-Ponty's descriptions of people incorporating objects into their bodily perception of space, Sudnow's description of *Breakout* recognizes a similar incorporation with the virtual paddle on the television screen he controls through the dial in his hand:

> Knowledge about the paddle's programmed subdivisions and angles no more truly aids the task at hand than a knowledge of physics could help you line up a certain point on a [baseball] bat with the ball in order to hit to left field. When a paddle or a bat is incorporated by the body, becoming a continuation of ourselves into and through which we realize an aim in a certain direction, such implements lose all existence as things you measure on rules. They become incorporated within a system of bodily spaces that can never be spoken of in the objective terms with which we speak of objects outside of ourselves. (1983, 122)

That Sudnow incorporates the videogame into his embodiment does not mean that he as a rational and intentional actor is the center of *Breakout*'s microworld, however. Several pages later he acknowledges the inverse to be true: "It's as if instead of truly incorporating the events of the screen within the framework of the body's natural way of moving and caring, the action on the screen must *incorporate me*, reducing or elevating me to some ideal plane of synaptic being through which the programmed coincidences will take place" (1983, 138–139, emphasis added). Sudnow does not simply "use" the videogame. Rather, he adapts to a distributed embodiment; he adjusts his posture and his movements to those required by the videogame.

Importantly, however, unlike the feather, car, walking stick, and baseball bat, *Breakout*'s paddle is not an actual, tangible object; it is a lit-up rectangular section of a television screen, responding to the input of the handheld knob in such a way as to be perceived as a paddle that moves in response to the player's own movement. Likewise, the ball is not a ball; the bricks are not bricks. Nothing is "actually" moving except Sudnow's fingers and eyeballs as well as the electron gun behind the cathode-ray tube television screen and the consequential makeup of electrons flickering fast enough for the human eye to perceive the rapidly changing lights *as if* discrete objects are moving across the screen space. Unlike Merleau-Ponty's instruments that we habitualize to "participate with the voluminosity of [our] own bod[ies]" (2012, 145), videogames "extend our bodies across a *material* divide, into screen space" (Klevjer 2012, 24, original emphasis). To understand how videogames are perceived by players is, centrally, to understand how the "virtual" worlds and objects of videogames are perceived (indeed, constructed) as worlds at all by the actual bodies that incorporate and are incorporated by them.

Why do *Grand Theft Auto IV*'s cars feel heavier than *Grand Theft Auto III*'s cars? A model of embodiment that focuses on the player as a discrete and autonomous subject cannot answer this question. Either literally or metaphorically or consciously, players do not simply step out of an actual world and into a virtual one. Conceptualizing the playing self as an intercorporeal and partial posthuman subject instead helps us understand how players engage with and perceive virtual environments *through* actual, sensuous flesh. The actual and the virtual are, to use Weiss's word, intercorporeal. There is a "virtual" world that is perceived by the videogame player, but it must be understood as embedded within the actual, not discrete from it. This section explores the ways a division between the actual and virtual is encouraged by the videogame player's desire to feel a sense of "immersion" in the virtual world and the ways that this immersion is always contingent on the actual body that never fully "enters" the virtual world but that is not entirely left behind either. Although the player does all they can to focus their full attention on the virtual world through the screen, a phenomenology of videogame experience can privilege neither the actual nor the virtual but must account for the assemblage of both—the incorporation of virtual paddles with actual hands—if we are to understand how that virtual world is constructed by the player in the first place.

The Virtual as Actively Constructed

The first-person videogame *Deus Ex* (Ion Storm 2000) begins with playable character J. C. Denton undergoing a training mission that acts as a tutorial for new players. A character in the game tells Denton how to use various tools. At one stage, this character tells Denton to use F1 to open his inventory. This instruction makes perfect sense to me, even though Denton does not have an F1 key on his body. The instructor is instead referring to the key at the top of my QWERTY keyboard. For Denton to open his inventory, I must press F1. Such splicings of the actual and the virtual in videogame play are entirely mundane. Few players would think twice about the weirdness of Denton being told to press the F1 key. Videogames regularly remind players of their intangibility through nondiegetic elements, on-screen prompts, glitches, and the simple fact that they rarely, if ever, hold the player's full attention (a notion explored in chapter 2). However, the explicit artificiality of virtual worlds is often obscured through the player's own desire for "immersion"—to experience the videogame as a diegetic, coherent, frameless world that they can step into and leave the "real" world behind.

The character's reference to a button on my keyboard does not hinder my ability to feel a sense of immersion in this virtual world because I, the player, refuse to consciously focus on such a disruption. Perhaps more accurately I should say that the character's reference simply *isn't* a disruption in the actual/virtual assemblage required for me to perceive the virtual world in the first place. I look "past" it as I look "through" the screen to the virtual world beyond the explicit artifice of the videogame play activity. As William Gibson describes cyberspace in the novel *Neuromancer* (1984), the virtual world is a *consensual hallucination* that the player must help to construct. As such, the player's desire for immersion poses a major challenge for the videogame phenomenologist looking to rearticulate videogame embodiment in such a way that the splicing of actual and virtual bodies and worlds can be appreciated. The act of videogame play itself often requires repressing a conscious consideration of the embodied experience that videogame play depends on and that we here wish to understand. We must look at what the player looks through.

The term *immersion* usefully describes the ideal sensation many videogames aim to imbue in their players: being transported to and enveloped in another world discrete from the actual world. As a consequence, however, immersion is often treated as an inherent attribute of the videogame form rather than as a perceptual strategy performed by an actual player engaging with input devices, screen imagery, and digital sounds.[4] Immersion has an immediate history in the rhetoric surrounding virtual-reality technologies and imaginings of cyberspace from the 1980s and 1990s, but its roots stretch back centuries to various artistic techniques. Creative works have long attempted to give an audience a sense of presence in the virtual world depicted through the artwork by obscuring the very frame of the artwork, from Leon Battista Alberti's window-perspective system deployed by painters since the fifteenth century to the panoramas of the nineteenth century and other more recent technologies, such as the stereoscope and 3D cinema (Lister, Dovey, Giddings, et al. [2003] 2009, 115–123). Immersion has strong connections to the baroque style and is dependent on framing devices and strategies such as the trompe l'oeil no less so than previous media forms.[5] Which is to say that although immersion is very much the intended experiential goal of many videogames (as it was of much Western art before them), such a goal is always dependent on actual, situated bodies viewing from *somewhere* and relies on formal framing strategies that direct and shape such seeing.

Immersion as the desired goal of virtual worlds is commonly conflated so that diegetic, immersive worlds become a pregiven attribute for many critiques of videogame play rather than a perceived quality emerging *from* play. Marie-Laure Ryan, for instance, in her extensive work on the role of immersion and interactivity in virtual-reality narratives, draws on Merleau-Ponty's work to highlight the apparent ease with which the user's actual body is set aside for a virtual body in a virtual world and how a world can be embodied and perceived through a virtual body as easily as it can through our own body:

The ultimate test of the material existence of things is the ability to perceive them under many angles, to manipulate them and to feel their resistance. When my actual body cannot walk around an object or grab and lift it, it is the knowledge that my virtual body could do so that gives me a sense of its shape, volume, and materiality. Whether actual or virtual, objects are thus present to me because my actual or virtual body can interact with them. (2001, 71)

Ryan here identifies the fluidity with which players pick up and discard bodies in their perception of a virtual world as well as the way virtual objects possess a kind of actual, imagined physicality through the player's incorporation of a virtual body. However, she sidelines the technological and corporeal materialities that allow such virtual engagements to be performed in the first place. Just how might *Grand Theft Auto IV*'s world feel heavy through my virtual body, for instance, if not through how I connect to that virtual body through my actual engagement with a physical controller and with responsive, animated images and sounds?

Just as the perceptual stimuli of our senses becomes the background against which all our conscious knowledge of the world is produced, our ability to feel perceptually immersed in a discrete, virtual world risks being considered as a pregiven attribute of digital media rather than the very constitution of virtual embodiment demanding our analytical focus. We risk taking for granted that our virtual worlds are round just as our ancestors once took for granted that our own world is flat. How we come to perceive the worlds in which we are immersed as worlds at all needs to be considered.

Even in the more enclosed virtual realities imagined by Ryan that are perhaps more aligned with wearing a virtual-reality headset than with holding a videogame controller, an engagement with virtual objects is still dependent on handling (or gesturing at) actual objects alongside viewing and listening to actual images and sounds. Ryan begins with immersion and then discusses what it means for the player to have stepped into such a diegetic world. Although such an experience of immersion by the player may very well be the aesthetic goal of many videogames, immersion as a critical and evaluative tool tends to obscure the full machinations of embodiment *across worlds* that videogame play constitutes.

A nascent attempt to account for this actual–virtual hybridity of videogame play can be seen in an extensive essay by videogame critic and designer Tim Rogers (2004) on the Japanese role-playing game *Mother 2* (Ape and HAL Laboratory 1994; released as *Earthbound* outside of Japan). *Mother 2* is a Japanese role-playing game, a particular genre of story-driven videogame that has the player lead a party around a map, fighting enemies and getting stronger as they move the narrative forward over dozens of hours. Released on the Super Nintendo console, *Mother 2* is a two-dimensional videogame that has the player view the world and its characters from a persistent, orthographic perspective (see figure 1.1). In his essay, Rogers (2004) synthesizes descriptive analysis and developer interviews to contextualize *Mother 2* within a broader comprehension of Japanese videogame design and aesthetics. Instead of talking about the videogame in broad generalizations, he focuses on specific moments of play to ground his insights. Significantly, in describing these moments, he restricts himself neither to objects and actions performed by the player in the actual world nor to objects and actions performed by the character in the virtual world but instead threads the two together in the space of single sentences.

One such moment is worth citing at length. Rogers concentrates on a house that the player is able to purchase in the village of Onett for $10,000

Figure 1.1
The "house with two walls" in *Mother 2* (Ape and HAL Laboratory 1994).

in-game dollars. However, as he notes, the player is unlikely to have access to this kind of money when the house is first encountered:

You can't buy the house during the game's ending, when you'll no doubt have more than $10,000 in the bank, because the real-estate agent is gone and the door is locked. You can't buy it past a certain point in the game, either, because once the endgame begins, Onett is invaded by aliens and plunged into eternal darkness until you kill the aliens. If you want to buy the house, you have to come back at some reasonably early point in the game. When you buy the house, the real-estate agent takes your money and leaves the doorway. He runs all the way off-screen. You are then free to enter the house. When you go inside, you find that it's a run-down shack with wooden floors and walls. A few boards are missing. With the power of its pixels, the game shows you that the mattress in the middle of the floor has a few springs popping up out of its fabric. The back wall of the house—the third wall, as it were—is missing, and we can see the lake in the distance. The fourth wall is already gone—that's the wall through which we, the player, see our heroes standing in this dilapidated shack. We're looking at, essentially, a house with two walls. (2004)

In this passage, Rogers does not distinguish between the player and the playable character (meshing the two in the common second-person term *you* that *Tearaway* [MediaMolecule 2013] comments on explicitly), or between *Mother 2* as a virtual world and *Mother 2* as software instantiated on a televisions screen. He instead richly threads them all together simultaneously, just as the *Mother 2* player experiences them. To develop insights into the value of the videogame and the creator's intentions, Rogers entwines the player's investment in real labor to produce the virtual money required to buy the house; the "power of the pixels" that depict the house as dilapidated; a real-estate agent that runs "off-screen" beyond the frame of the television set in the player's lounge room; and the missing wall through which the player views the world through their television screen.

By drawing together technologies, audiovisuals, and the pressures on the player's physical body to describe an embodied and local phenomenon of videogame play, Rogers is able to make broader observations on lead designer Shigesato Itoi's creative practices and to critique *Mother 2* as a work of popular art—not by distinguishing its virtual "content" from its physical instantiation as played form but by acknowledging that *no such distinction exists*. This acknowledgment is by no means unique within popular vernaculars around videogames; indeed, such fusing of the actual and virtual is necessary and everyday if a critic is to explain what the player "does" in a particular videogame. If the discreteness of the virtual word is presumed, how would one account for a real-estate agent running "off-screen" or for the "removal" of a wall that exists in the world so that I, viewing from my actual body in front of a television screen, can witness the virtual events? The real-estate agent is at the same time a character running away from my character's virtual body standing in the village of Onett *and* a sprite on a television screen looked at by my actual body sitting in my lounge. The agent is simultaneously perceived as both of these things, just as a fantasy novel is experienced as both a mythical kingdom of heroes and beasts as well as bounded paper and ink held in my hands. When I am present in the virtual world of a videogame, I do not perceive objects because my actual *or* virtual body can interact with them, as Ryan suggests, but because my actual *and* virtual bodies interact with them as aspects of a holistic embodiment across worlds.

Rogers extends the dilapidated *Mother 2* house into a metaphor of videogames as a two-walled medium. It is a powerful way to consider how the embodied player perceives the videogame as a necessary precursor to any constituted immersion, incorporating both virtual and physical materialities into their lived experience. Just like all prior media that strive to immerse the audience in a virtual world, videogames do not simply allow the player to "step into" a world that is waiting for them, regardless of the player's transcendent desire to do exactly this. Rather, immersion requires the player to actively construct the illusion of diegesis. Janet Murray, although in part using similarly sealed-off configurations of immersion in her "holodeck" metaphor, significantly understands immersion as a *desired* experience, not as an a priori phenomenon. Videogames and virtual worlds demand more than a suspension of disbelief; they call for the player to *actively make belief*: "because of our desire to experience immersion, we focus our attention on the enveloping world and we use our intelligence to reinforce rather than to question the reality of the experience" (1997, 110). Like Don Quixote tilting at windmills, *the player makes the virtual world make sense* by sealing off the gaps of incoherency the videogame leaves open, be that the ability to heal bullet wounds by leaning against a wall in *The Getaway* (Team Soho 2002), the ability to carry ten weapons at once in *Doom* (Id, 1993), the ability to reload a shotgun while climbing a ladder in *Half-Life* (Valve, 1998), or, in two-dimensional games such as *Mother 2* where environments are viewed from one set angle, the rendering of the fourth wall or ceiling invisible so that the player can view the interior, as in a three-walled theater set.

More accurate still, *Mother 2*'s missing fourth wall *does not exist*. It has not simply been made invisible but in a literal sense it does not exist while the player-character is inside the house. We are looking at, as Rogers rightly notes, a two-walled house in *Mother 2* when we enter the house with the missing rear wall. Just as Merleau-Ponty knows that the concealed faces of the cube exist because he can perceive the cube from different perspectives across time, the *Mother 2* player knows that the removed front wall "virtually" exists because they previously viewed it from the outside. The player must view this world from somewhere, from their corporeal position before a television screen, and thus they both literally and figuratively *must actively construct the fourth wall* in order to feel that sense of immersive diegesis and, in Melanie Swalwell's terms, to *partially become* the virtual actor (2008, 84).[6]

Virtual embodiment does not simply abandon the real body for a virtual one; the virtual body is a *masked* actual body (Murray 1997, 113): an actual body augmented—not replaced—by digital play. It is this need to view the videogame *from somewhere* that allows *Mother 2*'s real estate agent to play his prank: selling the player-character a house that is actually missing a rear wall. The character could have very easily noticed this house was missing its rear wall by simply walking behind it, but the player-character, fixed to a single viewing position, can only presume that the obscured surface exists from the limited perspective they have available to them. The virtual does not replace the actual but augments it. The player makes the world make sense. The player makes the world.

Identities and bodies are emergent splicings of partially human and partially nonhuman materialities. Following this, the virtual world itself is partial, which is what the very word *virtual* traditionally means; its diegesis is incomplete, never sealed off from the partially actual player who constructs the virtual out of screen imagery and digital sounds and plastic input devices. A sense of immersion in a virtual world is thus a desired, deliberate act of perception performed by the videogame player that is dependent not on the virtual world being autonomous from the actual but on the reflexive splicing of actual and virtual worlds. The terms *actual* and *virtual* remain useful for considering how videogames are actively perceived as producing other spaces beyond their flat, glass screens even as this terminology falls out of favor in broader digital media discourses, but only if we consider the actual and the virtual as co-constitutive in the moment of videogame play.

Videogame Play as a Cybernetic Circuit

To play a videogame is not simply to act in a virtual world but to incorporate technologies and audiovisual-haptic feedback that extend, restrict, and ultimately augment the player's embodied experience into complex assemblages of capacities and processes (Ash 2013, 34). Just as starting with the immersed player splits the virtual world and its bodies from the actual world and bodies that are fundamental to the constitution of the virtual, it also splits the videogame's content from the videogame's form. It reintroduces what Susan Sontag notes in her essay "Against Interpretation" as a Cartesian split that "takes the sensory experience of the work of art for granted, and proceeds from there" ([1964] 2009a, 13). Beginning a consideration of a videogame work with what happens "inside" the virtual world highlights a desire for an immediate experience of the videogame's content while ignoring the fact that this content, as Sontag explains in her essay "On Style," "is, as it were, the pretext, the goal, the lure which engages consciousness in essentially *formal* processes of transformation" ([1965] 2009b, 25, original emphasis). Sontag's categorization of the form/content split as Cartesian aligns a split between form and content (the actual and the virtual) with the mind from the body and the self from its world. Understanding virtuality as the player's unproblematic immersion "in" a virtual world reinstates a liberal subject that exists separate from the technological object: *using* the object rather than *participating with* it. Like an objective God, this subject experiences the virtual world from nowhere. The situated and embodied subjects that we are, however, experience the microworld from somewhere.

Immersion is a situated and sensorially dependent outcome of videogame experience, not its antecedent. Thus, to appreciate videogame experience is to begin with—rather than to presuppose—the sensorial and corporeal engagement of player with videogame. Such is the way to account for how the player makes sense of the videogame through a body that is an amalgamation of organic, technological, and audiovisual elements made in the moment of play by the videogame they are playing.

More so than the common understanding of videogames as uniquely "interactive," such a move better understands videogames as *intermediative*—a notion Hayles forwards to discuss the reflexive feedback loops between users and computers (2005, 31). Any easy distinction between agency that originates from the player or from the machine collapses in videogame play. Agency is instead distributed through the *circuit* of player-and-videogame. Various scholars have already deployed a notion of videogame play as "cybernetic" (Jayemanne 2005, 2017; Bogost 2006; Dovey and Kennedy 2006; Giddings and Kennedy 2008; Giddings 2009), building on the work of cybernetics, actor-network, and cyborg theorists such as Bateson (1972), Latour (1991), and Haraway (1991c) to conceive of videogame play as a material feedback loop of information and agency that flows between the machine and the player.

A cybernetic conceptualization of videogame play straddles the border between social and technological determinism to account for how both player and videogame have some mediating effect, some agency, over the other. Just as feminist theorists demonstrate how lived, situated experience accounts for a fuller spectrum of human experience than the patriarchal and colonialist transcendence of objective consciousness, cybernetic conceptualizations of videogame play highlight how the oft-privileged but niche pleasure of mastering a videogame—of dominating and "beating" it—is but a rationalist subset of the broader embodied pleasures of participating *with* a videogame. An active player is not the essence of videogame play that differentiates it from other media. A videogame player is at times afforded and at times constrained so that both activity and passivity—a flow of agency—give shape to the videogame experience. Players do not always act the way they wish with all the available information; they act in the ways a system allows them to act with the information the system provides. As the example of *Mother 2*'s house demonstrates, this configuration can allow the videogame to take advantage of the player, but being thus taken advantage of is not necessarily an unpleasurable experience. On the contrary, the pleasure of videogame experience is to be caught up *as part of* the experience, to constitute the experience that constitutes *you* in turn.

The importance of being sensorially caught up as part of the experience has long been known to videogame developers. Indeed, the most thorough exploration to date of how the circuit of player-and-videogame constitutes the player's embodiment was conducted not within academia but by videogame developer Steve Swink in his book *Game Feel* (2009), which forwards a preliminary understanding of how it "feels" to play a videogame. Swink is concerned with understanding what we mean when we say a videogame's controls feel "tight" or an assault rifle in an action game feels "meaty" or a car in *Grand Theft Auto IV* feels "heavy." His focus on the ways in which proprioception, or the preconscious sense of the position of the self in space, is projected into the virtual world exemplifies the circuit between player and videogame where inputs and outputs are made by both and action is initiated by neither. What the videogame puts out as audiovisual representation via the screen, speakers, and rumble motors is taken in through the player's bodily senses (sight, sound, touch); these senses send messages to the player's brain, which in turn influences output from the player's muscles toward the videogame hardware's input device. The videogame then again takes these inputs and alters the audiovisuals accordingly. In this model, the player's sense of self is caught up in and mediated by a circuit of organic, physical, and audiovisual actors and materialities, and the body through which the player perceives videogame play is reconstituted within the circuit.[7]

What a single moment of videogame play "feels" like is an embodied pleasure caught up in an intimate coupling of bodies. A car feels "heavy" in *Grand Theft Auto IV* through the way it perceptually "moves" on the screen and through what I hear from the speakers in tandem with the resistance of the thumbstick beneath my thumb—all alongside how I expect such a car to act. Significantly, neither the player nor the videogame comes first; each is created and mediated by the circuit. A cybernetic understanding of videogame play does not leave the player's body back in the actual world while focusing on the events of an insular virtual world; rather, it focuses on the meshing of materially different bodies into an amalgam cyborg body through which the player both produces and perceives the play experience.

Notions of videogame play as a set of embodied pleasures (Kennedy 2007) and kinaesthetic knowledges (Swalwell 2008) have been prevalent in understandings of videogame play for some time and have gained more recent interest with the parallel rise of both casual and gestural videogames (explored in the next chapter). But, importantly, comprehending such pleasures cannot start with an essential and stable player who is autonomous and distinct from the videogame in a way that risks reinscribing limited understandings of the essential human and its appendages (the player as fully present in the actual world as opposed to the fully "immersed" player present in the virtual world). This gets us no closer to appreciating the ways in which the videogame acts upon and shapes the player in turn. We must instead account for how the player is redistributed across a network of material information and actors and how they perceive the videogame from this redistributed embodiment.

The way we peer into *Mother 2*'s house, the way *Grand Theft Auto IV* feels corporeally heavy and grim, and the self-awareness of *Tearaway* as a world that is played *with* demonstrate the ease with which the player's attention flickers back and forth between the worlds and bodies across which their sense of self is distributed. To quote Laura Marks, "there's no need to say anything transcends this material life; it's enfolded in it" (2002, 179). The virtual does not exist beyond the actual but is enfolded within it. During videogame play, the player takes on a hybrid body that incorporates flesh, hardware, and virtual objects. Rather than worlds that are either "stepped into" or "acted upon," the feedback loop of videogame play is partial, distributed, and emergent—enfolding the actual with the virtual.

To recognize this fluidity of bodies and identities is to understand that virtual worlds, like human capability and identity, are not imperiled by the splice but dependent on it. How else are we to reach across two worlds at once? When *Grand Theft Auto IV* communicates a sense of sluggishness and heaviness, it does not do this solely through "my" bodily experience at an input device or solely through Nico Bellic's experience walking down a city street. It is in the mixture that is the two of us combined across worlds, in the distributed-but-situated embodied perspective, that the videogame player encounters and entangles with the videogame's work to produce a carnal sort of meaning. It is this spliced world perceived through a distributed presence that is the experience of videogame play, and it is here that the scholar interested in the textual impact of a videogame must focus their attention.

Locating the Videogame Text

Hideo Kojima's stealth-action title *Metal Gear Solid* (Konami 1998) regularly breaks the fourth wall to playfully comment on the liminality of virtual worlds. In one memorable battle, I as espionage expert Solid Snake fight Psycho Mantis, a terrifying man capable of mind reading and telekinesis. Every time I press a button to shoot Solid Snake's gun at Psycho Mantis, the psychic easily predicts the movement and dodges the shot—that is, until I unplug the gamepad from the Player One slot of the PlayStation console and plug it into the rarely used Player Two slot, bypassing Psycho Mantis's mind-reading ability that allows him to preempt my actions. "I can't read you!" wails Psycho Mantis as each shot hits him, quickly defeating him.

Just as Psycho Mantis is unable to read the player due to the player's actual, physical engagement with material hardware, videogame scholars have long been challenged by notions of "reading" videogames as texts. Where might the videogame "text" be located? If one analyzes the videogame as an actual, played phenomena, it is a question of performance, not textuality; if one analyzes the videogames as a rule-based, configurable world, it is a question of systems, not textuality. However, if we now consider videogame experience as a distributed play of bodies across actual and virtual worlds, then videogames *do* stand up to textual analysis, and such analysis can account for and accentuate the meanings and pleasures that emerge in the playing of a particular videogame. This reading requires, however, not only that we rearticulate videogame play to account for textuality but also that we rearticulate textuality to account for the embodied, formal instantiations demanded by all texts.

Playful Textuality

Videogames are more than virtual content; they are embodied and materially instantiated by the player. This means that if we are concerned with the textual significance of specific videogames, the object of a textual study must be the circuit of technologies and audiovisual signifiers that constitutes and is constituted by the player's body. David Surman makes a similar claim when he concludes his study of pleasure, spectacle, and reward in the fighting game *Street Fighter II* (Capcom 1991) by arguing that "when studied independent of one another the form and meaning arising from either *play* or *representation* leave us bankrupt. To create a picture of a player's textual experience, we must try to elect criteria within game design and gameplay where these aspects intersect" (2007, 219, original emphasis). Meaning emerges in the irreducible assemblages and feedback loops of light, sound, and gesture that players find themselves a part of and find to be part of themselves. Meaning emerges not just from what a videogame depicts in its virtual space but also through how that space is sensorially perceived by the player *as* a space. A textual analysis of a videogame must be able to account for the way a videogame physically feels through the synthesized work of hands-on-controllers, eyes-at-screens, and ears-at-speakers to produce specific embodiments for the player.

Perhaps the greatest difficulty in considering the textuality of the videogame form is the notion that videogames are uniquely interactive, whereas texts are essentially stable. An individual player's competency (or lack thereof) individualizes a videogame experience and destabilizes any discussion of what a particular videogame is expressing. Hayles provides a solution to this problem by showing how print-centric notions of textuality are responsible for assumptions that such instability is a problem to be solved rather than a fundamental aspect of all textuality. Print-centric notions of textuality have allowed "the text" as a stable and immaterial ideal to become disconnected from its always unstable material instantiation (2005, 92–95). The notion of the text as stable and immaterial, as nothing more than the order of words and punctuation, is challenged most directly with the rise of electronic texts built on a materiality of code that fundamentally differs from print media:

[Electronic] text is dynamically assembled on the fly, the text as "the actual order of words and punctuation" does not exist as such in these data files. Indeed, it does not exist as an artifact at all. Rather, it comes into existence as a process that includes the data files, the programs that call these files, and the hardware on which the programs run, as well as the optical fibres, connections, switching algorithms, and other devices necessary to route the text from one networked computer to another. (Hayles 2005, 93)

Thus, Hayles makes the same move for the text as being inseparably grounded in its embodied, material instantiation as she makes for our posthuman identities being inseparably grounded in our amalgam bodies. Texts, like bodies, are processes. Indeed, Hayles connects the two together, tracing a history that demonstrates how "the notion of the literary work as an ideal immaterial construction has been deeply influenced by a unitary view of the subject," and she suggests that "perhaps now it is time to think about what kind of textuality a dispersed, fragmented, and heterogeneous view of the subject might imply" (2005, 106). The videogame player is very much a dispersed, fragmented, and heterogeneous subject, and, hence, conceptualizing such a textuality—an *embodied* textuality—is not just timely for videogames but required.

Considering the player-and-videogame as an intercorporeal circuit perfectly situates videogames to take advantage of Hayles's calls for an embodied textuality that can account for the specificity of electronic texts, but it
also does not distance itself far from earlier conceptualizations of what a
text is. Roland Barthes, for instance, notes that "the metaphor of the Text is
that of the *network*" and that "the Text requires that one try to abolish (or
at the very least diminish) the distance between writing and reading, in no
way by intensifying the projection of the reader into the work *but by joining
them in a single signifying practice*" (1977, 161, 162, emphasis added). Most
relevant to the textuality of videogames is how Barthes considers this back
and forth of textuality as a sort of play: "The text itself *plays* (like a door, like
a machine with 'play') and the reader plays twice over, playing the Text as
one plays a game ... [and] in the musical sense of the term" (162, original
emphasis). Barthes's multifaceted approach to a playful reader and a playful
text echoes Vivian Sobchack's notion that film is a play of images and my
own suggestion that videogames are a play of bodies. The link of textuality to play in the musical sense, too, has been connected to the embodied
pleasures of videogame play, most provocatively in an essay by designer
and composer David Kanaga, where he notes that "the kind of meanings
that exist in music are the same kinds of meanings that exist, fundamentally, (but lying latent), in [video]games—they don't point at anything but
the experience itself, at the materials and interrelationships that form the
binding structures of that process" (2012).[8] Contrary to suggestions that the
play demanded of videogames resists any notion of textuality, to engage
with any creative work's textual meanings demands some sort of reflexive
play between writing (producing the experience) and reading (consuming
the experience). Textuality is a feedback loop.

Material Textuality

To engage with any text is an active and embodied engagement. To recap-
ture the immanent experience of engaging with that text in a written analysis is "to make the dry words retain a trace of the wetness of the encounter"
(Marks 2002, x). However, the idea that digital play is exceptionally
reactive—requiring configurative action and bodies to *do something*—was
and remains a central contention of videogame scholars trying to pin down
the particularities of videogame textuality. One of the earliest explorations
of digital media as texts, Espen Aarseth's book *Cybertext* understands digital texts as a form of "ergodic" literature that requires "nontrivial" effort
by the reader to traverse (1997, 1). By this, Aarseth means that a cybertext "focuses on the mechanical organization of the text, by positioning

the intricacies of the medium as an integral part of the literary exchange" (1). Although Aarseth is careful to note that any medium's text requires some form of mechanical interaction—a book's pages must be turned; a film must be played and looked at—he claims that ergodic texts are those in which the mechanical interaction is fundamental to the meaning they produce. Ergodicity thus "shifts the focus from the traditional threesome of author/sender, text/machine, and reader/receiver to the cybernetic intercourse between the various part(icipant)s in the textual machine" (22).

Aarseth makes a significant early contribution toward conceptualizing digital media as texts by highlighting their cybernetic nature and the fundamental way digital texts are constructed at the very moment they are interpreted, but a focus on the text's machinations risks overshadowing the equal importance of the digital text's signifying audiovisual representations. That is, Aarseth's focus on how the page is turned forgets that the page still has words written on it. Hayles makes this critique, too, when she notes that Aarseth's definition of text as any object with the primary function to relay *verbal* information "[leaves] out of account visual, graphic, sonic, kinetic, and other nonverbal signifiers" (2005, 37). Where immersion reduces the videogame to an essence of pure content (just the virtual world), ergodicity reduces the videogame to an essence of pure form (just mechanical interactions).

Although this dichotomy between mechanical and representational aspects is implicit in *Cybertext*, it is made explicit elsewhere, such as in Alexander Galloway's (2006) input-centric account of videogame action or in Aarseth's own claim that Lara Croft's presented gender in *Tomb Raider* (Core Design 1996) is irrelevant and that all that matters is what Croft allows the player to do (2004, 48; critiqued in Dovey and Kennedy 2006, 92, and MacCallum-Stewart 2014). Videogames become reduced to action, but it is a disembodied and *configurative* action that is unable to account for "looking" and "listening" as actions that are as central to the circuit of videogame play as the pressure of fingers against buttons and the interpretation of rule sets. Daniel Golding notes as much in his Michel de Certeau–influenced critique of how game studies discourses typically suggest a player who is looking down on the world from a godlike, all-powerful position and how this assumption obscures the actual, situated ways that players engage with videogames:

> Through the recurrent privileging of a configurable conception of the videogame, scholars have failed to sufficiently account for the played experience of videogames. As an underlying concept, configuration implies a user who has full and unhindered vision ... totalizing and isolating the videogame through a controlling perspective. It

has transformed the videogame into "The Videogame" like a proper name, providing a way of conceiving and constructing the medium on the basis of a finite number of stable, isolatable, and interconnected purposes. From above, through configuration, we encounter the videogame as a concept. (2013c, 30)

Rather than toward configuration, Golding looks toward navigation as more accurately accounting for the player's moment-to-moment movement *with* the videogame, always with partial, imperfect, and located knowledge (2013c, 42). Considering the player as navigating rather than configuring the videogame, argues Golding, offers the videogame scholar the ability "to think of the videogame from both the holistic 'from above' viewpoint of the strategies of designers and programmers, and also from the low-level, 'from below' viewpoint of the experiential tactics of the player" (2013c, 42).

Considering videogames as navigable rather than configurable brings videogame experience back to textual analysis so long as we pay attention to the significance of every text's material instantiation navigated by an embodied reader. By a text's materiality, Hayles means not just its physicality but also how its physical characteristics and its signifying strategies interplay; a text "has a body (or rather many bodies), and the rich connections between its physical properties and the processes that constitute it as something to be read make up together that elusive object we call a 'text'" (2004, 72). Thus, while Aarseth helps us appreciate how the textual interplay between player and technology that videogames make so explicit might function as ergodicity, Hayles repositions *all* texts as having a fundamental and meaningful materiality that requires an embodied engagement: "what matters for understanding literature … is *how the text creates possibilities by mobilizing certain aspects of its physicality*" (2005, 103, emphasis added). Videogames were never entirely configurable, and texts were never entirely stable. For videogames, like for all texts, how the audience embodies and incorporates the materiality of the work matters. For texts, like for all videogames, meaning emerges from the ultimately playful and unstable encounter between audience and work.

The videogame text is distributed across the player's physical body, the videogame hardware, and the virtual bodies and worlds of the videogame's audiovisuality. It is in the coming together of these heterogeneous materialities as embodied by the player that the videogame text is produced, and it is through this text that the videogame player is embodied. If the text is repositioned as a dynamically embodied entity rather than a disembodied essence detached from its material instantiation, "neither document, text, nor work would be considered immaterial," and our focus could turn to "how physical characteristics, verbal content, and nonverbal strategies work together to produce the object called 'text'" (Hayles 2005, 105). Videogames are not immune to textual analysis simply because they involve an active player; rather, their demand for an embodied engagement with both physical form and signifiers is itself textual.

Toward an Embodied Textuality of Videogame Play

Nico Bellic wants redemption. *Grand Theft Auto IV* makes it clear that Nico, like other immigrant antiheroes throughout the past century, came to America to start again, to leave a life of crime and violence behind. But *Grand Theft Auto IV* makes this redemption impossible for him. The videogame doesn't allow him—me—to start a business or get an honest job. Its programmed systems force Nico—force *me*—into a downward spiral of revenge that ultimately ends with the death of a person Nico loves. I can play the whole videogame again, make slightly different choices, and the outcome is different only in that a *different* person whom Nico loves dies. This is where the ultimate tragedy of *Grand Theft Auto IV* lies, where the gravity and gravitas come to rest. Within the player-and-videogame circuit of my playing *Grand Theft Auto IV*, I can make choices only within a particular, partial, and situated experience that is the coupling of myself with Nico Bellic. I can play with Nico's life, nudge it this way or that way, but my experience exists within—as part of—a system of corporeal possibilities and limitations. I don't just interpret *Grand Theft Auto IV* as a tragic story about Nico's poor life choices; I *feel it* as a tragic experience about my-and-Nico's inability to escape this system that both of us find ourselves in.

To describe the meanings that emerge in the complex, reflexive relationships between player and technology, player and character, actual and virtual worlds, an analysis of a videogame as a text requires not only a "synthesis of existing approaches, hybridizing methodologies for hybridizing media forms" as Jon Dovey and Helen Kennedy (2006, 84) call for, but an approach of syntheses, a methodology of hybridity. It requires an appreciation for the complexities and tensions and irreducibilities of the circuit of videogame play across worlds and bodies where the player and the videogame intermediate each other in reflexive loops. The videogame player exists in a doubled world, enacting and interpreting in a singular function—not a purification of player on one side and character on the other, subject on one side and object on the other, reality on one side and virtuality on the other, experienced on one side and interpreted on the other, but a play of bodies that dances across actual and virtual spaces. Videogames require an *all-at-once* notion of embodied textuality that accounts for physicality and signification, form and content, as irreducible and inseparable.

Neither immersion nor interactivity renders videogames immune to textual analysis so long as all texts are understood as requiring some embodied interaction, some splicing of material form with signifying strategies. The videogame text is located in neither the virtual world nor the actual world but in the perceptual ebb and flow of attention between the player's flesh, the videogame hardware, and audiovisual-haptic representation. It is in this circuit where the player has a corporeal engagement with the videogame that analysis must be grounded, accounting for the embodied player that constructs the videogame experience but not presuming that embodiment to be either essential or stable or presupposing the videogame experience it constructs. Through the *player-and-videogame* as a textual circuit, the videogame is perceived and experienced *by* the player-and-videogame.

Such an analytical focus demands that various worlds and bodies and the tensions between them are preserved, not resolved—brought into the light, not suppressed. With the videogame text located in the circuit, the challenge is then to focus on the back-and-forth flow across the actual and virtual worlds and bodies: the videogame text as played.

The tensions explored in this chapter point to what Dovey and Kennedy urge is a need to develop "a phenomenology of [video]games that takes account of both their textual and experimental properties" (2006, 93). The following chapters build on such an approach to comprehend videogame experience as meaningfully embodied. This approach does not separate text and user but demonstrates that they are *inseparable,* that videogame texts and the meanings they produce come into existence through recursive, dynamic, and spliced bodies—actual and virtual, flesh and machine. In this hybridity, the player's experiences are not just textual *or* just embodied but *textually embodied*. As in a hall of mirrors, when I play a videogame, I am both here and there, my own being reflected back to me even as it extends into this world through the glass. The player looking down onto the world of *Tearaway* is reflexively integrated into the world they look down on.

Videogame play is meaningful through the continuous construction and reconstruction of a cyborgian body through which the player occupies and perceives the circuit of videogame play—and through the experiences the player has by means of this body that is at once flesh, audiovisual, and hardware. If a videogame is textually experienced, that experience is perceived through the bodies that come together to mediate and determine some things about the other. This is possible only if both the human player and the videogame work are from the very start understood as interconnected—neither coming before the other but each constituting the other in ongoing processes.

To play a videogame is both to perform and to consume, both to act and to spectate, both to experience and to interpret. Videogame play is an embodied textuality. By starting with the experience of videogame play as it constitutes the player across worlds and bodies, an embodied textuality of videogames provides a way to describe the immanent meanings and carnal pleasures offered by a particular videogame: both the gravitas of *Grand Theft Auto IV* and the gravity.

2   Touching the Looking Glass

Apple has changed the videogame industry irrevocably, and the simple truth is that it has changed it without even really trying. It did it with a handheld device that has no buttons, no sticks and no ports for physical media.
—*Edge*, "An Accidental Empire" (2012)

As I step onto the bus every morning, I pull my iPhone out of my pocket and tap the "smart card" concealed in the rear of my phone case against the bus's card reader. I find a seat, plug in my headphones, and select what music to play from my phone's music-streaming application. I close the app, and the music keeps playing in the background as I flick across to a second page of apps and tap my finger on the mobile videogame with which I am currently enamored. At present, it is Michael Brough's roguelike *Imbroglio* (2016), but within a few weeks it will undoubtedly be a different game. To play *Imbroglio*, I hold the iPhone in my right hand, its weight resting in my palm and secured by my four fingers. My right thumb, meanwhile, rubs against the glass, swiping horizontally and vertically to move my character around the screen's space. *Imbroglio* is a turn-based videogame, so it doesn't require my undivided attention. The videogame has noises, but they are muted automatically by the phone in favor of the music playing from the other application. Between turns, I glance away from the device and look out the window to see if we are nearing my stop yet. Around me, without fail, other commuters are also glancing at their phones. Many are also sliding their thumb around the screen but perhaps instead to read statuses on social media sites or to read news articles. But many others, like me, are playing videogames. A businesswoman is playing a match-three puzzle game similar to *Bejeweled* (PopCap 2001) and *Candy Crush: Saga* (King 2012); an older man is playing a digital version of backgammon; two teenagers are staring intently at *Pokémon Go* (Niantic 2016), watching their avatars jog down an overhead map of the same street the bus is driving down, looking for pokémon to catch.

It was inevitable that videogames would appear on mobile phones—devices that bring together digital screens and haptic input—in one fashion or another, and they have had an ad hoc existence on mobile phones ever since Nokia began installing *Snake* on every Nokia handset since the 6110 in 1997. In Japan, videogames and social network sites have been a normal part of *keitai* culture since before the turn of the twenty-first century (see Hjorth 2003; Ito, Okabe, and Matsuda 2005; Chan 2008; Hjorth and Chan 2009). But it is the more recent rise in popularity of touchscreen-equipped "smartphones" led by Apple's iPhone alongside the parallel rise in popularity of "casual" videogames that in Western countries has most radically shaped just what contemporary "mobile videogames" are and how they function.[1]

The iPhone's designers made little effort to accommodate videogames. Apple was initially ambivalent toward the gamelike "applications" that began appearing on its App Store distribution front (*Edge* 2012, 76), and the device itself lacks any of the buttons traditionally required for videogame play. Yet videogames quickly accommodated to the iPhone, and the videogames produced for it can't help but be expressive of the ways in which mobile media is incorporated into the user's everyday life. The iPhone's increased computational power, larger screen, versatile touchscreen, and lack of any tangible buttons as well as the new distribution routes and regulatory processes offered by the App Store have fostered a broader and more eclectic ecology of videogames than any previous mobile device. Mia Consalvo notes in her study of mobile videogames' migration to the App Store that the iPhone—compared to previous mobile devices—provided mobile videogame developers with a common platform and a sizeable pre-installed base of potential customers (2012, 193). The iPhone is now home to hundreds of thousands of videogames—from social to single-player videogames, distracting to time-consuming videogames, casual to traditional videogames, publicly to privately played videogames, blockbuster to niche videogames, and corporately to independently produced videogames—each of which has to contend with the iPhone's specific technological affordances and constraints and its users' mobile practices.

As videogames incorporated the iPhone, so too have the users of mobile phones incorporated the devices into their everyday lives. Larissa Hjorth, Jean Burgess, and Ingrid Richardson claim that the iPhone "represents a distinctive moment both in the very short history of mobile media and in the much longer history of cultural technologies" (2012, 1).

Comparing this "iPhone moment" with the impact of Sony's Walkman music player several decades earlier (see du Gay, Hall, Janes, et al. 1997), Hjorth, Burgess, and Richardson claim that the iPhone "marks a historical conjuncture in which notions of identity, individualism, lifestyle, and sociality—and their relationship to technology and media practice—require rearticulation" (2012, 1). The iPhone—and by extension the countless other smartphones that have appeared in its wake, such as Samsung's Galaxy series[2]—marks the moment that mobile phones were no longer just telephones capable of other uses but multimedia devices that could afford a whole range of uses, one of which is making phone calls and another is playing videogames.

The increased number of convergent practices surrounding smartphone use sees multiple media practices incorporated into a single device. For Richardson, "the remediation of older forms of media into newer and mobile devices is a process of dynamic interplay between medium specificity and convergence, complexly embedded in the usability and intuitiveness of the interface" (2011, 421). Indeed, the iPhone's touchscreen interface and mobility are central to what numerous mobile scholars have focused on as the "hybrid" nature of such devices. As mobile media devices and "wearable screens" become increasingly ubiquitous and personalized, they penetrate and transform everyday cultural practices and spaces, "disrupting distinctions between private and public, place and space, ready-to-hand and telepresent interaction, actual and virtual environments" (Richardson 2012, 133).

I am particularly fascinated with the last of these distinctions. Chapter 1 highlighted how players themselves work to complete the virtual, actively perceiving it as discrete from the actual. Videogames played on mobile devices, however, explicitly challenge the entrenched dichotomy that sees the virtual world of the videogame—and consequentially the videogame play activity itself—as conceptually distinct from the player's actual world. Through the mobile videogame, videogame play instead becomes an "incorporated" and "nonexceptional" activity (Consalvo 2012, 193). I am acutely aware of this incorporation as I play *Imbroglio* on a small screen with a single hand, listen to my own music playing from a different app, and glance away from the screen every other moment to ensure I haven't missed my stop. The hybrid actual/virtual bodies of videogame players, as conceptualized by the previous chapter, always require hybrid actual/virtual worlds. Mobile videogames are important for how they draw attention to their own liminal state, providing an explicit opportunity to consider how all videogames evoke a sense of presence simultaneously both *in* and *at* virtual worlds.

The first section of this chapter expands on the previous chapter's discussion of the relationship between the actual and the virtual through literature that explores mobile media practices as constructing "hybrid worlds." Whereas much of this literature constructs its notion of hybrid worlds by contrasting mobile media with the "immersive" virtual worlds of nonmobile media, here I argue that the hybridity explicit to mobile videogames exists implicitly in all videogame play. The next two sections build on this argument through the close analysis of two different iPhone games: Rovio's blockbuster casual game *Angry Birds* (2009) and Action Button's niche game *Ziggurat* (2012). *Angry Birds*, as a "casual" smartphone videogame, is more exemplary of contemporary mobile videogames than the publicly played "augmented-reality" or "location-based" videogames commonly favored by mobile scholars. It demonstrates through its casualness how the mobile videogame player is able to perceive the screen space *as* a virtual world while remaining consciously aware of the presence of the actual world they are situated in and moving through. Here I am interested in how the hybrid worlds made explicit in mobile videogame play, rather than being a mere "distraction" from the player's everyday existence, demand a *co-attentiveness*, where the player pays attention to two worlds at one time. *Ziggurat* complicates this factor further as a smartphone videogame that, unlike *Imbroglio* and *Angry Birds*, impossibly desires the player's full attention to its screen space. Ultimately, this chapter demonstrates that what is specific about mobile videogames is not that they demand a hybrid, postphenomenological embodiment across worlds, whereas nonmobile videogame platforms do not, but that they draw attention to, render explicit, and provide an opportunity to unpack the hybridity of worlds and bodies that is fundamental to *all* videogame play, be it explicit or obscured. The iPhone does not flag a departure from traditional videogame play so much as it demands, to borrow from Hjorth, Burgess, and Richardson, that we *rearticulate* how we understand videogame play phenomena more broadly.

Actual/Virtual Hybridity and Copresence

As the previous chapter detailed, the relationship between the actual and the virtual is a discussion that predates videogames to account for the authenticity of depicted images in a range of media. For digital media and videogames in particular, the conceptualization of the virtual as a distinct world or reality reached popularity through the 1980s and 1990s with the rise of spatial conceptions of digitality such as virtual reality and cyberspace. Such concepts entered into public view "less through a revolutionary computer system than through a grand flourish of rhetoric" (Ryan 2001, 48), and the notion that videogames could allow us to step unchanged into different, fantastical, unreal worlds remains (and will remain for the foreseeable future) more a marketing dream than a lived reality.[3] The notion of the virtual as somehow distinct from the actual or physical is a concept deserving of scrutiny and skepticism, and the rise of pervasive and mobile digital media that we take "out there" with us into the world has seen the term *virtual* fall somewhat out of favor with media scholars. However, it remains relevant when considering the player's embodied perception of the videogame's microworld. As the previous chapter demonstrated, players seeking immersion actively make the videogame make sense as a coherent world—not suspending disbelief but actively constructing belief as they close off the fourth wall that the videogame necessarily leaves open to make engagement with it possible in the first place. Videogames do not allow players to step into virtual worlds, but they do allow players to actively perceive and interpret screen imagery, digital sounds, and haptic interfaces *as if* these things constitute an extended world of virtual bodies and objects.

Here, Martin Lister and his colleagues' etymological consideration of the virtual is useful. Looking at how the word *virtual* is used in everyday language to mean "pretty much" or "more or less" (for instance, "I have virtually finished writing this book"), they conceptualize virtuality less as an illusion to be contrasted against "the real" and more as something not yet complete ([2003] 2009, 124–125). Virtual worlds are *partial* worlds in need of the player's perceptual apparatus to bring them to life. The virtual is constructed through and dependent on the actual, but once the virtual is perceived *as if* it is a world, the actual in turn becomes dependent on it as the player's senses and identity become distributed across this actual/virtual embodiment. Videogame play is a complex interplay of actual and virtual worlds as perceived through a dually embodied player.

Mobile Media and Hybrid Worlds

Nonmobile screen devices typically draw the user's conscious attention away from their physical body and toward the virtual engagements depicted on the screen, thus obscuring the dependence of those virtual engagements on the physical. Mobile devices, however, are incorporated into the user's embodied existence as "wearable" screens (Richardson 2005). In particular, it is the mobility afforded by mobile phones—their ability to be taken along with us *out there* into our everyday lives—that highlights how such devices mediate our being-in-the-world rather than provide discrete "other" worlds and bodies to occupy. More than simply devices that are used alongside a person's day-to-day life, mobile phones *incorporate* day-to-day life and are incorporated into day-to-day life in return. Rather than devices such as videogame consoles and desktop PCs that sit in a particular place in the home, are arrived at, turned on, booted up, and used, mobile devices are always "ready to hand" in the Heideggerian sense: an unconscious reaching into my pocket and a somatically known gesture to unlock the screen are all that separates my morning commute from the virtual spaces of my smartphone.

The incorporation of mobile devices into everyday life is never neutral; our everyday life is at the same time incorporated into our mobile devices. Contemporary mobile devices commonly track our mobility through time and space with the use of location services such as GPS and vision technologies such as built-in cameras. Such components increasingly survey and draw attention to our actual, corporeal everyday life, while our everyday life is simultaneously interspliced with what is happening on our mobile screens. From these elements emerges the phenomenon of being present in both actual and virtual worlds at once, of being simultaneously here and there—a phenomenon constructively explored by others through the notion of "copresence" (Hjorth 2007, 370). We do not simply experience the world "through" the mobile device but also experience the mobile device as an incorporated aspect of our world.

In particular, it is the new modes of play afforded by mobile devices that are most often held up as being indicative of this copresence, such as location-based games (games that read the player's location in actual space via GPS and incorporate these data into the game) and augmented-reality games (games that read the actual space around the player through a camera or GPS and present it on the screen with an overlay of digital artifacts).[4] Richardson notes that location-based games "work to seamlessly combine the corporeal schematics of actual and virtual worlds as they are actively negotiated on-the-move, effectively creating a hybrid mode of being where the boundary between game and real life collapses" (2012, 143). Crucially, such location-based playful activities do not just read the player's actual, bodily location but also insist the player *engage* with these actual and often public spaces in alternative and playful ways. Jason Farman proposes that the embodiment demanded by mobile devices thus depends on "*a proprioceptive-semiotic convening of bodies, technology, and material space"* (2009, 2, emphasis added). Not coincidentally, this is also an apt way to describe the embodied textuality of videogames and suggests a broader relevance of the study of mobile media to the study of video-game play.

Casual Smartphone Games

Mobile practices—in particular mobile-videogame play—might insist that the user is present and active in two worlds at once, but the vast majority of iPhone games are neither location-based nor augmented-reality games. The most prolific—and profitable—of the videogames to appear on con-temporary smartphone platforms are *casual* mobile videogames. Casual videogames mark the proliferation of videogame genres and play styles that have emerged through the 2000s beyond those valued by a cultivated and masculine "hardcore gamer" demographic, which I historicize in chapter 6. The rise of casual videogames represents videogames becoming "normal," becoming incorporated into the everyday lives of players rather than an exceptional activity requiring a demarcated time and space. I explore and critique the notion of casual videogames in more depth in the following section, but here the vital distinction of a casual videogame is the *flex-ibility* with which it can be played. As Jesper Juul succinctly puts it, "A casual game is sufficiently flexible to be played with a hardcore time com-mitment but a hardcore game is too inflexible to be played with a casual time commitment" (2010, 10). On smartphones such as the iPhone, an incorporation of wearable and touchable screens into the user's body schema combines with casual game design's focus on a flexibility around the player's everyday life to create a powerful synergy between mobile-media platforms and casual-videogame design. Casual mobile videogames such as *Angry Birds*, *Cut the Rope* (ZeptoLab 2010), and *Candy Crush Saga* combine the smartphone's intuitive gestural interface, a low barrier of entry via digital distribution channels, the fact that many people already own and carry mobile phones with them throughout the day, and per-sistent connection to online social network sites to create a home on the smartphone for approachable and accessible casual videogames that differ dramatically from the "hardcore" videogames of console and PC platforms.

Although the casual videogames that are most representative of the videogames played on contemporary mobile devices do not incorporate the actual world as explicitly as the augmented-reality and location-based games favored by most mobile-media scholars, simply by being videogames played on a mobile device they cannot help but draw the player's attention to an actual environment and corporeal schema that nonmobile video-game platforms traditionally work to obscure (or at least work to render obscurable). The pervasive presence of mobile phones in pockets and bags as well as mobile videogames' amenability to being played for as little as a few minutes at a time (in stark contrast to most PC and console video-games, which take more than a few minutes even to commence) mean that casual mobile videogames are often played by a "body-in-waiting" in environments where the player is still paying some attention to the actual world around them even as they also pay attention to (and construct) the virtual world presented on the small, palm-size screen: sitting on a bus, waiting for a friend at a café, waiting for a commercial break to finish. Even when one is playing videogames, the engagement with a mobile phone is characterized primarily by interruption and split attention (Hjorth and Richardson 2009, 29–30; see also Carter and Björk 2015). Richardson notes insightfully that in Japan such casual games are sometimes understood as "*nagara* games" (2009, 220)—that is, games that are played *while doing something else.*

Chris Chesher (2004) explores how players are "held" in a sticky "glaze" by console videogames through their eyes on the screen and hands on the controller, but Hjorth and Richardson claim that casual-game players must avoid this "stickiness" so that they can split their attention between play and the other activities in which they are simultaneously engaged (2009, 30). This observation is in line with a similar statement made by Richard-son elsewhere that the players of mobile videogames seemingly do not wish to experience immersion in the strictest sense (2007, 210). Such claims are true insofar as a sensation of full perceptual transferal into a virtual world is not what most mobile videogames strive to achieve. Such claims risk, however, taking the actual-world presence that refuses to fade into the background in the playing of mobile videogames and privileging it to the extent that the construction of the virtual world through mobile video-games becomes a trivial distraction. Much of the literature that examines the hybrid embodiment revealed through mobile-phone practices do so by contrasting these "mobile" and "public" devices with "fixed" and "private" nonmobile devices such as desktop computers and dedicated videogame consoles. Most explicitly, Adriana de Souza e Silva depends on a "traditional distinction between physical and digital spaces" in order to conceptualize the hybrid space of mobile devices, going so far as to call desktop com-puters "static interfaces" that the user needs to be stationary to "enter" (2006, 264, 268). But as the next chapter explores in detail, the desktop-computer user does not sit "stationary" in order to "enter" the internet or a videogame, as de Souza e Silva claims in order to distinguish the mobility of mobile platforms. The desktop-computer user still engages bodily with a physical interface by moving through actual space. Although analyses of mobile devices have allowed constructive insights into the hybridity of actual/virtual worlds, they often simplify how nonmobile technologies are engaged with, ultimately polarizing the actual and virtual rather than blending them.

What is distinctive about videogames played on mobile devices is not that they hybridize actual and virtual spaces and bodies where previous technologies easily divided them but rather that they demonstrate that such a clear division never truly existed. Mobile videogames render explicit the splicing of perception across actual and virtual worlds and bodies that has always been central to the experience of videogame play. In videogames made for mobile devices, the player's attention is held in part by components of the hybrid world of play that nonmobile videogame platforms, in cooperation with their players, typically work to obscure. As Hjorth and Richardson rightly note, the actual world around the mobile-videogame player is ever present, and the player must be able to disconnect from the hybrid world of play at any moment. But that does not mean that the virtual world of mobile videogames is less important to the mobile player, that it is "merely" a distraction. I might not stop paying attention to the actual world while playing *Imbroglio*, but my attention is *also* held by the mobile screen.

Indeed, although mobile devices are most commonly theorized as devices that we take out with us into public spaces, they are also highly private, with one device typically being owned and used by a single owner. We use *our* phone on the bus, in the café, in bed, on the couch, on the toilet. We customize them with wallpapers and color cases and keychains, and we access them with personalized passcodes, gestures, or sometimes even with our individualized fingerprint. Further, unlike our televisions and computer screens, our mobile screens are typically too small for observers to watch easily,[5] and as Dean Chan shows in his study of Japanese mobile gaming, mobile videogames are commonly played in the home, just like their non-mobile counterparts (2008, 23). Instead of an attention/distraction dichotomy between fixed and mobile platforms, the explicitly hybrid worlds of mobile videogames demand an explicitly hybrid form of attention, where the player is paying attention to two worlds at one time. By complicating notions of distraction and attention in mobile videogames, we can better understand how the hybrid embodiment made explicit by mobile videogames is implicitly fundamental to all videogame play.

Paying Attention to *Angry Birds*

Since the first game launched with 63 levels in 2009, *Angry Birds* (see figure 2.1) has ballooned into a highly commercially successful and well-recognized videogame franchise. Although popularity is never necessarily synonymous with the quality of a creative work, the fact that *Angry Birds* has been able to hold the attention of so many players who feel no temptation to play a nonmobile videogame is worth exploring. *Angry Birds* is a quintessential casual smartphone game, one that is expressive of the iPhone as a videogame platform and of the videogame practices that surround mobile devices. A close look at *Angry Birds* reveals a complex set of practices and forms of attention shaped by particular design decisions. Unlike location-based or augmented-reality games, with their partial dependency on public spaces and mobility, *Angry Birds* combines a traditional videogame dependency on audiovisual design with intuitive touchscreen controls in a way that is representative of contemporary mobile videogames. As a casual smartphone game, *Angry Birds* disrupts stable conceptualizations of public/private, presence/absence, distraction/attention, and actual/virtual to show that hybrid worlds are not created as one world distracts the player from the other world but as the player's attention is held by two worlds simultaneously.

Figure 2.1
Rovio's *Angry Birds* (2009).

Angry Birds combines simple mimetic controls with the spectacle of simulated physics, a vibrant yet sterile visual aesthetic, and a dose of luck. I begin with a team of cartoon birds of a variety of shapes and color, queued on the left of the screen beside a giant slingshot. I am to send them crashing into the building-block forts to the right of the screen, creating spectacular collapses and destroying the snorting green pigs residing therein. Holding the iPhone in a landscape orientation with my right hand, I press my left index finger on the bird in the slingshot and slide down and to the left to pull back the slingshot. As with a real slingshot, the distance I pull the band back and the precise angle at which I pull determines the velocity and angle of the shot. I then release my finger from the screen, and the slingshot fires the bird toward the fortress with a squawking battle cry. The virtual camera zooms out as my bird flies, showing me the full trajectory of my chosen flight from slingshot to fort. These forts are made out of precariously balanced blocks of different shapes and materials (commonly glass, wood, and stone), and they often have weak points (such as a glass crossbeam in an otherwise stone building). If I can locate and accurately hit these points, I can bring the entire structure crashing down with a single bird. Regardless of where my bird hits, damage dominoes outward from where the bird makes contact with the structure, and I observe as my small input is amplified into massive damage. Depending on the type of bird fired, a second tap of the screen while the bird is in midflight will execute a special ability, such as splitting the bird into three smaller birds, increasing the velocity of the attack, or dropping an explosive egg. From these two simple interactions (firing the bird, using their special skill), countless different outcomes are possible from each bird on every stage. The ultimate goal of each stage is to destroy all the pigs on that stage (either by hitting them directly or by making the structures collapse on them) with my finite number of birds. A scoring system rewards me with points for each block and pig destroyed and with major bonus points for each bird left unused at the end of a stage.

Casual Games as Flexible, Mimetic, and Polished

Angry Birds marries the affordances of mobile media as incorporated into the user's everyday life with the typically desired experiences of casual videogame players. Juul (writing at a time when casual games were more predominately represented by videogames played in a PC web browser or on the Nintendo Wii console) traces several key features common across casual videogames: inoffensive and "nice" fiction; usability through an intuitive or mimetic interface; interruptibility; a balanced difficulty; and an excessive amount of audiovisual feedback (2010, 30–55). Each of these elements works to capture the player's attention quickly but, importantly, just as quickly allows the player to redirect attention away from the videogame.

However, the very term *casual* often obscures (and just as often genders) both the quality and extent of labor a player puts into a casual videogame (Taylor 2012, 241). The core audience of videogame players—along with critics, academics, and the developers of more traditional videogames— have historically dismissed casual videogames on mobile phones and social media as mere distractions that lack both the thematic and mechanical complexity of more traditional console and PC videogames. However, as Juul's extensive interviews demonstrate, casual-videogame players regularly devote just as much time and attention to the videogames they play as noncasual-videogame players devote to more traditional videogames, but that time and attention are commonly interspersed across shorter, more frequent play sessions (2010, 14). Whereas a player of a console videogame might sit and play one videogame uninterrupted for an hour, a player of *Angry Birds* is more likely to play for a total time of an hour across various five-minute sessions throughout a day. Significantly, then, a casual videogame does not simply offer an "easier" or "shallower" experience than a traditional videogame but an experience that is more flexible with the player's time. Just as a casual employee may still work extensive hours but on a more flexible roster, a player of casual videogames may play videogames with as much commitment as a player of noncasual videogames but do so more flexibly in a way that is more easily incorporated into their daily life.

Although Juul does not account for the rising trend of casual smartphone games, which was only nascent at the time he wrote *A Casual Revolution* (2010), videogames such as *Angry Birds* exemplify the attributes of casual games and the flexible forms of attention that he observes. It is worth looking in particular at the three features of interruptibility, usability, and polish as they are exemplified in *Angry Birds* to highlight how casual smartphone games demand forms of attention that account for both the actual and the virtual worlds of play as a hybrid whole.

By "interruptibility," Juul means that the player of a casual videogame can be interrupted with little consequence. Whereas many traditional console or desktop videogames depend on a prolonged commitment of time and attention from the player and on reaching a certain checkpoint before progress can be saved, casual videogames typically allow both brief and prolonged engagements. In *Angry Birds*, one level can often be completed in a matter of minutes, and, as in the vast majority of iPhone videogames, progress is saved constantly and automatically. If at any point I leave the application (to answer a phone call, to check a social media notification, to get off a bus, to continue watching a television show after a commercial break), I can come back later and start at the same level I left off from. During play, too, *Angry Birds* does not require my undivided attention. Once the bird is fired, I am free to look away from the screen for as long as I need to, and the game can continue unheeded. There is no time constraint on how quickly the structures must be destroyed. I am able to approach *Angry Birds* as something that can be put aside at a moment's notice through how it incorporates itself into my everyday life, as opposed to most console or desktop videogames, which more stubbornly demand I turn both my body and my attention toward the platform in a particular, concentrated manner.

That *Angry Birds*, like most casual smartphone videogames, can be just "picked up and played" is fostered not just by the swiftness with which the videogame both loads and closes again but also by the usability and intuitiveness of its interface, which must be easily understood by a player not willing to commit dedicated time to learning how to play. Whereas noncasual videogames commonly demand intricate and habitualized comprehension of complex input devices (explored in detail through the notion of "embodied literacy" in the next chapter), *Angry Birds* is successful with a broader audience through the immediate and tactile gratification it offers. The metaphor of using a slingshot to fling a bird across the screen with just enough accuracy to destroy a part of a structure requires no previous experience or specialist knowledge of videogames, just a basic understanding of how the iPhone's touchscreen functions and an intuitive comprehension of gravity. Just as I can throw a ball to another person more or less consistently without knowing the exact force behind my arm's movement, after only a little practice I can aim and lob my angry birds at the pig fortress with an unconscious knowledge of what trajectory they will take. The interface afforded by the touchscreen highlights what Juul calls "mimetic interfaces," which are a common feature of casual videogames (2010, 103). Juul is referring to those input devices that ask the player to imitate the actions being asked of their avatar on (or inferred by) the screen. Specifically, Juul is thinking of input devices such as Nintendo's Wii-mote, which asks players to swing their arms as though they are "actually" swinging a tennis racquet, or plastic musical instruments for videogames such as *Guitar Hero* (Harmonix 2005) or *Rock Band* (Harmonix 2007) that ask the player to imitate the playing of an "actual" instrument.

Such mimetic interfaces "are a backlash against [complex] and counter-intuitive game controllers" (Juul 2010, 108). A traditional gamepad controller, with all its buttons and thumbsticks and triggers, offers a competent player a more detailed and focused ability to navigate a virtual world, but it does not suggest a way to be played to a player unexperienced with such a device—it suggests a gestural language to be learned. Mimetic interfaces, in contrast, do not need to be learned prior to playing—or rather, the bodily habits they demand more closely align to those already learned through the player's everyday existence (swinging a tennis racquet, navigating a smartphone's touchscreen). They encourage experimentation and "playing around with" rather than optimal control.[6] Juul does not mention haptic screen devices such as the iPhone, but the inputs asked of a videogame such as *Angry Birds* still function in a mimetic manner, with the player's thumb used to "actually" pull back the elastic band of the virtual, bird-armed slingshot. That is not to say, though, that the iPhone's screen is inherently mimetic because many successful iPhone videogames do not use mimetic controls, such as *Ziggurat*, discussed later in this chapter. But the most popular and widespread casual iPhones games typically do deploy mimetic controls through either the touchscreen (*Fruit Ninja* [Halfbrick 2010], *Cut the Rope*, *Paper Toss* [Backflip 2009]) or the gyroscope (*Real Racing* [Firemint 2009], *Doodle Jump* [Lima Sky 2009]).

Mimetic interfaces draw explicit attention *to* the actual world and the player's positionality. That is not to say that the player's body is "more" incorporated into mimetic input devices than into traditional controllers—each demands a specific incorporation of the player—but that mimetic devices draw attention to the playing body incorporated in the play circuit in contrast to how traditional input devices work to draw attention *away from* the playing body. We see this distinction in *Angry Birds*, where the player "actually" pulls back and fires the slingshot with their real finger. This minimized action of a single finger does not imitate the actual bodily exertion required to fire a giant slingshot, but there is a clear, synonymous relationship between the player's gestures and the response from the slingshot. Graeme Kirkpatrick notes that when we use traditional gamepad controllers, the work of our out-of-sight hands is central to our connection with the videogame even as we might not consciously be aware of them (2009, 135). iPhone videogames complicate this connection in fascinating ways in that the player's configurative hands are not out of sight. The player's finger instead melds with and obscures the screen's glass by directly touching it, smearing fingerprints across it, fusing the work of the hands and the work of the eyes in a much more literal version of

Chesher's videogame glaze. *Angry Birds* draws explicit attention to the coming together of the player's body in actual space and the represented virtual space of the screen.

Yet the satisfaction offered by *Angry Birds*, like that offered by most casual videogames—indeed, practically all videogames—is heavily dependent on its audiovisuality, despite its mimetic controls drawing the player's attention to the actual bodies and devices that constitute its playing. Juul notes that casual videogames typically provide an "excessive amount of positive feedback in response [to the] player's actions" (2010, 45). He calls this positive feedback "juiciness," and it is closely aligned to what Steve Swink calls the polished element of how a videogame feels, referring to "any effect that artificially enhances interaction without changing the underlying simulation … [adding] appeal and [emphasizing] the physical nature of interactions" (2009, 5). The audiovisual design of *Angry Birds* gives the game a sense of physicality. When I draw the slingshot back, it makes a rubbery, stretchy noise, giving me a synaesthesic sensation of tension and tautness under my finger. The birds feel weighty as I watch them fly through the air on a slow parabola and hear them hit the structures with a satisfying "thud." I make a small input (dragging a finger), and the videogame offers the satisfaction of watching entire towers fall down via simulated physics, amplifying my input with excessive feedback. Thus, although the usability afforded by *Angry Bird*'s mimetic controls retains my attention in the actual world and the use of my actual body in ways that nonmobile videogames often downplay, the pleasure offered by *Angry Birds* also depends on my attention to the virtual world, to the audiovisual design that gives it a physicality distinct from but tied to the actual world. My attention is kept in player space, but it is also drawn by the audiovisual aspects that constitute the virtual space. In *Angry Birds*, the virtual world and the actual world *together* create the videogame experience.

Attentive Play Styles of Casual Games

The notion that the audiovisuality of *Angry Birds* is significant to the player's experience disrupts the notion that mobile videogames draw the player's attention *away* from the virtual world of the screen and toward the actual world of their day-to-day life. It suggests instead that both actual and virtual worlds occupy the player's attention simultaneously. However, despite being easy to "pick up and play" and just as easy to put down again, *Angry Birds* also has a scoring system that affords more committed, attentive play styles commonly associated with nonmobile and noncasual play. After each level, the player is given a rating out of three stars, based on how many points they scored. Points are awarded for causing massive amounts of destruction to the structures, and, crucially, large amounts of bonus points are awarded for the number of birds left unused at the end of a stage. In other words, bonus points are awarded for destroying all the pigs with the least number of birds possible. Many levels' three-star rating requires the player to find the absolutely perfect elevation and velocity that will completely destroy the pigs' fortress with a single bird. A desire to perfect the videogame and to compete against other players for high scores leads many players to play *Angry Birds* for extended, uninterrupted periods—not just in moments of public waiting but also during time sitting on the couch or in bed at home. As others have observed among other players (Rogers 2012; Thompson 2013), when I play *Angry Birds* I regularly find myself firing a bird, tapping the pause button, and pressing the "restart level" button in quick succession because I am immediately certain that I have fired with the wrong velocity to achieve a perfect game—just as I immediately know in my body when I have thrown a ball wide.[7] Casual smartphone videogames *can* be played by a body moving through the public world, but they just as often are engaged with in the same way that noncasual, nonmobile videogames are engaged with: privately and devoutly.

Angry Birds, like many mobile videogames, sits at the intersection of these tensions between casual and noncasual as well as between public and private play. The popularity of this focused, perfection-driven mode of playing *Angry Birds* is perhaps best observed in the evolution of the franchise's aiming system across the series. The original *Angry Birds*, released in 2009, offered no assistance to the player's aiming; the player simply had to pull back and hope they had aimed in roughly the right direction. After the first bird was fired, though, its trajectory would stay dotted through the air, and the player could use this line to better estimate the second shot. As the series progressed, different titles would show the first part of the trajectory ahead of the bird as the player pulled back, until, in *Angry Birds: Star Wars*, released in 2012 (Rovio Entertainment), the entire trajectory is dotted out before the player releases the bird, allowing pinpoint accuracy (see figures 2.2 and 2.3). Such an addition does not make the later games easier but, rather, allows the games to offer challenges requiring increasingly accurate shots.[8]

Angry Birds, as a quintessential casual mobile videogame, is not simply a distraction for the player but affords modes of play that demand an acute attentiveness to the virtual world and what is happening on the screen, even as the player remains aware of their corporeal being (the thumb obscuring the screen) and the actual world around them (their train approaching the

Figure 2.2
Angry Birds (Rovio 2009). Note the dotted trajectory of the previously fired bird and the complete lack of aiming assistance for the bird currently being aimed.

station, the television show they are watching). *Angry Birds* suggests that mobile casual games are not distractions but rather hold players' attention across both worlds for extended periods of time. Not distraction but *co-attentiveness* is indicative of how mobile videogame players engage with the hybrid worlds of mobile play. Hybrid worlds are not created in the way one world distracts us from another *but in the way the player's attention is held by two worlds simultaneously*. All videogame forms flicker; they all draw attention toward, through, and away from the hybridity of the worlds and bodies on which they all depend. What is special about mobile videogames is not that they create hybrid worlds (all videogames do this), but how they draw the player's explicit attention both toward and away from the hybridity of the worlds they create simultaneously.

Being Distracted by *Ziggurat*

Action Button's niche but critically successful videogame *Ziggurat* (2012; see figure 2.4) is both an antithesis of and direct response to *Angry Birds*. Whereas each *Angry Birds* title has an installed user base in the tens of millions, *Ziggurat* has at the time of writing less than ten thousand players

Figure 2.3
Angry Birds: Star Wars (Rovio 2012). Note the aiming assistance for the bird currently being aimed, showing the player exactly where this bird will fly.

on its Game Center leaderboards. Whereas *Angry Birds* is instantly inviting with its initially low difficulty and inoffensive visual aesthetics, *Ziggurat* is unforgivingly obtuse from the very start and presented in a gritty retro aesthetic of pixel visuals and discordant guitars. Whereas *Angry Birds* is an accessible casual game that also affords noncasual, attentive play styles, *Ziggurat* is a decidedly noncasual videogame that, due to its design for the iPhone, must still conform to certain tenets of mobile casual design. Most importantly, it is able to be played in short bursts to accommodate the constant pressures of the player's actual life. Although the earlier analysis of noncasual *Angry Birds* play shows that mobile casual games demand our attention to their screens, as do all videogames, looking at *Ziggurat* demonstrates with more nuance what actually distinguishes the co-attentiveness of mobile videogames from the forms of attention that allow an active and consensual sense of immersion on more traditional platforms.

Ziggurat has a conceptual heritage in *Angry Birds*. In 2012, when *Ziggurat* was released, designer Tim Rogers (quoted in the previous chapter for his analysis of *Mother 2* [Ape and HAL Laboratory 1994]), described on videogame journalism outlet *Kotaku* how his initial idea for *Ziggurat* came to him

Figure 2.4
Action Button's *Ziggurat* (2012).

when he played *Angry Birds* for the first time and felt frustrated by the sluggish, one-bird-at-a-time pace:

I wanted a "driving range." I wanted stuff to be falling down constantly, and I'm over here at this crazy distance, slinging birds at it. I imagined a game wherein a hero is against a wall at the end of a long tunnel. Enemies are coming at him. Maybe it looks like *Raiders of the Lost Ark*. Maybe they're bats. Yeah, that's good: bats. That way they can be at the top or bottom or middle of the corridor, and flapping and flopping in irregular paths. So you use slingshot controls to fire these for-some-reason-very-slow-moving bullets at these bats. You have to sit there and watch the bullets approach the targets. You have no limit to bullets you can shoot. Depending on your firing angle, you can sacrifice speed for accuracy. Speed knocks the bats back further. You're just—keeping a bunch of bats back. Okay—there it is. That's a video game. I put it into the idea vault. (Rogers 2012)

A year later Rogers saw someone playing *Angry Birds* on the train in the decidedly noncasual way described earlier: "he flung a bird; he let it fly for two seconds; he made a little sound in his nose; he tapped 'pause'; he tapped 'reset'" (Rogers 2012). That people wanted to play *Angry Birds* in an attentive way led Rogers to design *Ziggurat*.

In *Ziggurat*, I take on the role of the last human alive, standing atop a ziggurat—a massive, terraced pyramid— as the alien robots that killed everyone else in the world close in to end the human race. Different players approach the videogame's interface in different manners, but when I play,

Figure 2.5
Holding my iPhone while I play *Ziggurat* (Action Button 2012). I hold my phone in
my left hand and support its weight with my right hand's index finger. My right
hand's thumb slides back and forward to aim and fire the laser cannon.

I hold the iPhone in a landscape position with my left hand, locking the
other side of the phone between the base of my right hand's thumb and
index finger (see figure 2.5). Much like *Angry Birds*, *Ziggurat* is about slinging projectiles on arcs. Instead of the bats that Rogers first envisioned, an
endless army of robots must be confronted. Whereas *Angry Birds* allows me
to take an indefinite amount of time between each shot, in *Ziggurat* I must
fire constantly to manage the endless horde closing in from both sides of
the screen. To fire the laser gun, I slide my right thumb across the bottom
of the screen horizontally to determine the elevation of each shot. Holding
my thumb down on the far left-hand side of the screen has my character
(standing atop the ziggurat in the center of the screen) aim down the left
slope. As I slide my thumb to the right, the character raises the rifle higher
into the air until my thumb passes halfway across the screen, at which
point the character turns around and aims down the right-hand slope. In
place of a mimetic "pulling back" input to control the power behind each
shot, *Ziggurat* requires me to press on the screen to start charging the shot,
and the rifle fires once I release.[9] This requirement complicates aiming
because once I press my thumb to the screen, the gun starts charging, and
I must have the precise shot lined up in time to fire at precisely the angle
I intend. Complicating things further, the amount of charge behind each
shot will also determine the velocity with which it is fired. A fully powered

shot will be sent outward with great force, but a less-charged shot will drop down on a much sharper angle; a simple tap of the screen will dribble a shot that falls from the gun to my character's feet. The shot can be charged for as long as I wish, but, crucially, it is fully charged for only a split second before it depletes to a less-powerful stage. If I want to fire a fully charged shot, I must aim (slide my thumb) and fire (release my thumb from the screen) with a very precise rhythm, a steady melody of slide-release, slide-release, slide-release. While I am aiming and firing, the enemy robots approach up the sides of the ziggurat in tall jumps, and their heads grow and shrink to the same beat as my charged shots. Hitting a large-headed enemy with a fully charged shot will cause an explosion that will wipe all the enemies from the screen at once. Where *Angry Birds* is about "playing around" with one possible set of parabolas (the trajectory of the birds) to see what happens, *Ziggurat* is about pinpoint accuracy and paying careful attention to the interactions of a range of rhythms and parabolas at once: the gun's elevation, the shot's velocity, the size of the enemies' heads, the trajectory of the enemies' jumps. If a single enemy or even one of the slow laser beams the enemies fire at the playable character reaches the top of the ziggurat, the game is instantly over.

Inflexible Mobile Play

Most interesting, *Ziggurat* has no pause button. The game does not offer a running commentary of my score, only telling me after I die how many of the robots I destroyed. *Ziggurat* is not intended to be played while also doing other things; it desires my full attention for the duration of a single play session. Unlike when I'm playing *Imbroglio* or *Angry Birds*, if I reach my bus stop while halfway through a session of *Ziggurat*, my only option is to physically force my phone into sleep mode and hope to regain my rhythm once I have an opportunity to play again. Despite being a mobile videogame designed for mobile play (a touchscreen-specific interface and short game sessions only ever a few minutes long), *Ziggurat* is less interruptible than *Angry Birds*. Whereas *Angry Birds* does not have to be played in an attentive, noncasual way, that is the only way to play *Ziggurat*. A brief tutorial the first time I load the videogame teaches me how the firing interface works, but it is up to me to figure out for myself the complex, interlocking systems of charging of the gun, the meaning of the enemies' growing/shrinking heads, and the many extra components that the game adds as I progress. Such systems can be figured out only through extensive play—the player must gain a "feel" for them. This is in stark opposition to the instant accessibility and gratification of *Angry Birds*.

The fictional framing of alien robots closing in to kill the last human alive is also more aligned with the violent shooters of home consoles than the cartoon characters of most iPhone games. Despite both their genocidal and suicidal tendencies, the protagonist poultry of *Angry Birds* never seem less than comical in their endeavors. *Ziggurat*, meanwhile, works to evoke a sense of helplessness and urgency, more akin to early arcade videogames such as *Space Invaders* (Taito 1978) and *Missile Command* (Atari 1980). In *Ziggurat*, I will eventually die, and humanity will fall; my only solace is how many of the robots I take down with me. *Ziggurat's* background music is off-putting and discordant, including a high-pitch note that plays for an extended period of time. However, the audio of the game also offers key signals to the player, such as when particularly fast enemies are about to attack. This feature is significant because when playing in public, many players will either play without sound or while listening to their own music, so *Ziggurat* puts these players at a disadvantage.

Immersion as Distraction

Yet, despite all of these noncasual elements, *Ziggurat* is nonetheless a mobile videogame, created specifically with the forms of attention the iPhone affords in mind. Even if *Ziggurat* demands the player to be fully attentive to its screen space, it is still a videogame on a mobile device that will inevitably often be played by a body-in-waiting, by a player who will be explicitly aware of their actual surroundings and their actual body as it partially obscures the screen. Like *Angry Birds*, *Ziggurat* demands that the player pay attention to *both* worlds—it demands a co-attentiveness.

However, this stubborn prerequisite for co-attentiveness makes *Ziggurat* play all the more susceptible to the distraction that many mobile scholars mark as definitive of mobile videogame play. Hjorth and Richardson provide a description of distraction in relation to the telepresence offered by mobile devices: "[The term *distraction*] aptly describes how our attention becomes divided when we speak on the phone, send or receive a text message, or play a game on the mobile. It suggests that the locus of our perception is divided between the 'here' and 'there,' such that we can *know* different times and spaces simultaneously, an effect that shifts the boundaries of what immediacy is, and how it is defined and experienced" (2009, 30.) However, the *Ziggurat* player's or the noncasual *Angry Birds* player's attention is not necessarily "divided" between the actual and virtual worlds. Following Michael Arnold's (2003) observations, the player has to be Janus-faced—paradoxically fully attentive to both worlds at the same time. This is less a "division" of attention and more an amalgam of attentions.

The *Ziggurat* player cannot *not* be aware of both worlds: their actual fingers are touching the screen, obscuring the images that constitute the virtual world. Further, whereas a gamepad or keyboard suggests specific ways to be grasped by the hands, there is no set way to hold the iPhone to play *Ziggurat*. I prefer to hold my phone in such a way as to keep my right thumb free to access the whole screen, but other players I have conversed with hold the phone firmly in their right hand and use their left index finger to aim. Others hold the phone like a traditional gamepad controller and use each thumb to cover each slope. These different ways that the iPhone and *Ziggurat* can be incorporated into a player's body schema makes the player consciously aware of the role of their body in the circuit of playing *Ziggurat* in a way that console and PC videogames work to obscure by keeping the work of the hands out of sight. The *Ziggurat* player also has to be attentive to the world happening around them while they pay attention to (and construct) the world through the screen (the sun setting, the moon exploding, the narrative framing the action). Regardless of how intently focused I am on *Ziggurat*'s apocalypse, I do not want to miss my bus stop.

This is not to say that distraction is not a factor in *Ziggurat*. On the contrary, it is the demand for co-attentiveness that makes distraction all the more likely. Distraction is not a prerequisite of mobile videogame play so much as it is an inevitable consequence. Distraction is a break in the circuit. It is when one of the worlds—be it the actual or the virtual world—absorbs too much of the player's attention and breaks the co-attentive balance demanded by the play of bodies. Perhaps I am too attentive to the virtual world of *Ziggurat*, and I miss my bus stop; perhaps I am too attentive to the fact that my bus stop is approaching and get hit by an incoming projectile. Each occurs because my co-attentiveness to the hybrid world becomes unbalanced. Distraction is not paying attention to both worlds; it is when so much of my attention is held by one component of the hybrid world of play that the necessary and fundamental contribution of the other world is consciously obscured even as it continues unconsciously to contribute to the play experience. To be immersed *is* to be distracted. What distinguishes mobile play from that of more traditional videogame platforms is not a necessity for mobile videogames to be "merely" distractions—traditional videogames try very hard to distract us from our actual body and surroundings in their quest to have us feel a sense of immersion—but a demand for a precarious balance of co-attentiveness where the player is fully aware of the entire hybrid assemblage across actual/virtual worlds and bodies that all videogames demand.

The explicit ways in which mobile media practices hybridize the actual and the virtual through copresence provides an opportunity to account for how players do not simply step into the virtual worlds of videogames but instead actively construct virtual worlds through engaging with the particular images, sounds, and devices of different videogames. Much of the literature that addresses the hybrid worlds of mobile media does so in direct contrast to the supposedly "inert" bodies demanded of nonmobile media, but *Angry Birds* and *Ziggurat* complicate this distinction to show instead that the actual/virtual hybridity of mobile devices is not in contrast to the "fixed" devices of the home. Mobile videogames render explicit through their demand for co-attentiveness the full actual/virtual circuit that all videogames rely on but that traditional videogames work to obscure in their desire to have players focus their attention on the virtual world they construct through sight, sound, and touch. Just as the mobile videogame player is aware of the worlds and bodies that construct the player-and-videogame, we must account for how this coupling is assembled in those videogame experiences where the player themself works hard to push their awareness of it into the background.

3   With Thumbs in Mind

There's that world space over there, this one over here, and we traverse the wired gap with motions that make us nonetheless feel in a balanced extending touch with things.

—David Sudnow, *Pilgrim in the Microworld* (1983)

My housemate does not often play console videogames, but a childhood memory was triggered when they saw the copy of *Crash Bandicoot* (Naughty Dog 1996) on my shelf and insisted on playing. The intervening decades had not been kind to their muscle memory. They stumbled their way through the early levels, inexpertly jabbing at the PlayStation gamepad's directional buttons to move the titular character Crash to the left, then forward, then to the left again in a stop–start zigzag trajectory instead of the clear, soft curve of the jungle path they were meant to be following. They shuffled Crash to the edge of a bottomless chasm, looked down at the Play-Station gamepad in their hands (figure 3.1), then pressed X with their right thumb to jump before quickly holding down the Up arrow with their left thumb to move Crash—already reaching the apex of his jump—forward. Over the next chasm, a flying enemy drifted back and forward, blocking Crash's way. What the player must do here, I explained to my housemate, is move forward, then jump while continuing to move forward, then press Square while jumping forward to do a spin attack through the enemy so as not to lose forward momentum. These directions sounded matter of fact to me, but my housemate looked back with trepidation at their hands wrapped around the PlayStation gamepad in their lap, as though they were unsure how to connect my instructions to the buttons available to their hands. Both the X and the Square buttons (along with the O and Triangle buttons) are on the right-hand side of the controller, all requiring the pressure of the player's right thumb. My housemate backed Crash up and took a running leap with X, but before their thumb could travel the distance from

Figure 3.1
The DualShock 4, the gamepad input device used for the PlayStation 4, 2013.

X to Square, Crash had already smashed into the enemy and fallen to his death. How, my housemate asked, were they to press Square soon enough while still holding down X with the same thumb?

It was a good question. Despite contorting my thumbs effortlessly and unconsciously into such configurations during videogame play for more than three decades, I did not have an answer. I picked up a second, unused gamepad from the floor and pretended to play the videogame. Instead of allowing my eyes and senses to be drawn into the virtual world on the television screen, I looked directly at the gamepad and fingers in my lap and focused on the minute movements and twitches of my thumbs and fingers. I noticed how my right thumb sat across the action buttons: diagonally, with the tip of my thumb sitting at ten o'clock and its base joint at four o'clock. From here, when I imagined myself jumping and swirling as Crash, I noticed with some fascination that I did not shift my entire thumb to press the different action buttons separately, but instead my thumb *rolled*, down and then to the left, so that I first pressed X with the middle of my thumb to jump and then, without letting go of X, rolled my thumb to the side to push down Square a moment later with the top of my thumb, triggering the spin attack in midair. When I first explained to my housemate how to approach this challenge, I thought I "knew" what to do: jump and spin. Looking at my hands as I reenacted the scene, however, it became apparent that "I" consciously did not know what to do at all. The performance was somatic, proprioceptive. The knowledge was in my hands.

To intend toward the virtual world of a videogame, the player must move their body in a manner that the videogame hardware and software are primed to comprehend. "Input devices" are the translator through which the videogame comprehends the player. Input devices read the continuous movements of the player's body through space and translate this move-ment into digital code readable by the videogame software. For instance, the movement of a thumb downward might push on a button and alter the digital signal "Button = 0" to "Button = 1" and, in doing so, trigger some action by the videogame. But as I realized when watching my hands, most videogame play requires gestures more complex than simply trigger-ing a single input. Most input devices allow simultaneous inputs to produce more complex digital outputs, and, as a consequence, videogame players must habitualize different ways of moving their bodies at the videogame. Through the PlayStation gamepad, the close proximity of buttons allows me to roll my thumb against X and then Square so that Crash Bandicoot jumps and then spins a split-second later. The input device is the tether, the umbilical through which I am capable of poking the virtual world, the virtual's membrane in the realm of the actual, and a demand for bodies that move in particular, learned ways.

This chapter looks at how input devices become incorporated by playing bodies and how this incorporation of the input device is a fundamental aspect of experiencing the videogame. If videogames, as the previous chap-ters have argued, are an embodied textuality that are meaningful through the player's perception and embodiment of them as lived experiences across worlds, then they require a sort of *embodied literacy* where the player learns *how* to perceive and embody the videogame through particular gestures trained by particular input devices. In other words, a videogame demands a competency before it reveals its qualities, but that competency is itself not apolitical. The competencies demanded by videogames, this chapter dem-onstrates, are both fundamental to their expressive ability and exclusionary of anyone not able to obtain those competencies.

To incorporate a tool such as an input device into a body schema is to learn how to use that tool through repeated use. Following Henri Lefeb-vre, this as a form of *dressage*, of being "broken in," not unlike a dog or

a horse (2004, 39). Through repetition, dressage imbues in our self seemingly automatic or natural skills and movements as the very foundation
of social being. That is, social being has an embodied foundation in the
ritualized repetitions of everyday life—something Pierre Bourdieu (1984)
similarly identifies as the construction of our habitus. We are disposed by
society to hold our bodies in certain ways, and in so doing we habitualize
our selves. This dressage of the human body by everyday life is typically
invisible to conscious thought; it is of the body. Thus, the ways bodies are
"broken in" by habitus come to be seen as natural because "something
passes as *natural* precisely when it conforms perfectly without apparent
effort to accepted models, to the habits valorized by a tradition" (Lefebvre
2004, 38–39, original emphasis). Accents, performances of gender, which
side of the road we drive on, the direction we turn a bottle cap to loosen
it, the hand we instinctively put forward for a stranger to shake are learned
bodily actions naturalized and ritualized through repetition. Actions that
seem natural within a particular society—including the use of tools—are
taught through a repetition of use until they *become normal*. We "get a feel"
for them.

The cultural ramifications of habitus are already well established by gender theorists such as Iris Marion Young in her treatise on "throwing like
a girl" (1980, 2005b). The body is enculturated by habits, Young points
out in another essay: "Contexts of discourse and interaction position
persons in systems of evaluation and expectations which often implicate
their embodied being" (2005a, 17). Just who possesses the embodied literacies most videogames require has been historically demarcated along
gendered lines. As chapter 6 explores in more detail, because young men
were dominantly targeted by videogames throughout the last half of the
twentieth century, it is young men who are more likely than not to have
obtained the competency required to handle a gamepad or use the complex keyboard-and-mouse configuration needed to play most 3D videogames on a desktop computer. More accurately, the configurations required
by gamepads and by a keyboard and mouse have become more complex
alongside a maturing male audience implicated to already have some competency of these devices. It is crucial, then, in considering the embodied
literacies demanded of videogame experience to remember that such literacies are not possessed naturally but are entangled in cultural and historic
contexts.

The embodied literacy demanded of videogame players is thus two
things: a fundamental conduit through which the videogame reveals its
experiences to the competent player and the impassable wall by which

the incompetent player is excluded. To facilitate an appreciation of how a player becomes habitualized or "literate" in a videogame input device and what exactly their hands are doing down in their lap, this chapter first provides a broad introduction to how bodies take up tools generally and input devices specifically through a repetition of actions. These repeated actions habitualize the tool so that ultimately we do not think of the tool *as* a tool but as an incorporated aspect of our body schema: "the global awareness of my posture in the inter-sensory world" (Merleau-Ponty 2012, 102). The standardization of the QWERTY keyboard over the past 150 years provides here an exemplar of how this taking up of tools by the body is both culturally and economically mediated, producing a "hegemony of input" where dominant modes of input become habitualized and in doing so perpetuate their dominance through preexisting competencies.

The second section runs with this observation to highlight the importance of habitualization and the *learning* of competency of different videogame input devices. Although it might seem from casual observation that some people simply have a knack for playing complicated videogames that others do not possess, there is nothing natural about the movements required (and acquired) to engage with a videogame. They are learned, and they are taught. "Embodied literacy" is fleshed out in this section to account for how the ability to experience a videogame must be learned by a body and, crucially, how the most commercially successful videogames inevitably normalize just what bodily configurations videogames are conventionally primed for. Just as written languages allow for a great range of expressions while excluding those who are not literate in that language, the embodied literacies required of different videogame input devices allow great expression for those who are able to obtain competency in them but exclude those who are not. Acknowledging this competency is crucial for appreciating how videogame taste is formed and how particular videogame experiences come to be more valued than others.

Finally, and in this context, the chapter presents a phenomenology of one particular genus of input device: the gamepad.[1] The gamepad has been associated with videogames for more than thirty years since Nintendo released the Nintendo Entertainment System (or NES; Famicom in Japan) in 1982. Ever since players felt in their thumbs the "sticky friction" (Rogers 2010) of Mario sliding across the worlds of *Super Mario Bros.* (Nintendo 1985), jamming Left to futilely stop Mario sliding to the right, fingers have wrapped around gamepads of this heredity to act as the conduit through which the computer program reads the player's physical movements to poke into the virtual world. *Heredity* is a key term here because over the decades the gamepad has mutated from a simple device of six buttons (four direction buttons and two "action buttons") to more complex devices allowing up to twenty different individual inputs by buttons, triggers, thumbsticks, and touchpads. Although more accessible mimetic forms of videogame input such as motion sensors and touchscreens have garnered much attention in recent times for their accessibility and use of more of the player's body than just the fingers, looking at how gamepads over a series of decades became so complex and so inaccessible to those players not already competent provides an opportunity to explore how no videogame input device is "natural" in its incorporation of the human body that moves alongside it. Just as there is value in literature that remains impenetrable to those who don't know the required language, there is value in those forms of videogames that demand more complex competencies, even as they exclude those not inculturated in their use. What is important to account for is that all input devices require the body to bend and extend itself in particular, habitualized ways that are not naturally possessed but that must *become naturalized* before those videogames that require a gamepad umbilical can be competently experienced.

A Hegemony of Input

Tools translate particular gestural intentions into movements not possible by a body without the tool: the swinging of a hammer turns the movement of the arm into a similar movement that has enough force to push a nail into a piece of wood; the pushing on a bicycle pedal turns a movement of the legs similar to that required for walking into the rotation of a wheel, while the straightening and bending of the arms turns the handlebar so that another wheel rotates and steers the bicycle; a guitar translates the movement of fingers into a vibration of strings capable of producing music; a doorknob translates the rotation of the wrist and clawed fingers into the sliding of a metal bar. If digital computers are to comprehend the user's intentions and process them through binary code, they require tools that translate continuous bodily movements into discrete values for the computer to internally comprehend. They require input devices.

Input devices come in a vast array of forms: buttons, joysticks, motion sensors, blowpipes, computer mice, switches, gloves, pointers, treadmills, dials, trackballs, touchscreens, lasers, GPS, and many others. Each in its own way works to translate different normative bodily movements into digital code. A button translates the pressure of a finger into a simple off/on value. A computer mouse detects its movement through space across two axes as it slides across the desk and feeds these values to the computer so that the cursor, too, can move on its two axes across the screen space. A capacitive touchscreen such as that on a iPhone has an electrostatic field that the touch of flesh distorts, allowing the device to determine the location of that touch as numerical values. In each case, a body is expected to move in particular ways and, importantly, is expected to be *able* to move in particular ways. Before we can consider how players incorporate input devices, then, we must consider how input devices come to both configure and exclude particular body schemas.

Ready-to-Hand Tools

In chapter 1, we saw how Merleau-Ponty considers the human body and its "appendages" as dilating the body schema: the way that when I am driving a car, my proprioception becomes distributed so that I do not think "the car will fit in this gap" but know that "I will fit in this gap." Likewise, we saw in Bateson's discussion of the blind man and his stick the difficulty of distinguishing the man's sense of "self" as residing in either the flesh of the man or the wood of the stick exclusively. We can only say instead that the man's self is distributed across the man–stick apparatus as one becomes fully incorporated into the perceptually lived experience of the other; it is the man-and-stick that perceives the world. We then saw through Haraway and Hayles how all consciousness is constituted from and situated in such partial body-and-world constructions—we never exist apart from the world that constitutes us.

Neither the car nor the stick (nor indeed the computer) is "naturally" incorporated into the body. If I were to close my eyes and attempt to use the blind man's stick, I would fail to successfully navigate and perceive a world through it. I have recently begun to drive a car larger than the one in which I first learned to drive, and I now struggle to successfully park between the lines. I regularly overcompensate for the neighboring car, which is not as close as I think it is. I no longer know "I will fit in this gap" but think "I don't know if this car will fit in this gap." One does not simply pick up a tool and incorporate it through an effortless process. On the contrary, effort is precisely what is required. The incorporation of tools into embodied experience is learned and, more importantly, taught.

For a tool to be ready to hand—for us to be able to perceive the world *through* the tool rather than to perceive the tool as part of the world—we must first incorporate the tool into our body schema. This process is most vividly demonstrated when we attempt to use a tool that is similar to a tool we have used previously but that requires slightly different movements.

The new car I struggle to park correctly also has the stalks for the turn signals and windscreen wipers on the opposite side of the steering wheel than
my previous car. After driving this car for more than a year, I still regularly
flick the windscreen wipers on when I wish to signal that I'll be turning a
corner. I "know" intellectually which side the signal switch is on, but the
actions have become so normalized in my incorporation of the previous car
that this conscious knowledge has yet to sink to a level that overrides my
previous dressage.

Some tools are easier to incorporate than others. The movements
required to hit a nail with a hammer or to swing a bat are very similar to
other movements that an able-bodied human might already use their arm
for. A car, in contrast, requires a complex reconceiving of the body's size
and what ends different movements of the body will result in.

With the exception of mimetic input devices such as those discussed in
the previous chapter, most input devices for computers require movements
that have little logical connection to the intended action "within" the computer. When I press X on the gamepad while playing *Crash Bandicoot*, its
only relation to "jump" is that I already know that X makes the character
jump. When I move a pen to write the letter *a*, there is a clear connection
between the gestures of my hand and the shape of the letter produced on
the page; when I press the A key on my keyboard, there is no direct connection between the pressure of my finger against the key and the letter
produced on the screen. Input devices are a sort of second-order tools. They
act as mediators, in-betweeners, ambassadors of the virtual present in the
actual that translate human movement into quite different (but intended)
actions.

Or, rather, there *is* a connection between the gesture of pressing the A
key and the letter *a* appearing on screen, but only because I have pushed
the A key in that specific location on a QWERTY keyboard so many times
that it has "become natural" that this particular movement of that finger
will produce an *a*. But if I were to use a different keyboard with the letters in different placements, that connection between trained movement
and the production of the letter *a* on the screen would dissolve. The connection is one that has been trained into me through dressage, not one
that occurs "naturally." Players of console videogames will find a similar
anecdote in thumbstick inversion, where some players pull the thumbstick
toward themselves to look upward in 3D videogames, and others push the
thumbstick away from themselves to do the same. Most players struggle to
adapt to a configuration opposite to the one with which they are familiar,
even when they "know" what the controls are. As such, 3D videogames

with manual camera movement typically offer both options. An action at the computer's input device is learned, becomes part of how the body knows itself, and comes to feel as though it is a natural way of moving the body at the exact time that the body no longer has to consciously consider the input device it uses. At the same time, alternative modes of input that contradict the learned mode become explicitly *un*natural.

Learning QWERTY

Here we encounter a paradox of input devices: one must obtain a knowledge of them through repetition in order to use them, but one must use them in order to practice that repetition. If most input devices require movements that do not have a transparent correlation to the resultant actions they intend to produce, how might one know how to use them competently enough to begin practicing with them? Importantly, input devices have not appeared out of nowhere but connect to long histories of mediative tool usage and preexisting bodily configurations so that they might be used in some manner until they are learned to be use competently. The explosive popularity of Nintendo's Wii console in the mid-2000s among people who previously rarely touched a videogame console is owed to the ease and imperfection with which they could swing a motion-detecting Wii-mote in front of *Wii Sports* (Nintendo 2006), being able to play the videogame long before they really knew how to play the videogame competently.

The balance between new training and existing habits for input devices is exemplified in the persistence of the QWERTY keyboard still commonly used today as the primary mode of engaging with computers (and, indeed, with videogames). It is worth spending some time to consider how this "standard" keyboard became the standard historically through societal/ ritualized dressage. Thierry Bardini (2000) traces a history of the QWERTY keyboard in contrast to Douglas Engelbart's Chord Keyset device. On December 9, 1968, Engelbart gave a demonstration of a range of computer hardware and software innovations his team had made at the Stanford Research Institute. One of these innovations was the first computer mouse, with two wheels on the underside of the device, perpendicular to each other, tracking the user's movement across two axes (a later configuration of the mouse implemented trackball technology instead of separate wheels). Whereas the straightforward connection the mouse provided between the movement of the hand on the desk and the movement of a cursor on the screen has seen it become ubiquitous to modern computing, another device Engelbart showed that day has not been so well remembered. The Chord Keyset was a single-hand keyboard of five long, piano-like keys that allowed the user to input all the possible letters of the English alphabet with just one hand. The user would rest each finger on a different key and press them in different combinations to produce different letters, not unlike piano keys used to produce different chords. The device was demonstrably more efficient and faster than two-handed keyboards—once, that is, the user was adequately trained. For Engelbart, the need for training was not a problem because the device's design relied on a system that assumed the human user would be adequately trained before confronting the device (Bardini 2000, 58–59).

However, the Chord Keyset would be practically impossible to use prior to training because no clear correlation between the key combinations and the letters they produced existed. The training would have to be conscious and deliberate and dedicated. Bardini contrasts this history with the persistence (and ultimately the standardizing) of the QWERTY keyboard. Without knowing how to touch-type efficiently, one can still look at a QWERTY keyboard layout, find the button with A on it, and press it to produce the letter *a* on the screen. The keyboard can be used before training, and in using it, users can become trained *by using it*—that is, by the repetition required to ingrain a skill beneath consciousness.

This does not explain, however, why the QWERTY layout of buttons came into ubiquity, but not any of the other keyboard layouts that also existed in the 1800s. Created by C. L. Sholes in the early 1870s, the QWERTY keyboard was designed primarily to ensure keys that would be more likely to be used in quick succession were spread out across the typewriter to prevent typebars from jamming, but it was far from the only viable option. Indeed, a great range of key arrangements were proposed throughout the 1800s by different typewriter manufacturers (Bardini provides an extensive genealogy of these input devices and the direct inspiration these took from the piano). What made QWERTY so dominant was not a particular affection found within bodies for this particular layout, but that it was the keyboard layout that Remington implemented on its commercially successful typewriters in 1874. According to Bardini,

The reason why the QWERTY keyboard became standard was simply that "touch typing" and "all-finger typing" required a standard keyboard. QWERTY became that standard—not out of any inherent superiority in it as a technological innovation, but as a result of the stochastic nature of technological evolution. It was the keyboard employed by C. L. Sholes, and when Sholes and his backers went to Remington to secure mass production of their Type-Writer, which appeared in 1874, it was the keyboard they used. Because it was in use, it was used by serious competitors of

Remington in subsequent years, whose innovations lay in the machine itself, not the machine-user interface. *It became the standard because it became the standard. Something had to.* (2000, 74, emphasis added)

Today, we use QWERTY keyboards because we use QWERTY keyboards. The commercial dominance and sheer hegemony of the QWERTY layout and the practice of touch-typing evolved side by side to commodify bodies and produce a dominant habitus so that the layout persists long after the need to spread out typebars has become obsolete. Although alternatives such as the Chord Keyset would be more efficient once the user was adequately trained in them, too many resources and too much labor had already been invested in the QWERTY keyboard for this to happen. The QWERTY keyboard is what has become normalized through bodily repetition. It is the input device that has become standardized for typing not because of any natural intuitiveness of its interface but because an intricate range of historical, social, economic, and phenomenological pressures habitualized it and, in doing so, ensured that alternatives were—and are— less likely to be habitualized. It is the standard because it is the standard, and because it is the standard, alternative modes of computer input are not the standard.

Videogame Input Devices

One of the earliest digital games, *OXO*, was created by Alexander Douglas in 1952 for the Electronic Delay Storage Automatic Calculator (EDSAC) computer, simulating a simple game of tic-tac-toe against a computer-controlled opponent. Reportedly, *OXO* had the player use a rotary telephone to make their input, the nine digits corresponding to the nine possible grid spaces on the tic-tac-toe board. Years later, when William Higinbotham designed *Tennis for Two* (1958) for the Brookhaven National Laboratory's Donner Model 30 analog computer, he created two custom controllers attached to the mainframe by cables and to be held by the two players. When Steve Russell and his colleagues created *Spacewar!* at MIT for the PDP-1 in 1962, they found the switches located to the side of the cathode-ray tube screen awkwardly placed for a program that required the player's immediate reactions to the program's visual state, so they created wired devices consisting of buttons and switches for each player so the videogame could be played from in front of the monitor (Donovan 2010, 11). Since their inception and to the present day, videogames have always existed somewhere between parasitically adapting to existing input devices and having input devices produced for them.

Just as in the early days of typewriting a vast diversity of key configurations emerged before the QWERTY keyboard standardized a habitus, through the 1970s a vast range of input devices were created and implemented for different videogames. *Pong* (Atari 1972) had its "paddle controller," which had the player turn a dial clockwise and counterclockwise to slide an on-screen paddle up and down. *Missile Command* (Atari 1980) had a giant trackball that moved a crosshair slowly around the screen. Racing videogames implemented steering wheels and foot pedals to mimic the act of driving a car. Between 1976 and 1978, toy company Coleco released 14 different consoles to be plugged into a television, each with different videogames installed and different input devices to use with them, ranging from knobs to buttons, light guns, steering wheels, and other plastic instruments. Today, novel and unique videogame inputs are most commonly seen in videogame arcades, where the spectacle of the physical hardware is part of the attraction: dance mats, drums, giant light guns in the shape of sniper rifles, car shells that can be sat in.

However, also through the 1970s and into the 1980s, computers and thus the QWERTY keyboard and the mouse found themselves increasingly present in homes, providing another platform for videogames. Whereas many arcade videogames had input devices created specifically for them, the videogames produced for the PC worked within the existing limitations of the QWERTY keyboard, and thus many early PC videogames required text-based inputs. In the present day, different videogame genres have created their own conventions at the QWERTY keyboard. For instance, most contemporary first-person videogames played on a PC now use the W, A, S, and D keys for forward, leftward, backward, and rightward movement. These keys were chosen over the seemingly more conventional arrow keys because of, first, the close proximity of other keys for other quick actions (tapping R to reload a gun or E to open a door) and, second, so that a player can input directions with the left hand while using the mouse with the right hand to look in different directions with more nuanced accuracy than the four on/off arrow keys can possibly provide. This has not always been the norm, however, and one only has to go back to the early 1990s to find first-person videogames whose controls now feel alien and archaic. More recently, and as discussed in the previous chapter, the smartphone was never intended as a videogame platform, but videogames found a way to adapt to that input environment, with designers creating videogames such as *Angry Birds* (Rovio 2009) that rely on swiping and dragging and tapping gestures.

Input devices do not persist simply due to a natural intuitiveness with which the user's body takes them up—the abandonment of the Chord Keyset and the Wii-mote, on the one hand, and the persistence of the QWERTY keyboard and the gamepad, on the other, are evidence of this. Rather, input devices persist due to how readily they can be incorporated by bodies that have already been broken in through bodily repetition with similar input devices. This incorporation is determined in part by what devices are already commercially and culturally dominant, which in turn influences the design of not only future input devices but also the software (including videogames) that must fit within existing conventions and expectations (or deliberately flout them), thus allowing the dominant modes of input to further cement their dominance with each iteration.

Input devices produce a *hegemony of input*. Dominant modes of input produce a dominant habitus and imbue a competency that is seemingly "natural" to that dominant habitus while further marginalizing and atrophying alternative modes of input and the habits they require.

To Become Literate at Videogame Play

A few years before detailing his experience with videogames in *Pilgrim in the Microworld* (1983), David Sudnow offered an exhaustive account of the knowledge his hands acquired as he became a competent jazz pianist in *Ways of the Hand* ([1978] 2001). He describes the transition he underwent from relying on his eyes to determine where his fingers needed to go on the piano keyboard to allowing those keys instead to become "places towards which the appreciative fingers, hand, and arm are aimed" ([1978] 2001, 15). Sudnow gained a sense of the keys' locations in space by repetitively moving toward them, developing what he calls "an embodied way of accomplishing distance" (15). Jazz music, for Sudnow, is first and foremost "particular ways of moving from place to place. Without that motivated skilled accomplishment, there's no jazz for anyone to otherwise address" (127), and he came to believe through his acquired competency that the jazz pianist's handwork elucidates knowledges to the performer alone—knowledges not accessible to the listener—through their embodied experience (3).

The same can be said of the videogame: without the player's playing body coupled to the videogame through an input device, there is no videogame experience to consider otherwise. Although there is worth in understanding both jazz music and videogame play from perspectives other than that of the player (jazz music is listened to; videogames are increasingly spectated as often as they are played), the embodied experience of *playing*, of accomplishing the distances of the instrument or input device, is one that is known only to the competent performer or player. The account of jazz music Sudnow sees himself as being able to provide is that of the player who obtains competency within the body and who produces meaning through that body's competent performance.

Indeed, when Sudnow first encountered a videogame years later, he found a medium for finger work more immediate but no less intoxicating than the jazz piano. Within fifteen minutes of twisting the dial back and forth to slide the small on-screen paddle horizontally across the screen to play *Breakout* (Atari 1976), he was "no longer conscious of the knob's gearing" (1983, 39). In one vivid passage in *Pilgrim in the Microworld*, he describes his engagement with the screen as mediated by his fingers wrapped around the dial:

Line up your extended finger with the lower left corner of the TV screen a comfortable six feet away. Now track back and forth several times in line with the bottom border and project a movement of that breadth onto an imagined inch and a half diameter spool in your hands. That's how knob and paddle are geared, a natural correspondence of scale between the body's motions, the equipment, and the environs preserved in the interface. (1983, 37)

Sudnow understands his engagement with both *Breakout* and the piano as about a certain spatial awareness ingrained beneath consciousness, becoming habitualized as what Melanie Swalwell (2008) calls a "kinaesthetic knowledge." The key difference between playing *Breakout* and playing jazz piano, for Sudnow, is the quickness with which his body was able to incorporate the actions demanded of the videogame, whereas learning the flourishes and improvisations of jazz piano took many years. Sudnow notes how training is embedded into the very design of the videogames that require repetition and learning as precursors to progression (a notion that I consider further in chapter 5):

If you engage a human body through eyes and fingers in a precisely scripted interaction with various sorts of computer-generated events, what seem like quite complex skills are rapidly acquired by regular repetition. Sequences of events can be scheduled into readily mastered routines of progressive difficulty, and a program of timed transitions can be organized, *programming you*, in turn, at an economically desirable rate. (1983, 63, emphasis added)

What Sudnow identifies is a pedagogical model still deployed by most videogames today: confront the player with increasingly complex challenges to enforce the gaining of competency through the repetition of tasks.

Videogames extend, restrict, and reconfigure the player's body schema. *Crash Bandicoot* afforded my housemate certain intimate, active engagements with a fantastical world, but it also demanded certain bodily configurations *of* my housemate at the gamepad while denying others. It demanded the player wrap themself around the gamepad in such a way as to be able to produce both a jump and a spin-attack in quick succession with a single thumb's movement, and it refused to let the player progress until they had repeated this action enough times to perform it successfully. *Crash Bandicoot* made choices about the player's configuration even as the player made choices about *Crash Bandicoot*. Videogames reconfigure the body, and they are experienced through this reconfigured body.

A point worth repeating: until my housemate learned the correct way to move their thumb over the PlayStation gamepad, they could not adequately experience *Crash Bandicoot*. They could get *some* experience out of it—stumble through a few levels—but they could not experience the videogame as it is experienced by those who have been adequately habitualized by the input device (and who have maintained that training over the years) to the extent that it becomes ready-to-hand, a literally mindless conduit of the player's embodied experience distributed across the actual and virtual worlds of play with and as the body of Crash Bandicoot.

If videogames are an embodied textuality that express their meaning through the player's immanent experience, then the dressage required to incorporate videogames into embodied experience is a sort of *embodied literacy*. The remainder of this section explores the consequences of this requirement. What are the reverberations of videogames requiring a competency in order that they be engaged with? How does this requirement standardize particular videogame values and tastes while marginalizing others? What hegemony of input does it instill?

Sensitizing the Player

Considering input-device play as simply a matter of being broken in through dressage can risk trivializing the embodied knowledges learned through repetitive videogame play as simply mechanical and rote. One does not simply "use" a videogame. James Ash, following Heidegger, looks at how videogames *attune* players as "complex assemblages of bodily capacities and cognitive processes" (2013, 34). Looking particularly at the multiplayer component of military-themed, first-person shooter *Call of Duty 4: Modern Warfare* (Infinity Ward 2007), Ash observes that for players to become skilled at a videogame (that is, to be able to react near instantly based on the organization of actors in front of them at any one time), the videogame must "actively sensitize users to open their bodies to a variety of affective states" (2013, 28). Referring specifically to a gamepad's thumb-stick, Ash notes that "the material plastic of the thumbstick and its physical limitations for movement form the possibility space for the development of somatic memory to be developed in the body of the player" (37). Thus, to become literate at an input device for a certain type of videogame is not simply to be broken in through repetition but to become sensitized toward "particular forms of somatic and analytic attunement" (45). Videogames do not just train their players but prime them to affectively orient themselves to the videogame in a particular way.

The player's body is extended and reconfigured by the videogame and its hardware, but the adept player rarely consciously considers this exten-sion and reconfiguration. It is this "knowledge in our hands" (Merleau-Ponty 2012, 145) that allows the player to experience the embodiment demanded by videogame play as, "at least partly, a function of *not* looking at or thinking about our hands" (Kirkpatrick 2009, 131, original empha-sis). As a competent videogame player, I no longer look at the input device to ensure I am pressing the right buttons; I have instead incorporated the input device's spatiality and have learned the potential movements and configurations of my thumbs and fingers across it. Like the competent jazz pianist who "makes it up as [they] go along" (Sudnow 2001, 125) or the touch-typist who "incorporates the space of the keyboard into [their] bodily space" (Merleau-Ponty 2012, 146), I, a competent videogame player, do not "think" about how I am going to traverse the input device—my body has incorporated the input device so that, for example, I perceive my own action not as "pressing X" but as "jumping."

Videogames require a competency that is at once a learned physical behavior and a means of "reading" and engaging with the videogame's semiotics. To return to an example discussed in chapter 1, appreciating the heaviness of *Grand Theft Auto IV* (Rockstar North 2008) first requires me to be able to interface competently with *Grand Theft Auto IV* through the gamepad, to be adequately attuned to *Grand Theft Auto IV*. Truly, all languages require such a bodily competency. Merleau-Ponty speaks of the "gestural signification" of speech (2012, 184). For every word that I know, I possess an "articulatory and sonorous essence as one of the modulations or one of the possible uses of my body. … The word has a certain place in my linguistic world, it is part of my equipment" (186). As it is for spo-ken language, so it is for videogames, except now the gestural signification that demands a literacy is in my fingers, ears, and eyeballs rather than in the phonetic possibilities of my mouth. Videogames signify through the

gestures they habitualize in the player, and it is through these learned gestures that the "literate" player encounters a videogame's meaning.

An Embodied Literacy

[handwritten: can extend to other non-video game related concepts]

If videogame play is an embodied textuality where the player's incorporation of the gestural significations required of the videogame is both an
interpretative and somatic knowledge, then to play a videogame requires
an *embodied literacy*. The literate videogame player knows in their hands
the way around the conventional spatial syntax of the input device, has a
basic understanding of the performative grammar of different videogame
genres (how jumping works, how looking works, how menus work), and is
able to transport and adapt this literacy from one videogame to the next. In
contrast to the novice player who looks at the input device in their hands
and thinks, "Press X and then press Square," the literate player thinks,
"Jump and then kick in midair." The literate player does not have to learn
with each new videogame how to roll their thumb so as to push two buttons on the gamepad in quick succession but possesses such a gesture as
part of their repertoire. The novice player, who has not yet incorporated
the input device, distinguishes between the acts of their actual body at the
input device and the images moving on the screen; the literate player fuses
the two into a single, extended performance. Seth Giddings and Helen
Kennedy's autoethnographic retelling of their adventures with *Lego Star
Wars* (Traveler's Tales 2005) highlights this difference, describing how they
fumbled around pressing the wrong buttons (2008, 24), playing *with* the
videogame more than incorporating the videogame, as is intended of a
player with the learned literacy the videogame requires but they lacked.
Literate players, much like Sudnow's piano teacher, "develop a feel for it"
(2001, 28) that is then difficult to explain to others because the knowledge
has sunk beneath consciousness.

It is through a learned literacy of the fingers at the input device that the
videogame becomes textually legible to players. Just as one must learn how
to read before reading a novel, one must first become literate in the spatial
movements of fingers on the gamepad or at the keyboard and mouse before
the most conventional and widely played videogames will reveal their pleasures. To truly appreciate what the playing of a particular videogame offers
is first to understand how this embodied literacy is formed through the
player's attunement to particular input devices.

The risk here, however, is implicitly suggesting that until one knows
how to play a videogame, one can't possibly understand it. To an extent,
this is true, but being challenged to obtain a competency is itself key to

many videogame experiences. For instance, many videogames deliberately challenge the player's competency through experiences that strive to test and improve that competency over time. A simple example is the beginning of the first stage of *Super Mario Bros.*, which prevents progression until the player demonstrates their ability to successfully jump over an enemy. Until the player learns how to jump, they will run into the first enemy again and again. *Lego Star Wars*, meanwhile, as a lighthearted and comedic videogame, encourages the "incompetent" player to *play with* the videogame, allowing them, like Giddings and Kennedy, to have a meaningful experience with the videogame even as they struggle with the input device. In highlighting the gestural signification and consequential competency demanded of videogames, I want to stress the importance of not simply perpetuating the same hegemonic framings I am trying to discuss. Rather, the expressive potential of a given videogame is intimately tied to the player's incorporated knowledge of the input device.[2]

To claim videogames require a particular embodied literacy that is also a form of competency is thus not an apolitical statement. *Crash Bandicoot* never explains just how a thumb might roll from the X to the Square button quickly enough to perform a jumping spin attack. *Crash Bandicoot* does not just assume the player will repeat a single task until they habitualize the required action. Rather, it presumes the presence of a player who has *already* habitualized the required action through regular gamepad play, not unlike how a novel written in English assumes in its reader a preexisting literacy in English (as well as the bodily ability to view written words). If the dressage of everyday life produces social bodies that are bent to particular socially constructed experiences of the body, then we must consider what bodies are most likely to be bent toward the input devices of videogames and what bodily configurations the input devices of videogames are most likely to bend toward.

The gamepad came into popularity as an input device at the same time as the Western and Japanese videogame industries began to narrow their focus on a teenage male demographic, deliberately cultivating the consumer identity of the "gamer." What Graeme Kirkpatrick identifies as "a (gendered) gamer habitus" (2012) was formed alongside the birth and evolving complexity of the gamepad through the 1980s and 1990s. As the videogame industry focused squarely on a young, male audience, the gamepad evolved in such a way as to cultivate particular kinds of videogame experience that echoed experiences already normalized as masculine, and those who were most likely to engage with videogames long enough to habitualize using a gamepad were young men.

Whereas the commercial videogame industry is engaged in a constant rhetorical project of technological progress and "innovation," the persistence of the gamepad is surprising in its stability and conservatism. David Parisi (2015) points toward this stability as an "ergonomic branding" of players by the gamepad: players are taught how to configure their bodies at the videogame, and then future videogame hardware adapts to this configured body, not unlike the way the QWERTY keyboard has persisted long past the practical need to avoid mechanical typewriter jams. An explicit example of this desirable stability is provided by Teiyu Goto, the designer of Sony's original PlayStation and its gamepad controller. In an interview about the gamepad's design, Goto explained that Sony wanted to ensure that the large market of Nintendo's Super Nintendo console, Sony's main competitor, would feel familiar enough with the PlayStation to consider making the shift to the PlayStation: "[The Super Nintendo console] was a huge hit at the time, and naturally we wanted [Super Nintendo] gamers to upgrade to our system. ... That's why the management department didn't want the controller to be a radical departure—they said it had to be a standard type of design, or gamers wouldn't accept it" (in Gifford 2010). The gamepad became a standard because it became a standard. The hegemony of the gamepad input device became self-sustaining through a dominant habitus, so that particular videogames were created for a particular audience, who further habitualized that input device while other audiences continued to have little reason or opportunity to learn how to use that input device at all.

As Iris Marion Young explores in her influential essay "Throwing Like a Girl" (1980, 2005b), one's lived experience arises from the historical, cultural, social, and economic limits of one's situation. Just as dressage allows the ritualized to pass as natural, the feminine bodily comportment that causes some to "throw like a girl" cannot be explained by a natural and ahistoric feminine essence but by accounting for the situated lived experience and dressage of women in patriarchal societies. Likewise, videogame play through the 1980s and 1990s was naturalized through the gamer habitus as "for boys" in part through the demand of a preexisting habitualized knowledge of the gamepad. Indeed, it is only since the rise of mimetic and immediately accessible input devices such as motion sensors and mobile touchscreens that videogames have again begun speaking to a broader demographic. Of course, no shortage of women have always been competent at the gamepad and every other videogame input device, but this competency became normalized through a history of dressage as something men possess and women do not. The repercussions of this gamer habitus is explored in more detail in chapter 6.

This normalization can be demonstrated further through the regional specificity of embodied literacies. For instance, in the late 1990s and early 2000s it was common for PlayStation games made in Western countries to use the X on the gamepad as a confirmation button in menus and Triangle as a cancel button. Japanese videogames, however, used O as a confirmation button and X as a cancel button because in Japan a circle is the equivalent of a tick or checkmark. I recall playing Japanese videogames such as *Final Fantasy VII* (Squaresoft 1997) and often accidentally canceling a selection rather than confirming it, even long after I was consciously aware of the videogame's controls, because I was attuned to pressing X to confirm a decision. Marcel Mauss makes a similar observation on "the ways in which from society to society [humans] know how to use their bodies," describing how British troops in World War II struggled to use French spades (1973, 70–71). Japanese gamepad users were broken in through repetitions different from those Western gamepad users learned even though the gamepad itself was the same. The embodied literacies of an input device are not determined purely by the device itself; different embodied literacies at the same input device "became natural" in different cultures, just as different languages are "natural" for different cultures even though they use the same alphabet of symbols.

Competency produces conventions, and conventions produce competency, and the two combined produce taste. Bourdieu notes in his work on taste and class that different cultural or linguistic competencies are linked to different markets so that the acquisition of a competency "confers the self-certainty which accompanies the certainty of possessing cultural legitimacy, and the ease which is the touchstone of excellence; it produces the paradoxical relationship to culture made up of self-confidence amid (relative) ignorance and of casualness amid familiarity, which bourgeois families hand down to their offspring as if it were an heirloom" (1984, 66). The competencies of videogame play are no different. In accounting for the pleasures offered by complex, learned input devices, it is important to stress that it is the need for such learnedness that in part is responsible for the persistent critique of "core" videogames as inaccessible, exclusionary, and hegemonic across clearly demarcated, gendered lines (Juul 2010; Shaw 2011; Anthropy 2012). For the novice, contemporary gamepads are complicated and unintuitive, often having more than fifteen possible buttons to press by no more than four fingers. The gamepad, like all input devices, is a physical, corporeal language: some players have learned it from childhood, whereas others struggle to learn it as adults and remain excluded from both the production and consumption of its texts.

For the literate, using the input device is "natural," just as using a piano's keys is "natural" for the professional pianist; there is no conscious decision making about what buttons to press, but a learned mapping of the body to the input device, a knowing of distances that ensures fingers are in the right place at the right time. Each input-device iteration mobilizes "a haptic epistemology" (Parisi 2015, 10) that conserves and stabilizes an existing literacy for those already literate. It is the responsibility of those who are literate, then, to be reflective and critical of the language they use.

The final section of this chapter is an attempt to do just that. As someone who grew up playing videogames in the 1990s and 2000s, I was perfectly situated in my culture to be "broken into" the bodily demands of the gamepad—to have the opportunity to become literate in the gamepad and to access the videogames that demand such a literacy. By analyzing the aspects of the gamepad as they emerged historically, this final section allows both an appreciation of the specific pleasures and meanings that embodied literacy affords and a grounds to critique the hegemony of particular input devices that such a literacy inevitably instills.

Anatomy of the Gamepad

The gamepad, alongside the keyboard-and-mouse combo of desktop computers, has been a dominant mode of interfacing with videogames since it was first popularized with the introduction of Nintendo's NES (Famicom in Japan) in 1983 and of Sega's Master System in 1986, and it has persisted as a major influence on the embodied, lived experience of videogame play through the contemporary PlayStation 4, Xbox One, and Nintendo Switch consoles as well as through an increased presence of "plug-and-play" gamepads for PC videogames. The gamepad has undergone many deviations and mutations across the decades, but through the commercially dominant platforms a clear evolutionary lineage can be traced from the 8-button gamepads introduced with the NES to the 17-button, twin-stick, touchscreen-augmented gamepads that are the dominant conduit for contemporary consoles. Looking closely at the affordances and constraints of the gamepad's standard layout as it has evolved alongside an increasingly attuned and literate player is deliberately a selectively historical project, highlighting how the dominant gamepad has evolved and cultivated a certain familiarity in its competent users and an alienation in those not attuned to its needs. It also is a postphenomenological project, where neither the gamepad nor the player's hands can be considered separate from the other; the parallel and reflexive evolution of both gamepad and literate hands must instead be accounted for. To stress: this is a linear and somewhat determinist history, the type that inevitably sidelines and marginalizes nondominant experiences. In this case, however, such sidelining is the point: to demonstrate how a standard becomes a standard and then instills a hegemony of input that in turn shapes bodies and videogames alike.

The contemporary gamepad consists of three dominant types of inputs: action buttons, triggers, and thumbsticks.[3] All three are supported from within the gamepad by spring mechanisms that constantly return the button, trigger, or thumbstick to its default, not-pressed state (as opposed to a computer mouse that only ever moves relative to where it was previously moved). In other words, each type of input on the gamepad provides a physical resistance to my movements, a friction. Combining these different simple types of input allows for an intricate and complex variety of gestures on any given gamepad for any given videogame (see figure 3.2). Crucially, the way a videogame feels to play will depend on the very specific makeup of a particular gamepad controller: the strength of the springs beneath the buttons, the texture of the plastic buttons, the shape and size of the gamepad itself. Here, though, I am limiting the scope of my analysis to the shape and layout of gamepads in general, with specific examples from the most common and influential iterations that have standardized the gamepad in relation to my own literate, able-bodied hands. This limited analysis provides a platform on which other specific analyses of particular input devices can be performed and, more importantly, from which to appreciate the typically unseen and unconsidered but entirely learned actions and knowledges of the player's bodily movements that videogame play depends on and that the commercially dominant gamepads normalize.

Directional Pads and Action Buttons

In the early 1980s, the brick-shaped NES gamepad (see figure 3.3), echoing the input layout of Nintendo's earlier Game & Watch handheld devices, normalized the basic vocabulary of the gamepad that persists today. Unlike earlier joysticks or keyboards whose shape suggested they be rested on a tabletop or in a lap, the NES gamepad's buttons are too spread out to be covered comfortably by the digits of a single hand. Its layout instead suggests that it should be held with my two hands: each thumb resting atop the buttons positioned close to the edges of the device and my remaining

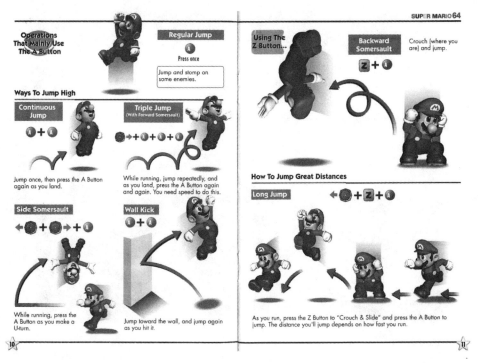

Figure 3.2
Some of the moves available to Mario in *Super Mario 64* (Nintendo 1996) through the combinations of different buttons on the Nintendo 64's gamepad, as explained by the game's manual. © 1996, Nintendo.

fingers resting beneath the gamepad both to support its weight and to push back against my thumbs' downward force. The NES gamepad consists of eight buttons: four directional buttons on the left, two action buttons on the right, and the Select and Start buttons in the middle. Each button has two states that can be read by the videogame software: "off" in its default state and "on" when I put pressure on them.

Under my left thumb is the cross-shaped "directional pad" (or "control pad" as it was previously referred to in Nintendo's own literature). Its name commonly shortened to "d-pad," this one piece of plastic can be pushed down at the four distinct, concealed buttons at its extremities, giving the impression of not just pushing a button inward but also pushing in a certain direction (up, down, left, right). The thumb rests in a small concave dome at the intersection of the four directions and rolls back and forth onto the four different buttons.

Figure 3.3
The gamepad controller for the Nintendo Entertainment System (NES), 1985.

The d-pad is historically responsible for the avatar's or cursor's navigation of the virtual space. Nintendo originally designed it for the Game & Watch version of *Donkey Kong* (1981) because it was the first Game & Watch title requiring both horizontal and vertical movement. The folding case of the Game & Watch also rendered a traditional joystick unfeasible (*Retro Gamer* 2016, 22). The NES's creator, Masayuki Uemura, explained in an interview why the designers translated the d-pad across to the NES gamepad instead of returning to a traditional joystick:

Naturally, we could have used a joystick but we were thinking of [the NES] as a toy and toys you put on the floor. Children might step on a joystick and it could hurt their feet … and break the controller! Also, when we played *Donkey Kong* Game & Watch we found we were only looking at the top screen. With a TV screen, you only look at that, not the controller. You need that sense, just using your fingers. (quoted in *Retro Gamer* 2016, 22)

In addition to contributing to a broader image of the NES as a toy rather than as a computer, the minimal d-pad allowed players to "just use their fingers" and, thus, encouraged them not to think about how they were moving their body.

The four directional buttons move my character relative to my orientation to the videogame world through the television screen. For instance, in a videogame presented from a side-on perspective, such as *Super Mario Bros.*, Left and Right correspond to "back" (toward the beginning of the level and the left-hand edge of my television) and "forward" (toward the end of the level and the right-hand edge of my television), whereas Down causes Mario to crouch, and Up is used to climb beanstalks. In a videogame presented from a top-down perspective, however, where the camera is looking down on my character and the world from a bird's-eye or isometric view, such as *The Legend of Zelda* (Nintendo 1986), the four directions correspond to the cardinal directions of the television screen "map" (Up moves north toward the top edge of the screen; Left moves west toward the left edge of the screen; and so on). More recently, the d-pad has shifted to a secondary role with the normalization of thumbsticks, as discussed later in this chapter.

Under my right thumb sit the two action buttons, named B and A from left to right. These buttons are circular with a flat, smooth surface, able to be pushed only directly inward toward the gamepad's plastic casing as the springs beneath them constantly push back. Action buttons are typically linked to specific actions: run, jump, shoot, talk, buy, rotate, accelerate, punch, kick, and so on. Like my left thumb, my right thumb rests diagonally between the two buttons, ready to roll one way or the other and to press down either or both of the buttons at a moment's notice. The basic behavior demanded of the NES controller (movement with the left thumb, action with the right) persists as a default setting to this day in all dominant gamepad designs.

The simple layout and minimal buttons of the NES gamepad belie a dormant potentiality. Each button, although having only two states, can read player input at three different moments in time: the moment the button is pressed, the moment the button is released, and while the button continues to be held down. Each button can be tapped (pressed quickly so that it immediately bounces back to its "off" state) or held (pushed down for a prolonged period) for different effects. In *Super Mario Bros.*, tapping and releasing A allows Mario to jump a short height, and holding A pushes Mario slowly toward a much greater height; tapping B will allow Mario to shoot a fireball if I possess the right items, and holding B allows Mario to move at a faster pace if a directional button is also held down. Indeed, I can press any two buttons on the NES gamepad at one time, with the significant exception of opposing directions on the d-pad because the plastic casing that covers all four buttons see-saws so that it cannot bend in two opposite directions at once—if Left is being pushed down, the casing will have raised too high over Right for the latter also to be pushed. I can, however, push two *adjacent* directional buttons with a single roll of my left thumb diagonally from the center of the d-pad, often allowing for more navigation options, such as walking Link northwest in *The Legend of Zelda* or making Mario duck and slide beneath a low block.

Combining taps and holds of various buttons on the gamepad with one or both thumbs is as fundamental to performing more complex actions in gamepad-controlled videogames as being able to press multiple piano keys to produce a chord is fundamental to performing a piece of music or stringing together different modulations of the human voice is fundamental to producing a word. By ingraining complex gestural patterns, I can do things *while doing other things* and build up a repertoire of combined behaviors and abilities. For instance, the ability to jump *across* a chasm or *onto* the head of an enemy (as opposed to jumping straight up) is fundamental for many videogames, requiring me to combine a knowledge of virtual distances and momentums with a sequencing of buttons beneath the thumbs. To return to the example of *Super Mario Bros.*, Mario must first gain horizontal momentum, requiring me to hold down Right on the d-pad with the left thumb. Then, while keeping Right held, I must hold down A with the right thumb as Mario reaches the edge of the chasm so that he is now moving right and up. The chasm may be so wide that Mario must get a running start for his jump, which requires me to hold down Right *and* B and then *also* to roll my right thumb onto A once Mario reaches the ledge.

More complex still are the small, proprioceptive adjustments I make with each of Mario's jumps as I become attuned to his body and its capacity for movement. I do not always jump Mario the maximum possible distance but learn to release A at just the right time to have him land on a precarious floating block or on an enemy's head or perhaps even to have him shift directions midjump from right to left to slow the jump's momentum. I cannot say, however, for just how long one must hold each of the buttons to make the jump that I make perfectly every time. I cannot answer the question "How high can Mario jump?" even as my body knows precisely when to release A. Whereas the body constantly renegotiates the hand's speed and distance from the object it is reaching for in our navigation of corporeal space, here what Sudnow observes as the *"common pulse to unite the two differently distanced moves"* between his two hands at the piano ([1978] 2001, 95, original emphasis) exists not just between the two hands on the gamepad but between those hands and the perceived movement of screen imagery that construct the illusion of a virtual world. My proprioception is

distributed. As I become literate in videogames that require the incorporation of a gamepad, my body develops a capacity for Mario's body and its
abilities in relation to my own capacity to navigate the gamepad in my
hands.

In 1990, when Nintendo released its next console, the Super Nintendo
Entertainment System (SNES or Super Famicom in Japan), four action buttons now sat beneath the right-hand thumb (see figure 3.4), with Y and X
added above and to the left of B and A, respectively, in a diamond configuration. Four action buttons continue to be the conventional design on current gamepads, keeping the same lettering on both Nintendo and Microsoft
gamepads (albeit in different positions, with B/A and X/Y swapped around)
and using Triangle, Square, O, and X on Sony gamepads. These two extra
buttons allow for an even greater combination of actions as the right-
hand thumb may be rolled between any two neighboring buttons, but the
somatic configurations required remain similar. New possibilities also come
with new restrictions, however, in that the thumb may not so easily roll
between two action buttons diametrically opposed, requiring a moment to
move the thumb up from one button, across the plastic divide, and down

Figure 3.4
The gamepad controller for the Super Nintendo Entertainment System (SNES), 1990.

onto the button that triggers the opposite action. For instance, when playing the 3D platformer *Spyro the Dragon* (Insomniac 1998) on Sony's PlayStation (whose gamepad, as noted, uses Triangle, Square, O, and X in place of B, A, X, Y), holding Square (the left-most action button) allows Spyro to begin a ramming run if that hold is combined with a d-pad direction. I must use this ramming run to chase down speedy thieves who have stolen dragon eggs. I am often tempted in these challenges to press O (the right-most action button) once Spyro nears the thief in order to execute his flame attack and ideally end the chase prematurely. However, in the time it takes my thumb to lift from Square (canceling the ramming run) and travel to the diametrically opposed O, the thief has almost always rushed out of range of the flames, suggesting that these challenges are intended purely as tests of speed and navigation.

Most important in the addition of these two extra action buttons is the beginning of a clear trajectory of the gamepad toward greater complexity in a way that assumes an existing familiarity with previous iterations of the gamepad. Assuming that the player has already become attuned adequately to the two-action-button NES gamepad, the SNES then works to further attune this player to new behaviors and capacities. More complex behaviors are now asked of a player presumed to be competent.

Shoulder Buttons and Triggers

The SNES gamepad also introduces "shoulder" buttons L (for "Left") and R (for "Right") on the top of the gamepad. The shoulder buttons are most easily reached with my index fingers, requiring me to reconfigure my hands at the gamepad. I no longer tuck all nonthumb fingers beneath the gamepad but instead wrap my index fingers around the upper curve of the controller to rest atop the L and R buttons (see figure 3.4). Significantly, the very shape of the SNES gamepad is altered from that of the NES gamepad to facilitate this incorporation, replacing the square-cornered brick with a rounded, "dog-bone" shape, better affording the multiple joints of the index finger to curve around its edges. As already explored with respect to the d-pad and the action buttons, shoulder buttons can be either tapped or held and can be used in combination with any of the other buttons on the gamepad.

Before the introduction of thumbsticks, shoulder buttons commonly allowed the index fingers to provide some kind of secondary action or adjustment of the dominant actions mapped to the action buttons beneath the thumbs. Placed on a perpendicular surface to the action buttons and d-pad, the shoulder buttons move along a different axis when pressed, pushing "inward" relative to my body more than "downward." In two-dimensional videogames, this movement often corresponds to a clockwise/counterclockwise orientation in virtual action relative to the player's fingers. For instance, in the on-rails space-flight videogame *Star Fox* (Nintendo 1993), I hold down L or R to rotate the ship either counterclockwise or clockwise 90 degrees to fit through tight spaces, the top of the ship rotating to point toward the left or right side of the television. As the ship is held sideways through the shoulder buttons, the thumbs on the d-pad and the action buttons are still able to maneuver, shoot, and drop bombs. Similarly, in the exploratory platformer *Super Metroid* (Nintendo 1994), L and R are used to aim the protagonist's gun diagonally up or down to fire at enemies above or below the avatar, again suggesting movement on a different axis than that provided by the d-pad, a rotation in relation to the player's side-on perspective of the videogame's world.

The gamepad for Sony's PlayStation console, released in 1994, adds two additional shoulder buttons, named L2 and R2, beneath L and R, now renamed L1 and R1, so that each of my index fingers is responsible for two buttons. Whereas my thumb easily rolls across multiple action buttons, the lankier index finger more commonly must be lifted off one shoulder button and placed on the next. As such, few videogames demand both shoulder buttons on a single side of the gamepad to be pressed at the same time because it would require both my index and middle finger of each hand to be wrapped around the edges of the gamepad, leaving only my pinkie and ring fingers underneath to support its weight.

Microsoft's Xbox console, released in 2001, then normalized the conversion of these secondary shoulder buttons into "triggers." Requiring an action not dissimilar to pulling the trigger of a gun, the triggers require much longer actions to be fully pressed but also register multiple values between fully not pressed and fully pressed. Whereas typical buttons record a whole integer value of either 0 (off) or 1 (on), the trigger is translated by the videogame as a decimal float value between 0.00 (fully off) and 1.00 (fully on), allowing for more nuanced interpretation by the videogame of the pressure exerted by the player's index finger. For example, a partially pushed trigger might return a value of 0.32, and pushing it slightly harder might increase that value to 0.65, which allows for virtual actions intimately connected to the pressure of plastic beneath flesh, such as slowly accelerating a car instead of slamming the foot (and finger) down.

Thumbsticks and Dual Embodiment

The role of action buttons, shoulder buttons, and d-pads shifted significantly with the introduction of thumbsticks, first on the Nintendo 64 console in 1996 but primarily through the dual-thumbstick layout with Sony's DualShock gamepad released for the PlayStation console in 1997 (see figure 3.1 for the PlayStation 4's DualShock 4 iteration), a layout that persists as the most common on contemporary gamepads. Like a miniature joystick on which the thumb rests, the thumbstick can be rotated in a 360-degree dome around a default, upright position to which it will return if the player lifts their thumb. The thumbstick translates this rotation into float values between –1.00 and 1.00 along two axes of movement, communicating to the videogame just where the player's thumb is holding the stick (for example, a bit to the left and forward is –0.5, 1). This more nuanced control across two axes coincides with the rise of 3D videogames on home consoles. As the left-or-right movement of the d-pad couples with Mario in *Super Mario Bros.*, the slow, circular turns of 3D Mario in *Super Mario 64* (Nintendo 1996) maps symbiotically with the tight arc of the Nintendo 64's thumbstick. Dual-thumbstick control in particular introduced the now common allowance for nuanced, symbiotic movement of both the avatar's body *and* the virtual camera simultaneously, as had been normalized for PC videogames years earlier with the mouse under the right hand moving the camera in relation to the position of the character, and the W, A, S, and D keys under the left hand moving the character in relation to the position of that camera.

The significance of dual-thumbstick control and the affordance of a dual embodiment of both camera and character are perhaps best illustrated in the genre of first-person videogames, where the camera and the character are most convergent.[4] As the literate player becomes attuned to dual-thumbstick control and to an embodiment of both character and camera, they are able to look in any direction with the right thumbstick while continuing to move in the "same" direction with the left thumbstick by rotating it complementarily to the new orientation of the camera. To look over the character's shoulder while continuing to walk forward, for instance, I rotate the right thumbstick clockwise to turn the character's head (my viewpoint), while my left thumb at the same time rotates counterclockwise so that the character's body continues to walk in the same direction in relation to the turning head. The complex combination of avatar and camera movement across two thumbs simultaneously, one's movement relative to the other, is of fundamental significance to the embodiment afforded to the player as both acting character and viewing audience by conventional contemporary gamepad play and the spatial navigation of 3D worlds. It is also one of gamepad play's most complex and difficult-to-learn behaviors.

Through the 2000s, as 3D navigation has become more ubiquitous in console videogames, the thumbsticks are the new resting place for the literate gamepad player's thumbs, which has relegated the d-pad and the action buttons to secondary functions because they now need to be reached for instead of lying readily under thumbs. At the same time, the importance of the shoulder buttons and triggers has increased, always already under my index fingers even as my thumbs rotate around the thumbsticks. Primary actions such as shooting guns and accelerating vehicles have shifted from the action buttons to the shoulders. Action buttons meanwhile are used for secondary actions where a quick (but delayed) movement of the thumb away from the camera-controlling right thumbstick is negligible, such as a quick switch from one weapon to the other in *Halo* (Bungie 2001) or choosing to enter a nearby car in *Grand Theft Auto IV*. The d-pad, however, has become almost tertiary and sometimes entirely unused because the left thumb is rarely free to disconnect from the left thumbstick, which determines character motility. The four directions of the d-pad have increasingly become hotkeys to quickly equip a character with different items without having to enter a menu screen or, alternatively, for snappier navigation of menu screens—tapping Down five times on the d-pad is much quicker than pulling the thumbstick down five times. The introduction and normalization of thumbsticks radically shifts my incorporation of the gamepad, yet the gamepad's lineage and hegemony persists as I adapt my learned movements and bendings.

Actions beyond Play and Play beyond Actions

Toward the center of the NES gamepad are two much smaller buttons, labeled "Start" and "Select." These buttons demonstrate the significance of button location on the gamepad relative to the resting position of the player's thumbs, as well as the significance of the shape and texture of buttons in communicating potential action to the player. Start and Select exist predominately for actions external to the virtually projected world of the videogame, such as pausing the game or accessing an options menu. Just as their actions are removed from the diegesis of the videogame's projected world, so too are the buttons removed from my typical incorporation of the gamepad. To press either Start or Select, I must reach with my right or left thumb respectively, lifting it entirely from its usual resting position over the action buttons or d-pad (or on later gamepads over the thumbsticks). The

Start and Select buttons themselves are thin and narrow, not communicating the full-rounded responsiveness of the flat action buttons or the clear directionality of the d-pad. They feel *removed* from playful action because they are removed from the thumbs' resting zones.

Importantly, the immediate feedback of buttons, triggers, and thumbsticks is not the only manner through which players perceive gamepads. The most explicit example of this broader perception is vibration, where small motors installed inside the gamepad cause it to vibrate in response to on-screen action. Varying intensities of vibration are used to communicate a vast array of physicalities, such as a sudden jolt when two cars collide in *Grand Theft Auto IV*; a trembling shockwave of a nearby colossus's footstep in *Shadow of the Colossus* (Team Ico 2005); or a constant juttering to communicate to the player that they have left the road and are driving through the garden in *Mario Kart 8* (Nintendo 2014).[5] Although a full analysis of gamepad vibration is beyond the scope of this chapter (see Parisi 2015 for such an analysis), the vibration is no less significant to the player's perception through the gamepad than fingers pressing buttons.

A Cultivated Gamepad Literacy

The layout and design of the gamepad and the particular movements and configurations it demands of me not only translate my actions into the videogame but also translate the possibilities, affordances, and texture of the videogame back to me. The resistance of a thumbstick, the urgency of a double tap, the complex combination of action buttons and d-pad express something about the played videogame as it is perceived by me as a literate player. Such engagements are literally out of sight and out of mind but fundamental and primary to the embodied experience of videogame play. The gamepad is a gestural signification of the videogame in the hands.

Although I have focused on each gamepad input type as it was standardized chronologically to the evolving gamepad and incorporated into the literate player's habitus, it bears repeating that this chapter is not intended as an exhaustive historical account of all gamepads. Such an account would demand analysis of the countless significant deviations by various companies, such as the Atari Jaguar's unwieldy 17 forward-facing buttons; the Sega Saturn's 6 action buttons as opposed to the now conventional 4; the Nintendo 64's three grips, allowing, at least theoretically, the ability to be held in three different ways; the Sega Dreamcast gamepad's ability to be expanded with plugged-in devices and LED screens; the countless third-party gamepads with "auto" or "turbo" switches that drastically augment the player–gamepad–videogame relationship; and customized gamepads such as Ben Heck's modified single-hand Xbox 360 gamepad for one-handed players, who are traditionally excluded by the normative demands of two-handed gamepads (see Heck 2006). From a phenomenological perspective, too, this study is inexhaustive because it fails to account for the significance of "inverting" movement and looking controls; the presence of "southpaw" options in many videogames that swap the use of the left and right thumbsticks; the ability to configure and remap actions across buttons generally; and the numerous ways nonnormative bodies adapt to gamepad play.

Here, I have not attempted to account for *all* player embodiments across *all* videogame play (or even across all gamepad play) but have demonstrated how the dominant conventions of gamepad design and its features have persisted and homogenized in a clear trajectory from the NES to the recently launched PlayStation 4, Xbox One, and Nintendo Switch consoles to attune players to particular behaviors and cultivate certain embodied literacies. Just as the QWERTY layout became the standard keyboard layout due to a convergence of cultural, phenomenological, and economic imperatives, the gamepad has perpetuated its dominance since the 1980s, habitualizing and commodifying players' gestures. Unlike the QWERTY keyboard, however, gamepads have grown increasingly complex. Where the NES gamepad consisted of 8 different buttons, the PlayStation 4 gamepad has 21 different modes of input. The gamepad perpetuates its own hegemony of input not just through standardization but through encroaching complexity, making it increasingly difficult to gain an embodied literacy at all, while at the same time opening up new forms of gestural signification to those who are literate.

To be literate at gamepad play is to know in your fingers how to jump Mario across a chasm and how to turn a corner in a first-person videogame; it is to perceive virtual spatialities and physicalities through the resistances, textures, distances, and movements of plastic under thumb and finger. Such a literacy does not come naturally but is instilled through the ritualized repetition of behaviors and the sensitization of the body. As playing bodies bent themselves toward the gamepad, later iterations of the gamepad bent themselves toward literate playing bodies, each perpetuating the attunement of the other in reflexive cycles that historicized (and commodified) the circuit of player-and-videogame. Just as most pianists spread their fingers in similar (if personalized) manners to play a chord regardless of which specific piano they stand before, the configurations and movements described in this section form the building blocks of literate gamepad play.

To play a videogame with a gamepad in particular is to look "with thumbs in mind" (Sudnow 1983, 21). Before conscious thought, I feel the videogame as a combination of digital sights and sounds, the resistance of plastic and rubber against thumb and index finger, and the traversal of space between buttons and thumbstick. Although a cursory glance would suggest the gamepad user is more inert and less bodily involved than the player dancing before a motion sensor or the commuter swiping at a mobile touchscreen, deeply ingrained embodied literacies are at play, taught over years of repetition, that directly couple the gamepad user's body schema to the images and sounds that constitute the videogame's virtual world.

To understand the pleasures and meanings that emerge from a particular videogame is to understand that videogame as it is played by a competent body wrapped around an input device: hands tapping at a keyboard, waving at a motion sensor, clutching a joystick, smearing a touchscreen, or, more often than not, wrapped around a gamepad. Such movements commonly go unobserved by videogame players and scholars alike, but they produce through their habituation both the pleasures and the hegemony of dominant input devices. Interfacing with a gamepad—being configured by the gamepad—is not secondary to an intellectual engagement with the videogame's virtual world but the vital umbilical through which an intellectual engagement with the virtual is made possible. It is through the competent handling of the input device that the "wired gap" (Sudnow 1983) is traversed so that we can "poke around" the virtual world. But hands do not work in isolation. We also "peer into" virtual worlds, as the *Tearaway* (MediaMolecule 2013) narrator says. The next chapter turns to the other half of this equation: the eyes-on-screens and ears-at-speakers that are looking and listening as the fingers dance across the input device.

4 To Feel Sights and Sounds

[Playing in the] mud is a more important game to study than chess.
—David Kanaga, "Music Object, Substance, Organism" (2014)

Maybe the point was just to have your part in creating the noise?
—David Sudnow, *Pilgrim in the Microworld* (1983)

Four and a half minutes into Fatboy Slim's song "Right Here, Right Now" (1998) the pace slows; music and vocals alike fade away as the song heads toward its second and more pronounced crescendo. In Dylan Fitterer's videogame *Audiosurf* (2008), this fadeaway is rendered as a spatial journey up a slow hill, the track painted in cool blues and purples as my spaceshiplike avatar slows its ascent to match the pace of the music. For several beats, the song's volume is reduced to almost silence, and the track curves upward, almost vertical, and gives me the distinct feeling of being on the precipice of a roller coaster's plunge. A moment later the drum rolls, and as the beat and rhythm and lyrics come rushing back, I plummet down into a tunnel of bright reds and yellows. Through it all, I must flick the computer mouse left and right, quickly and precisely, to avoid and collect the various blocks that begin to congest the road as the music intensifies.

In *Audiosurf*, I "play" music in a most literal sense, with songs translated into videogame spaces, sights, and actions. This translation in itself is not significant; no shortage of "rhythm games" translate music into videogame play, such as *Rez* (United Game Artists 2001), *Amplitude* (Harmonix 2003), and *Rock Band* (Harmonix 2007). However, whereas these videogames consist of a finite and predetermined number of songs, each with a visual component carefully crafted by a designer, *Audiosurf* algorithmically generates its tracks from any MP3 file it is given. No designer created the track for "Right Here, Right Now" with its hills and plunges associated with the flow of the music; *Audiosurf* pretranslated the digital data of the music being played—the song's tempo, rhythm, melody, and volume—into a videogame space that can be played. To play a song in *Audiosurf* is to experience that song's texture through senses other than listening; it is to see the song, to traverse it, to touch it.

In addition to the act of contorting hands and fingers at an input device, the acts of looking and listening are themselves vital components of the experience of videogame play. In the embodied textuality of videogame play, the moment-to-moment feel of a videogame through my perceptual apparatus distributed across worlds is meaningful. How the videogame looks (how I view), sounds (hear), and feels (touch) creates the foundation through which I perceive the videogame as a world and interpret its systems, rules, and themes. Whereas chapter 3 explored this relationship through the embodied literacies of a player wrapped around an input device and the incorporation of tangible buttons, thumbsticks, and springs into the player's body schema, this chapter is concerned with the irreducible symbiosis of this gestural signification with audiovisual engagement.

The particular literacies demanded of different input devices create different embodied experiences; however, such a claim captures only part of the bodily engagement demanded of videogame play. Tapping a button on a gamepad not connected to a videogame is not inherently meaningful; it is just a button. Videogame experience depends on a hybrid sensorial engagement of using a motor gesture to push a button *while* looking at a screen depicting moving images as virtual objects and spaces *while* listening to sounds and music. When I pull the right trigger of an Xbox gamepad to fire a sniper rifle in *Halo* (Bungie 2001), I have a tangibly different experience than when I pull that same right trigger to fire a plasma rifle in the same videogame. The former, with its small, enclosed "o" crosshair, white tracer, and loud "crack!," feels singular, powerful, and precise; the latter, with its broad "> <" crosshair depicting an area rather than a specific point, its blue globs of plasma, and its high-pitched but wavering noise, feels messy, physical, and alien. To focus solely on the player's bodily action *at* the videogame (pulling the right trigger with an index finger) is to tell only half the story of how videogame play is embodied and experienced. The other half is audiovisual.

In *Audio-Vision* (1994), Michel Chion draws attention to the "audiovisual illusion" of sound cinema (5). Sound provides *added value* that "enriches a given image so as to create the definite impression, in the immediate or remembered experience one has of it, that this information or expression 'naturally' comes from what is seen" (5). However, the very notion that the sound is an "added" value to the more fundamental imagery of cinema "is what gives the (eminently incorrect) impression that sound is unnecessary, that sound merely duplicates a meaning which in reality it brings about" (5). The convergence of audio and visuals in cinema *produces* meanings that are not inherent in the visuals alone. Likewise, for the videogame, the convergence of audiovisuals with the mechanical foundations of the simulation produces meanings that are not innate to those mechanics by themselves. No videogame mechanics actually exist for the player's hands to configure separate from their audiovisual-haptic instantiation.[1]

The physical act of pressing a videogame button is dilated to take on a broader embodied significance through the sounds and visuals that are produced in the pressing. Here, we locate specifically the copresent player straddling the hybrid actual/virtual world already theorized broadly in chapters 1 and 2, where actual physical engagements and audiovisual representation fuse into an amalgam experience across worlds and bodies. In the spliced circuit of videogame play, the senses are extended and constrained by both material hardware *and* audiovisual representations.

Music-centric videogames are directly concerned with having the player's experience of music augmented by a synthesis of kinaesthetic input and audiovisual output. In this chapter, I look at several such videogames to explore this sensorial convergence that is central to all videogame experience. First, I bring together Merleau-Ponty's notion of the banality of synaesthesic sense experience with Steve Swink's work on "game feel" to better understand how the videogame's audiovisual output converges with the player's gestures at the input device to produce a distributed and irreducible sense of perception and proprioception. The next section explores this convergence through David Kanaga's work, which sees more than a coincidence in the joint use of the verb *play* in reference to music and videogames, and through Graeme Kirkpatrick's comparisons between videogame play and dance. The final two sections then turn respectively to the abstract and phenomenological experiences of *Audiosurf* and Stephen Lavelle's videogame *Slave of God* (2012) to explore how audiovisual feedback is fundamental to how the player perceives the pressing of buttons and engagement with videogame mechanics—that is, to how the videogame *feels*. *Audiosurf* exposes a musicality to videogame play that produces an aesthetic experience through bodily performances. *Slave of God* complements this musicality of play by providing what might be described as a purely perceptual experience. A short videogame that has the player navigate a nightclub from a traditional first-person perspective, *Slave of God* overwhelms the player's senses with a barrage of nearly incoherent sights and sounds. Through an immediate engagement with sights and sounds "in themselves," this videogame suggests a need to account for looking and listening as essential components of videogame play in their own right, not just in relation to the body's movements with an input device.

Everyday Synesthesia and Game Feel

When David Sudnow first became entangled with *Missile Command* (Atari 1980), he was fascinated by the synergy of his hand's movements and the screen imagery dancing before his eyes: "as you watch the cursor move, your look appreciates the sight with thumbs in mind, and the joystick-button box feels like a genuine implement of action" (1983, 21–22). Looking, listening, and touching mingled to create alternative and convergent perceptual apparatuses: "Punctuate a moving picture? I'm no painter and don't dance in mirrors. But here I could watch a mysterious transformation of my movements taking place on the other side of the room, my own participation in the animated interface unfolding in an extraordinary spectacle of lights, colors, and sounds" (1983, 23). Even with the relatively low fidelity of *Missile Command*, Sudnow immediately realizes the pleasure of videogame play as not simply one of action but of being caught up in a visual and aural spectacle—both intimately as a participant and remotely as an audience. Grasping at this physicality he detects in audiovisual videogame play, he calls videogames "instantaneously punctuated picture music. Supercerebral crystal clear Silicon Valley eye jazz" (135). I love these terms for how they reach toward a fundamental irreducibility of how videogames are sensorially perceived. How they look, how they sound, and how they feel cannot be easily or constructively distinguished. They are "punctuated picture music," they are "eye jazz"; they provide visuals for the ear to listen to and sounds for the eye to look at. They provide audiovisuals for the body to feel.

Everyday Synesthesia

Merleau-Ponty would find nothing odd in Sudnow's seemingly jumbled assessment of videogame experience. Rather, he takes issue with the common language used to describe the experience of each of the senses as ever being discrete: "I say that my eyes see, that my hand touches, and that my foot is aching, but these naïve expressions do not convey my genuine experience. They already present me with an interpretation of it that detaches it from its original subject" (2012, 220). Each sense is itself, he argues, *"a thought subjugated to a certain field"* (225, original emphasis), and it is through the simultaneous experience of all the available sensorial fields that an object's form is perceived by a body. Like Chion, Merleau-Ponty exemplifies this ambiguity of sensorial experience with the example of "an auditory rhythm [fusing] cinematic images together [to give] rise to a perception of movement whereas, without an auditory contribution, the same succession of images would be too slow to provoke the stroboscopic movement" (237). As the audible plays a shaping role in producing the visual in the cinematic medium, so too does the audiovisual play a shaping role in producing the sensuous in the videogame medium.

The sight of sounds and the hearing of colors exist as phenomena. Such synaesthesic perception, argues Merleau-Ponty, not only exists in medical cases but is also the general rule of sense experience. In everyday lived experience, our senses work together as lenses through which we perceive the world around us, and it is only in the language of conscious thought that perception is subjugated to its distinct fields of sight, sound, smell, touch. In a longer passage I want to quote in full, Merleau-Ponty provides a series of examples of what he understands as the way the senses intercommunicate to open onto the structure of things:

> We see the rigidity and the fragility of the glass and, when it breaks with a crystal-clear sound, this sound is borne by the visible glass. We see the elasticity of steel, the ductility of molten steel, the hardness of the blade in a plane, and the softness of its shavings. ... The form of a fold in a fabric of linen or of cotton shows us the softness or the dryness of the fiber, and the coolness or the warmth of the fabric. ... [T]he movement of visible objects is not the simple displacement of color patches that correspond to them in the visual field. In the movement of the branch from which a bird has just left, we read its flexibility and its elasticity, and this is how the branch of an apple tree and the branch of a birch are immediately distinguished. We see the weight of a block of cast iron that sinks into the sand, the fluidity of the water, and the viscosity of the syrup. Likewise, I hear the hardness and the unevenness of the cobblestones in the sound of a car, and we are right to speak of a "soft," "dull," or "dry" sound. ... Finally, if I alternately bend a steel bar and a lime tree branch with my eyes closed, I perceive between my two hands the most secret texture of the metal and of the wood. (2012, 238–239)

Just as two eyes function together to create single, unified vision, we perceive objects through all our available senses working together.

Merleau-Ponty here points toward an everyday synesthesia. The different senses are lenses that open up onto different facets of the world, and the world is perceived through an entwining of the senses. This is of particular importance to understanding how the virtual worlds of videogames are perceived in the synergetic system of player-and-videogame, where the hardness and brittleness of glass, the unevenness of cobblestones, and the fluidity of water are conveyed on a television or computer screen through animations and textures and sound effects and are engaged through a virtual body navigated by an input device. Through the resistance of the same gamepad thumbstick, one vehicle in *Grand Theft Auto IV* (Rockstar North 2008) can feel heavier than another. I perceive the weight of these virtual vehicles in no small part through how they look and sound on the screen. The properties of objects in videogames, tangibly perceived by the player, communicate their tactility through an entwining of how they look, how they sound, how they feel.

Game Feel and Juiciness

Videogame designer Steve Swink proposes the concept of "game feel" in an attempt to model this entanglement of sight, sound, and touch. Swink defines "game feel" as "real-time control of virtual objects in a simulated space, with interactions emphasized by polish" (2009, 6) and describes the experience of game feel as "to see through different eyes, hear through different ears and touch with a different body" (25). Although he was writing a handbook for an audience of videogame developers, his work remains to date the most robust consideration of how videogame play "feels." In particular, his definition of "polish" (touched on briefly in the discussion of casual mobile videogames in chapter 2) is telling:

> Polish refers to any effect that artificially enhances interaction without changing the underlying simulation. This could mean dust particles at a character's feet as it slides, a crashing sound when two cars collide, a "camera shake" to emphasize a weighty impact, or a keyframed animation that makes a character seem to squash and stretch as it moves. Polish effects add appeal and *emphasize the physical nature of interactions*, helping designers sell those objects to the player as real. (2009, 5, emphasis added)

Here Swink draws attention to the crucial role of audiovisual elements in videogame design. Just as Chion notes the "added value" that sound brings to cinema, polish elements are "artificial" insofar as they do not affect the "mechanics" or rule structure of the underlying simulation. But they *do* affect the player's perception of the physicality or tactility of objects in the videogame. That is, they *do* affect the player's experience.

   Although Swink's nod to the artificiality of polish and to the "underlying" simulation does echo a traditional view of videogames as fundamentally mechanical and superficially audiovisual, he is careful to counter this view when speaking in terms of how the player *experiences* the videogame: "if all polish were removed, the essential functionality of the game would be unaltered, but the player would find the experience less perceptually convincing and therefore less appealing. This is because—for players—simulation and polish are indistinguishable" (2009, 6). Like the sounds of cinema (Chion 1994, 5), polish does not merely duplicate existing meanings in the "underlying" videogame mechanics; it *creates* meaning. Indeed, the very notion that mechanics are more fundamentally formal to videogames than audiovisuals makes little sense. Without the tangible audiovisual-haptic form that constitutes the videogame's content, its mechanical systems wouldn't exist at all. When considering how videogames are experienced by players, the videogame's mechanical function cannot be meaningfully distinguished from the audiovisuals that constitute the virtual world. Form and content must instead be flattened and understood as a singular, all-at-once experience of videogame play.

Swink is not the only one to highlight the fundamental significance of how it feels to engage with a videogame. As discussed in the context of casual mobile videogames in chapter 2, Jesper Juul draws from earlier work by game designer Kyle Gabler to discuss "juiciness" as excessive positive feedback that grants the player "an immediate, pleasurable experience" (2010, 45). Juul's example of a videogame with juiciness is *Peggle* (Popcap 2007), with its vibrant colors and exaggerated sound effects. Simply dropping a ball into a pachinko-like machine can, when the player hits the final red peg, creates an overture of music and rainbows and fireworks (see figure 4.1). Similarly, in Halfbrick's mobile videogame *Fruit Ninja* (2010), the simple action of swiping a finger to slice fruit in half is enhanced with the feedback of seeing the fruit split at my touch, the *swoosh* sound of the blade cleanly passing through the fruit, the *splat* of juice against the wooden background. By contrast, when my reflexes overreach my intent and send my finger flying into a bomb, the bomb does not slice in half but for a moment gives a sense of solid resistance before it explodes and removes a life. Through a literal performance of juiciness, *Fruit Ninja* feels satisfying to touch.

In 2013, Jan Willem Nijman, half of two-person development team Vlambeer, discussed his commitment to making videogames feel good in a lecture titled "The Art of Screenshake." Starting with a basic prototype of a sidescrolling shooter, Nijman gradually added more and more effects to the videogame while keeping the underlying mechanics of shooting, jumping, and moving the same. Bigger bullets, sound effects, and animations tangibly alter the feel of the videogame, as do "screenshake" and "lerp" (short

Figure 4.1
The audiovisual overture of hitting the final red peg in *Peggle* (PopCap Games 2007).

for "linear interpolation") camera effects. The term *screenshake* refers to a common visual effect that rattles the screen space in response to particular events, such as the firing of a gun or a large explosion. The term *camera lerp* refers to effects on the virtual camera's movement wherein the camera lags behind the avatar's movement rather than keeping the avatar fixed in the center of its gaze. Each of these effects function as explicit remediations of televisual media, selling the tangibility of the videogame events as though they were being captured by a physically grounded and imperfect camera rather than by an arbitrary virtual viewpoint. The result is a videogame that feels tangibly different to engage with as each new effect is added, despite the unchanging input of fingers-on-keyboard.

"Game feel," "juiciness," and "polish" are significant forbears to appreciating the embodied and irreducible pleasures of videogame experience. Yet the intended audience of the accounts referenced earlier, with the exception of Juul's work, is the videogame developer, which renders them too prescriptive for my focus on the played experience of videogames. Game feel, for instance, is restricted in its need to quantify itself as a property that some videogames possess and others do not. Because Swink wrote his book *Game Feel* primarily to help developers detect and create game feel and necessarily limited it in scope to those videogames that he saw as providing real-time control, spatial simulation, and polish, he explicitly excluded many videogames from his conception of game feel (2009, 76–80). To limit game feel as a thing that some videogames possess and others do not restricts the concept's usefulness here because I am less concerned with game feel as a reproducible attribute and more with accounting for how any particular videogame feels to play. Rather than excluding a videogame for a supposed lack of real-time control, I find it more useful to understand what *does* make a videogame feel a certain way to play.[2]

Across these discussions of game feel and juice, a crucial point emerges: the audiovisual flesh is as significant as the mechanical skeleton when considering how a player experiences a videogame. To appreciate how a videogame feels, to perceive its material form, is to appreciate the irreducible sensorial experience, wherein the resistance of springs beneath buttons, visual flourishes, audio cues, *and* mechanical organization combine to provide tactility, texture, and tangibility to the screen imagery.

As we perceive our world through the different facets of our senses simultaneously, we perceive the videogame not as audiovisuals detached from actions but as sight, sound, and touch simultaneously. An appreciation of videogame play cannot assume the fundamental intelligibility of the videogame experience but must instead account for the sensorial and embodied perception and subsequent feel of playing a certain videogame. To make sense of videogame experience, we must, following Susan Sontag's advice for art critics, "learn to *see* more, to *hear* more, to *feel* more" ([1964] 2009a, 14, original emphasis). One cannot separate the mechanics of *Halo*'s sniper rifle from its audiovisual depiction because without this depiction there would be no sniper rifle for the player to otherwise perceive. Audiovisual representation does not just give context to videogame action; it *constructs* videogame action.

A Musicality of Videogames

Videogames are not *just* digitalized nondigital games; they are audiovisual playspaces. Before and while the videogame player "acts" in a strictly mechanical or gestural sense, they look at images and listen to sounds *as an irreducible part of* the play experience. Although much scholarly work around videogames distinguish between acting and viewing—such as

Alexander Galloway's claim that "play is absent" when the player stands inactive on a street corner in *Shenmue* (Sega AM2 1999) (2006, 10)—no such distinction is truly possible. If a player is required to do nothing but look and listen for a period of time while playing a videogame—such as during a cutscene or while waiting for another player to complete their turn—they are still actively engaged with the videogame as an audiovisual playspace.

The immanent and corporeal engagement the body has with the material, audiovisual-haptic form of the videogame as an embodied textuality is irreducible and meaningful in this irreducibility. In a discussion on the bodily operation of expression, Merleau-Ponty makes a similar point about the "in-itself" nature of music:

The musical signification of the sonata *is inseparable from the sounds that carry it*: prior to having heard it, no analysis allows us to anticipate it. Once the performance has come to an end, we cannot do anything in our intellectual analyses of the music but refer back to the moment of the experience. During the performance, the sounds are not merely the "signs" of the sonata; rather, the sonata is there through them and it descends into them. ... The signification absorbs the signs. (2012, 188, emphasis added)

There exists no essence, no "content," of the experienced music detached from the sounds that are the music. Videogames are similarly temporal. There exists no essence, no content, of the experience of videogame play detached from the audiovisuals and haptics that produce it. The perceptual experience does not refer to the videogame; rather, the videogame is there through that experience.

The irreducibility of music and the sounds that constitute it provide a useful analogy for comprehending the irreducibility of videogames and the audiovisuals that constitute them. In particular, the close ontological and phenomenological relationship between music and videogames is of central concern in the writings of videogame developer, composer, and critic David Kanaga. Across a number of esoteric essays written since 2011, Kanaga explores the close formal relationship between music and videogames, working from the hypothesis that both forms are subsets of a broader form that he has come to call "shifting possibility spaces" (2013). He takes as his hypothesis the notion that both videogames and music are "played": even if we treat music and videogames as discrete media, "it is hard not to be curious what is this PLAY that music and games have in common" (2013).[3] He argues that although videogames "are called games by habit," the material requirements of the medium of *videogames* (as opposed to the medium of games) do not demand goals or mastery; rather, "we can *move* or *play* in videogames—not much more can be said definitely. I am interested in a *formalism* ... that builds from this premise, that regards this movement in much the same way that musical movement is regarded, which has meanings, but meanings which are unspeakable, which are living in the material itself, and which mean very little divorced from the context" (2013). Kanaga argues for the playing of videogames, as a shifting possibility space through which the character can move (and with which the player uses movement to engage), to be understood much like the playing of musical compositions or instruments through their "degrees of freedom, or haptic capacity to be *played*" (2013).[4] Just as Sudnow understands both playing jazz music and playing videogames as "an embodied way of accomplishing distance" ([1978] 2001, 15), Kanaga sees both music and videogames as kinaesthetic in their pleasures, but a kinaesthesia symbiotically tied to vision and sound.

Shifting Possibility Spaces

To highlight such an intimacy between the forms of videogames and music is not to suggest the two should be collapsed together or their obvious peculiarities ignored. Neither Kanaga nor I wish to replace the conflation of "videogame" and "game" with a new conflation of "videogame" and "music." Rather, we are each arguing that a shared ontology allows fresh insights into how players engage with and experience videogames as fundamentally audiovisual. Just as has already been done extensively for videogames and nondigital forms of play, Kanaga shows how the language and concepts developed around music over centuries (rhythm, harmony, melody, pitch, timbre, etc.) can deepen our understanding of how materially different types of works are "played with" as possibility spaces. For instance, on the playfulness of Wassily Kandinsky's painting *Transverse Line* (1923), Kanaga writes:

Allow the line connecting our pupils to the picture to be the "avatar" or "player character" in the playspace. "Line of sight," "Line of attention," etc. ... Drift *intentionally*, from one spot to another, and feel the light-affects change as [the] zone of the picture you are focused on comes in and out of focus. The matrix in the upper-left corner can be massaged with the eyes somewhat, like flicking fingers through the teeth of a comb—brlrlrlrlrlrlr—rhythms slowing down some as gaps between lines increase, speeding up as they close together—maybe pitches changing likewise (faster rhythm = higher pitch, when *zoomed into*). Looking at other sections may feel totally different—colors to me often feel more like harmonic zones, whereas lines feel like rhythmic contours. It is worth spending some GOOD TIME with these pictures, like the amount of time you might spend with a little flash game, and to drift through them and feel the music/affect of the different points and their interrelations. (2013, ellipses in the original)

Through required bodily engagement, different creative works—including videogames—can be played with, and this play has its own rhythms, melodies, a timbre.

Videogames have a particular rhythm of movement: an "input-*microrhythm*" (Kanaga 2013) that flows through—that *is*—the fluctuating feedback loop of input and output, input and output between player and videogame, the pleasure of acting and the pleasure of being acted upon. This "input-microrhythm" gives a videogame its timbre. As a C-sharp played on a piano sounds different from the same C-sharp played on a guitar because each note is produced through different material qualities, so, too, does walking on each different surface in the platformer *Super Mario 64* (Nintendo 1996)—grass, stone, ice, and so on—feel different: "the mechanics of a game can be likened to an instrument in a piece of music; the *feel* of those mechanics (or how they interact with the world ...)[,] being the feel of instrument, is an experience which has everything to do with timbre" (Kanaga 2011, ellipses in the original). A C-sharp is a C-sharp, and Mario walking is Mario walking. But producing different C-sharps on materially different instruments feels different, and the different surfaces that Mario walks on feel different. How a particular videogame feels to play in its blending of instrument and audiovisual feedback, Kanaga enticingly suggests here, can be considered that videogame's timbre.[5]

Kanaga is interested in videogames, like music, as played form. As performed. As *touched by* and *touching* the player. As having *unspeakable* meanings that cannot be divorced from the experience and feel of embodied videogame play. The triple jump I can perform in *Mario 64* by tapping A on the gamepad again and again at the precise moment Mario touches the ground, at just the right rhythm, is an unintelligible pleasure. It is innately satisfying for me the same way playing one chord after another is satisfying for the musician. I tap the button at the right rhythm, and the plastic pushes back against my finger, and Mario makes more excited sounds with each subsequent jump, ending with the crescendo "wa-hoo!" and a cartwheel on the third jump. Rather than attempting to understand *why* pressing these buttons in this order in this videogame is meaningful, we need to be able to describe *how* pressing these buttons in this order in the context of this particular audiovisual output is innately expressive. To be caught up with (that is, to move with) the sights and sounds *is* the point.

Understanding videogames as shifting possibility spaces shifts the focus away from videogames as strictly goal-driven activities toward videogames as a more open-ended form of expression. This is seen most clearly in Kanaga's own videogame work. In *Proteus* (2013), a relaxed wandering game that Kanaga worked on alongside designer Ed Key, the "music" is embedded in the environment; the musical sound effects of flowers and birds and trees and stones and crabs allow each player's particular movement through the space to perform a different composition. The player simply walks, looks, and listens, and "these mundane acts of the senses, so routinely overlooked in favour of the more complicated interactions that video games can offer, become paramount in *Proteus*" (Golding 2013a, 108). At the other end of the spectrum, *Dyad* (Right Square Bracket Left Square Bracket 2012) is an overwhelming and intoxicating arcade experience that Kanaga worked on alongside designer Shawn McGrath, which throws the player into a much more restrictive possibility space, but one that is still focused on forms of movement producing different engagements with music. In *Panoramical* (2015), which Kanaga created with Fernando Ramallo, the player produces the landscape they angelically fly over, twisting dials and sliding faders on a MIDI (musical instrument digital interface) music controller or using the keyboard and mouse to augment both the videogame's soundtrack and landscape as one synaesthesic whole.

Other developers, too, explore this synthesis of "playing" videogames and "playing" music. Iain Snyder's *UN EP* (2013) provides a variety of toylike screens in which different inputs from the player create different aural and visual outputs; there are no goals or win states, simply a space in which music can be "played *with*" (Snyder quoted in Lucas 2013). The *Rock Band* and *Guitar Hero* (Harmonix) franchises are well known for letting players play at playing songs—not playing the songs per se but holding their bodies in the performative posture of a guitar-toting rock star and re-creating a gesturally simplified version of guitar play—and often provide breaks in songs for the player to improvise freeform "solos." Hu Wen Zeng's mobile videogame *Piano Tiles* (2014) has the player rapidly tapping black tiles and avoiding white tiles to stay alive. As the player taps, a piece of piano music plays, giving the bodily sensation of acting out a virtuosic piano performance with two fingers. What Kanaga's work and these musical videogames suggest is that more than goals or challenges or narrative, what a videogame formally requires to provide a meaningful experience is audiovisually depicted spaces and objects that can be played with—some "eye-noise" to become a part of.

Play and Dance

Whereas videogames such as *Rock Band* are more concerned with "playing music" in the sense of simulating the role of "music performer," a better analogy for the experience cultivated by videogames such as *Audiosurf* and *Rez* might be playing with music as a dancer plays with music: matching bodily movements and visual spectacle to musical movements and sounds rather than to specific instruments or notes, capturing the *sensation* of music in the player-dancer's gestures. Kirkpatrick traces a parallel between dance and videogame play, sensing a similar importance of bodily movement to each form and a similar difficulty in interpreting "meaning" from such movements:

Like dance, video games are caught up in a paradoxical refusal of textual or discursive meaning, although anyone who has attended a dance performance knows there is an inherent ephemerality about this vanishing content and that its very transience is somehow essential. … Both practices create methodological difficulties. Meaning interpretation requires skills of exegesis and linguistic or textual analysis focused on idea but dance and games present bodies in motion. (2011, 120–121)

The metaphor of dance is enticing, but Kirkpatrick's use of it becomes confused when he mentions "anyone who has attended a dance performance" as though playing a videogame is equivalent to *watching* a dance performance. Videogame players are not attending a dance performance; they are dancing. They *are* the performer (albeit one still in training through ongoing dressage), and what might be ephemeral to the observer of a dance recital is embodied and felt by the dancer as the rhythms of their body incorporates the rhythms of the music.

Kirkpatrick's interest in dance and *bodily* movement in the strictest sense leads him to reject conceptualizations of videogame play as a cybernetic circuit and of the player as constituting a cyborgian subjectivity and instead to prioritize the social context of the playing (organic) body (2011, 150–151). This prioritization, however, elides the fact that the "dance" of videogame play is a dance *with* the machine and *with* audiovisual representations. Indeed, in a vivid description of playing *Pac-Man* (Namco 1980) to demonstrate "the principle that video games contain dance moves" (2011, 127), Kirkpatrick highlights this himself:

Pacman [is] surrounded by ghosts who are bearing down on him along all the available paths. Only by *pirouetting* on the spot can he wait for one ghost to turn off at a junction, which opens an escape route. The player's body, especially their hand and arm, must transmit just the right forces at exactly the right time to pull this manoeuvre off successfully. Pacman is programmed never to be stationary so keeping him on one spot requires rapid alteration of the directional controls. This performance is normally accompanied by great, Bergsonian hilarity, or at least relief, because it is such a feat of poise and timing. (2011, 127, original emphasis)

This is a beautiful description of videogame play, but although Kirkpatrick is right to point out the primacy of movement and the "priority of form" (2011, 128) it suggests, his own description contradicts his dismissal of cyborg subjectivity. The "dance moves" of the player's hand and arm in playing *Pac-Man* are meaningful as such only in the context of the arcade joystick, the visually represented maze and ghosts and avatar, and the various sounds *produced* by the combination of these elements. If the player were to play *Pac-Man* on a different platform, these bodily motions would be altered by the different mediations of the player's body, such as perhaps the need to slide a thumb over a gamepad's d-pad or swipe an index finger over a smartphone's touchscreen rather than jerk an arm to and fro to move an arcade machine's joystick. The body that the player dances with is produced with the videogame. Despite the contradiction, Kirkpatrick's drawing together of dance and videogame play remains significant, with the caveat that the player dances *with* the videogame, not just *at* the videogame.

Kirkpatrick claims that "we should recognize that there is not one organizing meaning that suffuses the activity [of videogame play], but that its primary moments are just meaningless" (2011, 151). The notion of individual bodily movements being "meaningless" (in a strictly intelligible or interpretative sense) is compelling for paying attention to how it feels to play a videogame, where minuscule but rhythmic bodily twitches and gestures synthesize the playing body not just with the movement of the music but with the virtual avatar's spatial movement. What is important is not to be able to explain why a videogame is thematically meaningful but to be able to describe how that videogame is meaningfully perceived and constituted. The remainder of this chapter looks at two videogames that stress the urgency of this approach. Like the musician or dancer, the players of *Audiosurf* and *Slave of God*—indeed of all videogames—produce shapes, sounds, rhythms, colors, and forms that provide a synaesthesic texture and tactility to the worlds they both perceive and produce.

Playing Songs in *Audiosurf*

Dylan Fitterer's videogame *Audiosurf* exemplifies the mundane synesthesia of videogame play, where audiovisual engagement is inseparable from and fundamentally entangled with mechanical systems and gestural movements. In *Audiosurf*, the player's spaceshiplike avatar moves forward automatically down a track while the player slides the mouse to move the avatar left and right, picking up or avoiding different-colored blocks along the track to gain points in a basic match-three block game happening at the bottom of the screen (see figure 4.2). Different characters with different abilities can be chosen, but each is always simple enough to be played with a single hand on the mouse. One character allows the colored blocks to be picked up and placed in different columns; a different character can destroy all the blocks of a single color.

Yet, despite this minimal bodily incorporation, *Audiosurf* provides a captivating engagement through the way it allows players to "ride your music," as its slogan promises. "Music" and "videogame" are inseparable at the most ontological level in *Audiosurf*. The videogame's algorithms read an MP3 file selected from the player's computer and translate that audio file into a 3D track to be "played." A quiet song will translate into a gradual, relaxed, uphill climb in soft purples and blues; a loud, intense song will be all downhill plummets in reds and oranges. A song with a fast beat will be bumpy and jittery, tossing the player's avatar around; a song of lonely acoustics will provide smooth valleys and hills. The aural experience of listening to music is translated into an experience of spatial movement and haptic twitching.

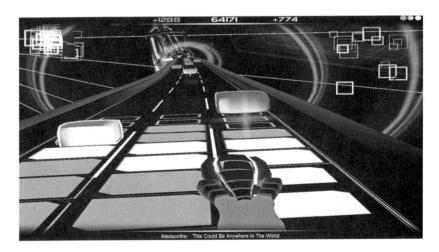

Figure 4.2
Audiosurf (Fitterer 2008). As blocks are collected, they enter the grid. Blocks disappear when three or more of the same color are adjacent, and the player receives points relative to the number of blocks in the grouping. If the player overfills a column of the grid, they lose points.

Tempo becomes acceleration and gradient; volume becomes warm and cool colors; percussion instruments are transformed into tunnels; cacophonies of instruments playing at once become congested traffic jams of blocks that need to be frantically and deliberately collected or avoided.

When a musical track produces an *Audiosurf* track, each block is generated by different noises in the song. Loud and intense parts of a song will be congested with high-scoring "warm" red and yellow blocks, whereas a quieter section will mean sparse, "cool" blue and purple blocks. For the "mono" character, though, all but a few blocks are grayed out, to be avoided rather than collected, allowing for a more relaxed surf focused less on scoring or optimal play and more on simply moving through the music. Fitterer has explained in interviews how this collection or evasion of the blocks is meant to suit different personal engagements with music: "For some people it's more of a zone-out relaxing experience, playing with the mono character. If you play it with the pusher character, it's more of this hopped-up, intense-focus, high-alert kind of experience, and that's kind of what I want from music" (in Wilburn 2008).

More important than the blocks is the shape of the track, which Fitterer explains is formed by frequency analysis:

The basic gist is that when the music is at its most intense, that's when you're on a really steep downward slope, like you're flying down a rollercoaster in a tunnel. When the music is calmer, that's when you're chugging your way up the hill, watching that peak in the distance you're going to reach. And music is not all about just going uphill and downhill; lots of music has speed bumps and waves that you ride, so that's all pulled out of the song. (in Wilburn 2008)

The videogame's audiovisual design and its "underlying" mechanics are ultimately inseparable. Indeed, it is literally from underlying audio data that the mechanics of any one particular course emerges. Yet *Audiosurf* is less concerned with a mathematically accurate mapping of music to videogame than a desire to capture the feel of music in videogame form. I flick my wrist left and the right to collect blocks as two distinct notes play, and the satisfaction of this rhythmic flicking is its own meaningful action, even as it remains unintelligible, not unlike tapping my finger along to my favorite song. It synthesizes my incorporation of the mouse with the sounds of the music to provide the chance "to be part of the noise" (Sudnow 1983, 4). To play a song in *Audiosurf* is to experience that song's form through sensorial fields other than hearing.

Audiosurf, whose tracks are derived algorithmically from the player's own music collection, is concerned primarily with ensuring that experiencing a

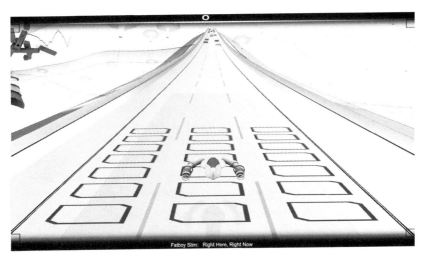

Figure 4.3
The slow, gradually fading-in intro of Fatboy Slim's song "Right Here, Right Now" in *Audiosurf* (Fitterer 2008).

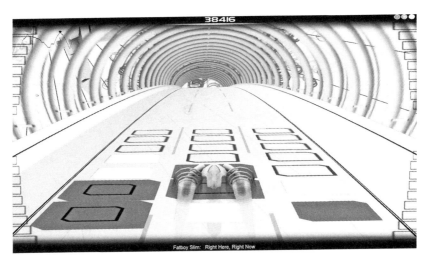

Figure 4.4
Reaching and about to plunge off the second climax of Fatboy Slim's "Right Here, Right Now" in *Audiosurf* (Fitterer 2008).

song through the videogame has a feel relatable to experiencing that same song simply as music. Fatboy Slim's "Right Here, Right Now," as already discussed in the introduction to this chapter, progresses through three movements, with the conventional climbs and drops of house and dance music, where a repetitive and slow rhythm gradually builds to eventually explode in a cacophony of noise and beats. In *Audiosurf*, this progression is translated into two distinct mountain climbs and sudden, steep plunges. But moment to moment, too, the shifts between the song's movements are intense. The song fades in gradually from silence, with lyrics ("Right here right now" repeated again and again), synth, and increasingly loud percussion. In *Audiosurf*, the gradual introduction of instruments causes my ship to accelerate and the road to become increasingly cluttered with blocks as the drum kicks in (see figure 4.3). A minute in, the music that has only just started to build drops away, leaving only the repeating lyrics, slowing me back down again to a near standstill for just a moment before the music returns suddenly atop the first drop. Through the middle of the song, the music becomes bouncier, and the lyrics change to the longer line "Waking up to find your love's not real," also repeated again and again. In *Audiosurf*, this section of the song becomes one of constant ripples rather than smooth climbs, with the cadence of the lyrics creating a bouncing path of small hills. The path smooths out again at the four-minute mark when the lyrics fade and the synth quietly returns, beginning the next slow climb toward a climax before, again, the final crescendo rushes in for the final two minutes of the song. In the game, this second climb-and-drop is conveyed as a sudden, jarring about-turn as the fast, bouncing red and yellow track suddenly swings back upward and turns a cool purple; little traffic populates the road, and the camera pulls back from my avatar to reveal the long climb ahead of me. As the music speeds up again toward the climax, more traffic fills the uphill climb, with rows of blue and purple blocks; collecting or avoiding each block gives a visceral sensation of the music becoming more crowded, of building toward something. At the very peak of the second and final climax, a moment of silence occurs before the drums bring in the plunge (see figure 4.4). This moment makes my avatar jerk to a stop at the very precipice of the hill as the blocks ahead of it plummet down, a sensation not unlike watching the first carriage go down a roller coaster before your own. After I go over the edge and the song explodes into its final act, valuable reds and yellows clutter the road, and I must slide the mouse back and forward rapidly and deliberately to survive the onslaught without overflowing the grid. This final act is differentiated from the first downhill slope by an occasional distorted cymbal crash, which manifests as a row of red blocks, an easy way to score points amid the clutter. With each cymbal crash, then, my hand twitches to intersect this row of high-scoring blocks, evoking how I might jerk my body to this particular moment of the song in a nightclub. As the six-minute song finally comes to an end, the last downhill rush plateaus out at the moment the final "right here" fades away with an echo ("Here here here here …"). As the camera pulls back and I see the flat, near-empty track ahead of me, I feel almost a sense of relief, as if I have come out alive on the far side of an obstacle course.

In contrast to Fatboy Slim's dance music, Bon Iver's song "Skinny Love" (2007) is a slow acoustic song. There is no percussion to push the song forward; the song instead relies solely on regular guitar strums of varying volume and soft vocals. In *Audiosurf*, this sound is translated into a wave-like track that undulates as the player climbs small crests and then surfs down the far side of them as the guitar chords fade—up and down, up and down. This is most pronounced in the chorus, where the iambic feet of the lyrics ("and I *told* you to be patient / and I *told* you to be fine") has the player climb to a small peak, rush down a hill with the word *told*, and then ride a half-pipe back to another peak in time for the next line. Just as this song is much slower and more straightforward than "Right Here, Right Now," so too is its *Audiosurf* manifestation. It is a shorter track and a much more consistent one, without dramatic change or congestion. Blocks in the visualization are much more sparse, and a single block often sits atop each crest of the chorus, so that collecting them feels akin to tapping along with the song. The pace allows me to more deliberately collect different colors rather than frantically scurry as I do for "Right Here, Right Now." The more relaxed pace does not render "Skinny Love" a less interesting song to play in *Audiosurf*, however. "Skinny Love" still plays like "Skinny Love" sounds: slow, melancholic, and sing-songy.

A vast diversity of movement and play sensations intimately tied to the chosen song are available to the *Audiosurf* player. The music is not laid over a core, predetermined visual track to give it a certain flavor, but the track and other elements themselves emerge from the audio data in a mingling of forms that I experience through my incorporation of the videogame by means of convergent sensorial fields: my eyes on the screen, engaging with lines and colors and movement; my ears hearing the song and the video-game's sound effects; my hand flicking the mouse to and fro and click-ing buttons to move blocks. Just as Merleau-Ponty insists one perceives the world synaesthesically through different sensorial fields, *Audiosurf*, by translating the sensation of performing a song (playing, dancing, listening, etc.) into "playing" a videogame, communicates the phenomenological sensation of engaging with that song through different sensorial fields across different embodiments of different media. Through sight, sound, and touch, a dance song still feels like a dance song, and a soft acoustic song still feels like a soft acoustic song.

Audiosurf foregrounds the inseparability of the experience of the eyes and ears with the experience of the moving body in videogame play. That "Right Here, Right Now" and "Skinny Love" feel distinctly different to engage with in *Audiosurf* suggests that what the player does and how it feels to do that are fundamentally caught up with what the player looks at and listens to. How a videogame *feels* to play is constituted by how audiovisual and haptic engagements come together to create that sensation of movement as an unintelligible expression that is ephemerally meaningful in the moment of play. If videogames are incorporated as much as they are interpreted through an embodied textuality where perceived content emerges through performed materiality, then to understand how and why different songs played in *Audiosurf* feel different—and why this feeling is meaningful in and of itself—is to understand the transient and corporeal played meanings of movement, of sensation, of being-in-the-world that produce the platform for the necessary intelligible, conscious engagement with a videogame to become possible.

Overwhelmed in *Slave of God*

Although *Audiosurf* provides an example of the formal importance of movement to videogame play and the importance of audiovisual engagement to the timbre or feel of that movement, it still functions safely within the accepted paradigm of real-time control. The immediate and direct relationship between player input through the mouse and the videogame output of audiovisual representation is the core experience—the focus remains squarely on the player's "action." This direct manipulation of the sounds and images of the videogame is certainly crucial to the experience of videogame play, but no less important is the parallel significance of the videogame player's engagement with audiovisual elements that are not necessarily connected directly to real-time control. Examples of these engagements, often overlooked or downplayed in scholarly analyses of videogames, include the spectacle of a prerendered cutscene; the theme song playing over a videogame's final credits; the satisfaction of watching units fulfill their orders in a turn-based strategy game; and the presentation of a videogame's opening splash screens.[6] These engagements with audiovisual elements are not directly mediated by the player's haptic inputs but remain crucial elements of the player's engagement with most videogames. The final section of this chapter explores what it means to consider looking and listening in themselves as significant acts of videogame play, using the videogame *Slave of God* as a particularly salient example.

Stephen Lavelle's *Slave of God* places me in the body of a person at a nightclub. Controlled with conventional first-person controls on a keyboard and mouse, the game requires that I move the character around the various spaces of the nightclub, from the dance floor to the bar to the men's bathroom. Although the game has a conclusion, its dominant experience is one of self-paced exploration. What is significant and most immediately striking about Lavelle's game is the audiovisual depiction of the space. From the moment I click on the quiet and minimal menu screen to start the videogame proper, I am hit with a barrage of lights and sounds. Ripples of color quiver and convulse across the walls and floor, not necessarily proportional to the perspective from which I am viewing them. Wavering lines jump and jitter flatly across perpendicular walls, blurring like a 3D movie viewed without the right glasses. The colors of certain objects, such as people or cocktails, spill out beyond their object's borders to smear like watery paint. Focusing is difficult; the videogame hurts my eyes. The space itself feels inconsistent, constantly shifting and morphing with the colors in kaleidoscopic patterns. Meanwhile, the music is loud and raving, a simple dance

Figure 4.5
Having a drink and watching the dancer in *Slave of God* (Lavelle 2012).

Figure 4.6
Trapped on the dance floor in *Slave of God* (Lavelle 2012).

loop stubbornly repeated again and again, but also morphing and shifting into quieter or louder versions depending on where I am in the club. Near the dance floor, the colors are at their most dominant and the music is at its loudest. If I walk my character into the center of the dance floor, our vision locks onto another dancer, so that A and D on the keyboard no longer allow me to sidestep left and right but only to rotate around this other dancer. My camera involuntarily spins and blurs and further distorts the entire screen, trapping me in the dance (see figure 4.6).

Slave of God feels like a nightclub. merritt k notes that the videogame's unique style "chooses to emphasize *intensity of feeling* in order to create an experience that is in a way 'truer' than a photorealistic representation might be" (2014, original emphasis). That is, *Slave of God* is concerned more with *feeling* like a nightclub than with *looking* like one. Cara Ellison similarly describes *Slave of God* as being

wonderful at capturing the way music muffles and meanders in the brain when you are drunk under flashing lights; it's a sort of a little prayer to a one-off experience, something halfway from a nightmare to a delirious hallucination in the mind of someone who has been abandoned. The music weaves in and out and changes to adapt your environment down corridors and by the DJ stand. Better still, *Slave of God*'s eye-searing art stylings are angular bright primary colours, burning themselves onto the back of your pupils like laser camera film. Your view, controlled by your mouse hand, is constructed so that it gives a lazy fisheye vision that could only ask you to feel inebriated. (2013)

Across these two accounts, we see the focus on how *Slave of God* feels to play through engaging with its sights and sounds. In Ellison's description in particular, we see the focus on the synthesis of how the videogame looks, how it sounds, and how it inscribes itself onto the player's body: vision controlled by a hand in such a way as to convey a sense of inebriation, colors that sear the player's eyes.

Developer and critic Robert Yang, meanwhile, is critical of the trend to casually describe synaesthesic videogame experiences such as *Slave of God* as simply "like being on drugs." Analyzing *Slave of God* in relation to his own in-development nightclub videogame, Yang sees such understandings of *Slave of God* as lazy and incomplete: "There aren't any interactions or parts about using drugs, and so any imagined link to drugs is obviously a metaphor for some other feeling. And yet, to so many people, that's what they take away—'it's an acid trip simulator'—which is an incredibly basic reading at best, and represents a profound lack of imagination at worst" (2014). "Like being on drugs" does not adequately describe what it is like to play *Slave of God*. At the same time, to play this videogame *is* like taking drugs insofar as its goal is to affect a physical, corporeal change in the player's embodied sense of self, and so it is this corporeal change that the simile "like being on drugs" becomes a shorthand for describing. Many early scholarly sources also compare playing videogames more broadly to taking drugs. For instance, David Sudnow (1983) and Sherry Turkle (1995) highlight the "addictiveness" of videogames and comment on the fact that *user* is a term that can connote either videogame players or drug takers. Although such drug metaphors are reductive, the ease with which they are deployed to understand videogame play emphasizes the corporeal change of embodied experience that each videogame strives to offer.

Through its dizzying sights and sounds, *Slave of God* aims to overwhelm the player's senses, to warp them as the player navigates the space, bumping off walls, searching for the bathroom, becoming trapped on the dance floor. As Ellison notes, the game communicates that sense—that *feeling*—of being lost, confused, and disorientated in a club.

There is little for me to "do" in *Slave of God* other than navigate its space. I can urinate in the men's room, dance on the dance floor, pick up drinks from the bar, and, eventually, stumble out onto the street at dawn as the sun rises. Yet with its lack of challenges or "interactions" in a traditional sense, *Slave of God* is exemplary of Kanaga's observation that what most defines the videogame form is presence, movement, and sensation. The "meaningless moments" Kirkpatrick identifies in dance are literalized here as the player is caught up with sights and sounds to stagger around and be overwhelmed by the nightclub. My ability to move the character through the nightclub space is vital for the disorientating sensation that *Slave of God* provides. Yet the sensorial engagement of its sights and sounds are not connected solely to what I am able to "do" in this world in a strictly configurable sense. There is something innately meaningful in my direct engagement with these eye-searing colors and repetitive, droning beats. Here, looking and listening are themselves playful acts.

Before the videogame player "acts" in a strictly mechanical or haptic sense, they actively look at images and listen to sounds. It is important, then, to account for looking and listening as bodily acts in their own right. Such a move can be made through work on the phenomenology of other visual media. For instance, Vivian Sobchack's work on cinema frames viewing *as* acting and addresses explicitly the way the *act of viewing* "implicates both *embodied, situated* existence and a *material* world; for to see and be seen, the viewing subject must be a body and be materially in the world, sharing a similar manner and matter of existence with other viewing subjects, but living this existence discretely and autonomously, as the singular embodied situation that makes this existence also a unique matter that matters uniquely" (1992, 23, original emphasis). In particular, as the title of her book indicates, Sobchack is interested in cinema's "address of the eye" as a "visual transcendence in bodily immanence" that allows "both the spectator and the film to imaginatively reside in each other—even as they both are discretely embodied and uniquely situated" (1992, 261). Similarly, Laura Marks writes on the "haptic visuality" of video, where "the eyes themselves function like organs of touch" to produce a dynamic subjectivity between looker and image (2002, 2).

Don Ihde, too, looks distinctly at viewing as an act through both reading and moving-image culture. He notes how reading is a structured perception that "normally, carries with it a dampening of bodily motion, a fixed place for its object, an enhancement of the visual, and the privileging of an elevated or overhead position" (1993, 86). For Ihde, reading is a way of being-in-the-world that audiovisual technologies such as television and cinema obscure because although they are still commonly "*viewed* from a usually *fixed* position," they "now begin to vary the 'text' with that which 'moves' and which develops a virtual 'movement' of bodily positionality"

(1993, 86, original emphasis). Such paradoxical entwinings of discretely embodied actors that Sobchack, Marks, and Ihde observe in cinematic spectatorship are amplified in the embodied, across-world demands of videogame play.

The "meaning" of *Slave of God* is not solely in its mechanical systems or allowed player actions; it is in the inexpressible and intensely physical sensations experienced by both player and character fused together: the way it feels to be lost in a nightclub, to be overwhelmed by the lights and music. Indeed, one of the locations the player can "discover" in the club is a back corner that can be retreated to, where the colors ripple less violently and the music softens. In the distance, the dance floor and bar still flash and pulse, but they are distinctly *over there*. I experience corporeally the relief of finding this back corner: a physical relief to escape momentarily the constant barrage of colors and music that *Slave of God* offers. To give my eyes and ears a respite.

Although previous inquiries into the embodied aspects of videogame play have been right to draw attention to the very visible ways bodies engage with interfaces, it is important to also account for *the act of viewing* and *the act of listening* as themselves active bodily engagements with the videogame text. Looking and listening are not passive lenses through which we let the world in, but active ways we intend toward the world. To call a cutscene "noninteractive," as is common in both popular and scholarly videogame discourses, is inaccurate because the player must explicitly and directly interact with the moving images and sounds through the intentional acts of viewing and listening. When I sit in the back corner of *Slave of God*'s club, I, as a player, am "doing nothing" with my hands, but I am still fully engaged in and incorporated with the videogame. To fully appreciate videogame experience, then, is to understand the synthesis of these bodily engagements. It is to understand what it means to engage with images (moving or still), movements (physical or virtual), and sounds (effects or music) as a simultaneous encounter with a videogame's textual form through different sensorial fields. It is through these different aspects of the same synaesthesic experience that the videogame is tangibly felt.

Conceptualizing the entanglement of player and videogame as a cybernetic "circuit" or as a feedback "loop," illustrated by Swink's model of interactivity discussed in chapter 1, is perhaps too straightforward even as it quite rightly favors neither player nor videogame as a primary actor. Rather than there being a single, unidirectional flowing loop of input and output, arrows must also shoot back and forward between eyes and screens, between ears and speakers, between hands and controllers, between controllers and screens, between hands and eyes, between ears and controllers. Rather than a cybernetic circuit, it is more of a cybernetic *web* that the player finds themself assimilated into and their senses flayed across.

The audiovisual aspects of videogame play are not just the "skin" or "flavor" of the videogame's "core" mechanics but are foundational to the experience of videogames in their own right. Looking and listening do not just happen simultaneously with the player's physical movements against an input device but contribute equally to the experience of videogame play as sensorial and corporeal: eyes engage with screens, while muscles engage with input devices, while ears engage with speakers as different fields of the perceptual engagement with a videogame's form. This accounting of the audiovisual aspects of videogame play opens up the opportunity to better understand what the player experiences in a videogame in those moments not accounted for under the moniker "real-time control"—that is, what the player is doing when they are supposedly not doing anything: watching a character summon a mythical beast in *Final Fantasy VII* (Squaresoft 1997), standing on a street corner in *Grand Theft Auto IV*, listening to the narrator in *Bastion* (Supergiant 2011), hiding in a locker in *Alien: Isolation* (Creative Assembly 2014), watching the sunrise in *Minecraft* (Mojang 2011), waiting for an item to restock in *Tiny Tower* (NimbleBit 2011), or simply trying to focus on a corridor in *Slave of God*. To put aside these moments of videogame play is not to reach toward some core, essential "gameness" but to fail to appreciate the full embodied experience of engaging with a particular videogame.

To play a videogame is not just to act but also to see and to hear and, above all, to perceive. Just as Merleau-Ponty shows how the different sensorial fields open up different perspectives of the forms of different objects in an everyday synesthesia, so too do videogames use sights and sounds not merely to flavor virtual worlds and objects but also to fundamentally construct them. The way a car looks heavy when it collides with a truck in *Grand Theft Auto IV*, the way *Hotline Miami* (Dennaton Games 2012) sounds fast paced, and the way performing under pressure feels stressful in *Heavy Rain* (Quantic Dream 2010) are fundamental to understanding how engaging with each of these videogames is meaningful and pleasurable. As *Audiosurf* shows explicitly, audiovisual design is not an interchangeable skin pulled over core mechanics but a fundamental facet through which the player is able to engage with the videogame at all. Further, as *Slave of God*'s overwhelming sights and sounds demonstrate, not all engagements with a videogame are funneled through an input device; there is a more direct back-and-forth engagement with eyeballs and screen as well as with ears and speakers *alongside* the engagement between hands and controller. Each complements and builds on the others, none more primary than the others but all together building up the rich tapestry of the videogame experience that has a felt, corporeal meaning perceived by the embodied, distributed, sensing, and performing player.

Across the previous chapter and this one, what it means for a player to be entangled with a videogame has become clear. Bodies move against input devices, eyes track images and lights, and ears attune to musical rhythms and audible textures to redistribute embodiment dynamically across bodies and worlds. Rather than reduce or essentialize the phenomenon of videogame play to a core "gameness," the embodied experience of playing a videogame is a particular, messy, fleshy engagement with an audiovisual-haptic form.

5   Repetition, Failure, and Permanence

[Video]games ... very much mirror how we remember things. A strict progression of chronology, suspended frames, moments that work in this linear way, like moving from stage to stage or level to level. And then there is the wish that you could do things differently, that you could go backward and fall in love or linger one more moment at a bedside or make just a little bit more time for someone or something, and so when games give us all these lives, these cheat codes, these branching directions where we can experiment with multiple or parallel endings—it's really a shame that real life, from this isolated vantage, doesn't work that way, that time doesn't work that way. ... Games are about time travel, is what I'm saying. Every game is.

—Jenn Frank, interview (Rhodes 2012)

I have been playing *Minecraft* (Mojang 2011) for two hours. When I started this session, I left the small house I built for myself in the hope of finding a new cave to explore. I found a small opening under a mountain in a direction I had not previously ventured and went inside. Despite the small opening, the cave unfurled into a vast and complex system of caverns and dungeons that had been produced by *Minecraft*'s algorithms when the world was first created. It takes about twenty minutes for the sun and moon to cycle through the sky in *Minecraft,* and several of these twenty-minute days pass while I am beneath the surface. I remain underground with my tools, collecting stone and precious minerals such as iron, gold, and even diamond to take back to my base to craft into stronger and rarer tools and instruments. After two actual hours, my inventory is bursting at the seams, my character carrying as much as they can. I abandon my steel axe to empty up the inventory slot for another sixty-four pieces of iron. I use up all the wood I brought with me to craft new torches and to replace my damaged tools, and the empty slots left in the wood's wake are filled with coal and mushrooms and diamonds. I am heading back to the surface to place all my treasures in chests for safekeeping when I spy one last vein of diamond that I missed on the way down. I hop down to it and hastily chop the first block away with my pickaxe while standing on it. Beneath it, though, is not a cube of stone; beneath it is nothing. I have chipped away at the ceiling of a hidden and vast pool of lava. There is no time to react. I fall into the lava and promptly burn to death.

Death is typically no more than a nuisance in *Minecraft*. You respawn back at your base, albeit empty-handed: anything you were carrying is dropped where you died, and to recover it you must walk back to that spot. However, dying in the lava means all my diamonds, all my gold, all my iron, all my tools burn away. They all are gone. The loss stuns me. I sit there looking at the screen of my laptop for several minutes. Eventually, dispirited, I quit the game and walk away from my computer. Every previous death in the videogame had felt so trivial, but now I feel the retrospective *wasting* of two hours of real labor and the permanent destruction of those resources like a physical, actual loss: I will never get those treasures back, and I will never get that time back. It will be a while before I can bring myself to return to the game.

A playable character's death is typically inevitable and uneventful in videogame play: a temporal glitch in the system's efficiency brought around by the player's incompetence (Pias 2011, 173), an inevitable and intermittent interruption to the player's experimentation (Atkins 2007, 239), a pedagogical tool used by the videogame to teach the player how they should be playing (Sudnow 1983, 162). Playable character death is a mistake to undo and a lesson to learn. The character dies, and the player continues from the previous checkpoint or save point. Perhaps the player first has to spend a few seconds watching the character graphically, spectacularly die, as in *Dead Space* (Visceral 2008) and *Tomb Raider* (Crystal Dynamics 2013). Alternatively, the character might "respawn" at a different location within the videogame's world, the actions of their previous incarnation still intact. The player will often be punished financially, maybe losing some in-game resources or currency, as in the *Grand Theft Auto* and *Pokémon* games.

The most common resource lost in the death of the playable character is time: the time that the player spent directing the character through the videogame since the previous checkpoint or the time they spent accumulating the resources that were taken away upon a previous death. Even when the character is resurrected, the time and labor the player invested in the character's previous incarnation may not be. When I fall into *Minecraft*'s lava and watch all my diamonds burn to nothing, the extreme and sudden sense of real loss I feel is primarily for those careful hours spent mining and working that are now going up in smoke. Character death acts as a fulcrum for the experience of temporality in videogame play, around which rhythms of progression and repetition hinge.

In this chapter, I use the experience of character death as different videogames portray it to consider how videogames constitute temporality for the player, imbuing actions and potentialities with different sensations of permanence or impermanence. Merleau-Ponty insists that time should not be understood as "an object of our knowledge, but rather a dimension of our being." Time is "neither a real process nor an actual succession that I limit myself simply to recording. It is born of *my* relation to things" (2012, 438, 434, original emphasis). Our embodied presence in any current present is always in relation to perceived pasts and perceived futures in such a way that "consciousness unfolds or constitutes time" (Merleau-Ponty 2012, 437). We have already seen how videogames use repetition and dressage to imbue and police habitual skill in the playing body. If we are embodied in the actual/virtual world through both the playable character with its stop–start repetitions and our corporeal body with its on-flowing rhythms, what happens to our sense of time when that body is regularly ripped apart and restitched together?

To understand the embodied textuality offered by videogames requires an appreciation of how time is not only experienced but *constituted* in the cybernetic web of player-and-videogame. As the *Minecraft* anecdote shows, the potentiality of pasts and futures is ever present in videogame play, returning and repeating or lost forever around the phenomenon of character death. Character death—or, more broadly, the potential of failure—is often central to the player's experience of videogame time. To play a videogame as a playable character is often to play *with* that character, to figure out what it can and cannot survive. To play a videogame is to consider "What if?"

Early in *Tomb Raider's* (2013) story, our hero Lara Croft doesn't die while paragliding through a forest at breakneck speed. But if she *were* to die here—if I failed to react to the videogame's challenges adequately—a cutscene is triggered showing me Lara gruesomely impaled on a tree branch. But then, after a short delay as the game reloads at the previous checkpoint, she is okay and ready to try again and again until I gain the competency to do it how it is "meant" to be done. In the open-world role-playing game *The Elder Scrolls V: Skyrim* (Bethesda 2011), my character would never consider massacring a whole town. But I can save my game, go on a rampage until the guards inevitably take me down, and reload my saved game to continue with what my character would "actually" do in an "authentic" timeline. In

Barry Atkins's words, the player "plays with the possibility of avatar death at any given moment" and navigates "a complex relationship between life and death and a past, present and future of ruined bodies as he or she moves intermittently through game space" (2007, 239). To play a videogame is to play with different timelines as authentic and inauthentic through death, memory, and failure.

The complex embodiment across worlds and bodies that is the play of bodies of videogame experience demands an appreciation of time as a complex assemblage of cyclical and linear *rhythms*, where failure and repetition become crucial components of progression and completion. As the discussion of dressage and embodied literacy in chapter 3 has already suggested, through repetition and failure multiple pasts and lost futures converge on the present play experience to intermediate each other through muscle memory, genre conventions, retries, "Game Overs," seriality, and wasted time. To play a videogame is to overwrite invalidated pasts and to peek at alternative futures. Just as the player does when completing the virtual world, they work to downplay the "inauthentic" timelines in their desire to experience videogame play as holistic and continuous. But these other timelines do exist and contribute to the ongoing videogame experience, and they thus must be accounted for. Lara Croft didn't die, but she also *did* die—dozens of times.

The first section in this chapter moves toward an understanding of embodied videogame time through Henri Lefebvre's work on rhythm and repetition. From that section, the remainder of the chapter turns toward phenomena of character death specifically. The second section looks at conventional notions of failing and repeating a videogame task, starting with the arcade game convention of chasing "coin drops," before it moves on to explore how various videogames strengthen or lessen the impact of death and repetition through creating different relations to the time the player has committed to the videogame thus far. Common across these examples is a commitment to death as a form of experimentation or inauthentic spectacle for the player as they play *with* the character and not just *as* the character. In contrast, the final section looks at the phenomenon of "permanent death." Permanent death contrasts with the conventional experience of character death as trivial and temporary and instead ends the player's session of a videogame with the death of that character, putting extra pressure on the player to *never* fail, to *never* repeat. This particularly consequential type of character death is dependent on the investment of the player's actual time to provide a sense of tension while the character lives and a sense of actual loss once the character dies.

However, as this chapter ultimately shows, what the player perceives as "temporary"/"inauthentic" and "permanent"/"authentic" temporalities is ambiguous and intermingled. Appreciating the embodied textuality of videogame play requires us to understand how temporality is constituted during videogame play by both those moments of inauthentic failure and experimentation as much as by those moments of authentic progression that "actually" happened.

Repetitive Play, Rhythmic Play

Cloud, the primary playable character of Squaresoft's role-playing videogame *Final Fantasy VII* (1997), does not know that his close friend and companion Aeris is about to be killed by the game's antagonist, Sephiroth. Nor does Cloud know that moments later he will find himself in a battle with the powerful monster Jenova-LIFE. How could he know? These events haven't happened yet. Nevertheless, Cloud is prepared for this battle he is unaware of because I, the player of *Final Fantasy VII*, remember well the encounter that is about to happen. Minutes earlier I had watched Aeris die in a prescripted, animated cutscene, and then I commanded Cloud and his comrades to fight Jenova-LIFE. It was a short-lived affair because the moment Jenova-LIFE cast the powerful, water-based move "aqualung," my entire party was killed instantly, sending me to a Game Over screen. From here, I returned to *Final Fantasy VII*'s main menu and accessed my saved file, written on the PlayStation memory card, and started playing again from the last place that I saved: several moments before Aeris's death. Now Aeris is about to die again, and, again, there is nothing I can do about it. But now I know about the fight with Jenova-LIFE, and I have equipped Cloud with an item that renders him immune to water-based attacks, effectively making him invincible against Jenova-LIFE. In the diegesis of *Final Fantasy VII*'s virtual world, Cloud does not "know" he is about to fight a monster that casts aqualung, but I know. I remember the fight that has yet to happen, and I have prepared for it.[1] To play a videogame is often to remember events that are yet to happen and learn from mistakes that are yet to be made.

Videogame time's constitution across the actual and virtual worlds of the play circuit is intricate and malleable. It is a topic that has received its own dedicated study (Jayemanne 2017). Here it will suffice to account for how the player perceives the parallel progression and repetition of time through the copresent embodiment of actual and virtual worlds and bodies: how the player comes to see events around character death as happening either "before" or "after" or most crucially "*instead of*" previous and future played events.

Actual Time and Virtual Time

In *Half Real* (2005), Jesper Juul, within his broader conceptualization of videogames as a binary of "real rules" and "imagined fiction," forwards a preliminary understanding of the function of time in videogame play. He identifies two parallel timelines existing in any play event: "play time," or the actual progression of time spent engaging with the videogame, and "fictional time," or the depiction of time progressing in the diegesis of the virtual world (141–156). These two timelines occasionally map onto each other in a straightforward, one-to-one, "real-time" ratio. For instance, in the racing videogame *Gran Turismo* (Sony 1997), it takes me two actual minutes to complete a lap of the racetrack, and in the virtual world's depiction of time it also takes two minutes. Meanwhile, in an abstract game such as *Tetris* (Pajitnov 1984), nothing in the virtual world suggests a different scale of time than the time it takes to play the game.

In many other videogames, however, time is "scaled" between the play time and fictional time. When I play the sports videogame *FIFA '15* (EA 2014), I complete an entire soccer match in a number of minutes. In the strategy game *Civilisation* (MicroProse 1991), years and centuries pass as I sit at my computer during a single play session. In the *Minecraft* anecdote that began this chapter, every twenty minutes a full day and night cycled across the virtual world.

Juul's observations of two simultaneous and interrelated flows of "real" play time and "imagined" fictional time are a fruitful starting point. However, the identification of two parallel flows of time—one actual, one virtual—remains too linear to adequately account for the complex but everyday back-and-forth cycles and stop–start repetitions of time across worlds. For instance, Juul struggles to account in his model for how a videogame might present a flashforward or flashback in time because, seemingly, "to describe events-to-come would mean that the player's actions did not really matter" (2005, 147–148). This anxiety of the player possessing enough autonomous agency that they *could* break something with their actions is common, and many videogames consciously and explicitly play with it. For instance, *Metal Gear Solid 3: Snake Eater* (Konami 2004), a prequel set decades before the earlier *Metal Gear* videogames, claims a "time paradox" Game Over if the death occurs of either the playable character or any antagonists present in the chronologically later games. *Assassin's*

Creed (Ubisoft 2007) claims a "desynchronization" if the player fails to successfully reenact the actions their character's ancestor already performed centuries in the past.

Many videogames, even at the time Juul was writing, had already successfully incorporated flashbacks into their play, denying a narrowly linear notion of videogame time subservient to player agency. *The Legend of Zelda: Majora's Mask* (Nintendo 2000) has the player weave a temporal path back and forth across the events of a three-day period; *Half-Life* (Valve Corporation 1998) and its two expansions, *Opposing Force* (Gearbox 1999) and *Blue Shift* (Gearbox 2001), thread together the simultaneous narratives of three characters, each occasionally overlapping (but incapable of altering) the events of the other; more recently, *Thirty Flights of Loving* (Blendo 2012) has no inhibitions about throwing the player back and forward in time through instantaneous cuts to produce abbreviated and cinematic perceptions of videogame space (see Golding 2013b). By deliberately narrowing the scope of the player's possible actions in such a way that they are unable to "break" anything in their time travel, these videogames play with time in intricate ways, but they are not exceptional.

Time as it is perceived and constituted in videogame play is not straightforward enough to be mapped onto two linear, progressing arrows as though time "itself" might exist discretely from the player-and-videogame's constitution of it. Juul himself encounters this problem when he concedes various "violations of game time" (2005, 151), such as the way diegetic time runs at an accelerated pace in *Grand Theft Auto III* (DMA Design 2001) even as the player's actions continue in "real" time: driving a taxi around a city block can take simultaneously twenty seconds *and* twenty minutes, which means the three-minute song playing diegetically on the car's radio technically takes three in-game hours to reach its conclusion. Juul calls such violations "incoherent time" and suggests that such videogames *flicker* between real time and game time—for example, *FIFA* as "a real-time game of 2×4 minute [halves] and an imagined full-length soccer match of 2×45 minute [halves]" (2005, 151, 152). The notion of videogames, as a play of bodies, flickering between actual and virtual foci—the player's attention fluctuating between worlds—is entirely apt. Just as actual and virtual spaces are not discrete but entangled and caught up with each other, so too are actual and virtual temporalities. Violations of game time such as those Juul identifies are not contrarian cases of incoherency but rather indicative of the embodied experience of time in videogames as constituted by two bodies acting as one across symbiotic worlds.

Synchrony and Diachrony

To account for videogame time is to account for interconnected, overlapping, and differently paced temporalities. Darshana Jayemanne provides an intricate and comprehensive account for this complexity and simultaneity of videogame time when he explores videogames as *performative multiplicities*: "a balance between potential and act that offers the possibility of thinking beyond the limits of any particular definition or unit of performativity" (2017, 134). As part of a philosophical project exploring the role of framing devices in videogame play and narrative, Jayemanne points toward "diachronic" and "synchronic" elements of play as fundamental to videogame time, where the diachronic performances of different players (and different plays by the same player) synchronize and then diverge at different stages of a videogame, and it is in the muddle of the two (the diachronic tendencies of synchrony and the tendency of diachrony to lead back to synchrony) that the "weft and warp of a videogame's temporal fabric" is constituted (2017, 270).

The *Minecraft* vignette of this chapter's introduction provides an example: all players of the game's survival mode similarly start at dawn with no items in an unexplored world. Most *Minecraft* players' opening actions will overlap: obtain wood, make a pickaxe, obtain coal for lighting torches and stone for crafting better tools. However, as time progresses, different plays will move toward diachrony as each player sets their own goals in their own world. But over even longer play times, all plays will move back toward some sense of synchrony as most players will obtain certain rare items and work toward certain overlapping broad goals even as their own world and moment-to-moment actions remain wildly different. Time in videogames is plural and multiple—defined as much by what did *not* happen or *could* have happened or happened but was then overwritten by what *actually* happened. Jayemanne (2017) suggests an ultimate nonlinearity of videogame time, of its habit not just to progress ever forward but to ebb and flow rhythmically and to turn in on itself. Through character deaths, saved files, checkpoints, action replays, Let's Play videos, walkthroughs, skippable cutscenes, lag, fluctuating framerates, and countless other phenomena, time travel is a banal feature of videogame play.

Videogame time folds back in on itself as players return to the past, jump forward into the future, and create multiple variations on a single event. In one play session with *Final Fantasy VII*, I rewind time and fight Jenova-LIFE multiple times. Videogame time is less the constantly progressing arrow than an arrow that spirals around onto itself. As Juul acknowledges in his more recent *The Art of Failure* (2013), videogame play is as much about repetition as it is about progression. Characters die; players get Game Over; players pause the videogame; players go away for a week and then come back; players play a videogame a second time; characters and players combine to fight different instances of the same enemies and face incrementally difficult versions of the same challenges time and time again between the beginning and end of a videogame—if the videogame even has an "end." Failure and repetition are more often than not a vital component *of* progression. As I fail and repeat a videogame, I learn more about the videogame and how to handle it both literally and figuratively; I become more attuned to its rhythms and capable of progressing farther the next time.

Repetition is also of crucial importance to the visual logics of many videogames, where repeated assets with minor deviations are commonly used to signify different characters or enemy types (for instance, the differently skilled green and red Koopa Troopas in *Super Mario Bros.*). Across two essays looking specifically at *We Love Katamari* (Namco 2005) and the *Pokémon* games, David Surman (2008, 2009) explores the significance of this visual repetition through the notion of "serial aesthetics." In videogames, time does not constantly progress in a straight line, with the past left behind and the future somewhere ahead of us; rather, it loops back in on itself, with past experiences and future expectations both mingling and mediating the present playing of the videogame.

Rhythmic Play

Repetition and progression, synchrony and diachrony point toward a notion of videogame *rhythms*. Videogames provide "an *aesthetic of repetition*, similar to that of everyday life" (Grodal 2003, 148, original emphasis). Indeed, it is the embodied rhythms of everyday life as explored by Lefebvre in *Rhythmanalysis* (2004, originally published in French in 1992) that provide a useful foundation for thinking about progress and repetition in videogames. Time is constituted—is lived—as rhythmic through the embodiment of "cyclical" processes and "linear" repetition:

Cyclical processes and movements, undulations, vibrations, returns and rotations are innumerable, from microscopic to the astronomical, from molecules to galaxies, passing through the beatings of the heart, the blinking of the eyelids and breathing, the alternation of days and nights, months and seasons and so on. As for the linear, it designates any series of identical facts separated by long or short periods of time: the fall of a drop of water, the blow of a hammer, the noise of an engine, etc. (76)

Cyclical processes are often connotatively perceived as favorable in their "worldliness" or "naturalness," whereas linear repetitions are perceived as monotonous, tiring, and tied up with labor. Lefebvre, however, stresses the interdependency of both in the rhythms of the body and everyday life and hence in the body's constitution of time.

Time in videogames is likewise constituted by the embodied player's involvement in cyclical and linear processes. Whereas a constant, cyclical flow of play is commonly seen as ideal, with the player's ability and the challenges of the videogame escalating in turn in the much-lauded notion of "flow" in videogame design, derived from the work of Mihaly Csikszentmihalyi (1990), this flow is not merely a constant progression forward but is always already caught up with failure, death, and the stop–start repetition of habitualization and dressage. The rhythms of playing a videogame—the means through which the player's body adapts itself to and incorporates the passing of time during play—are found in the coupling of cyclical processes and linear repetition, each of which intersects and splices the actual/virtual divide. For the videogame player, there is a constant, cyclical process of passing levels, loading screens, cutscenes, and the fluctuation of agency and power between player and machine (Giddings and Kennedy 2008, 30) as well as of inputs and outputs across the cybernetic circuit of player-and-videogame (Swink 2009, 64). But cutting across these cyclical processes are the linear repetitions of failing and trying again; the repeated switching on and off again of digital buttons to perform the same stop–start actions on one level after another; the duplicated instances of assets; the bodily interruptions of sustenance and defecation (Apperley 2010, 40).

Thomas Apperley draws on Lefebvre extensively in his own discussion of videogame rhythms, but for different ends. More concerned with the everyday situations and actual context in which videogames are played, Apperley grounds his research in the rhythms of the videogame situation through an ethnographic study of the videogame-playing body in internet cafés, highlighting a range of contextually specific ways the circuit of player-and-videogame is influenced by "external" rhythms: time zones, toilet breaks, meals, work schedules, and so on. Apperley is wary of cybernetic understandings of videogame play, such as the understanding I forward here, warning that they can be "inward-looking" and "closed" and that cyclical rhythms instead suggest that "the physical needs of the gaming body, and the ways that meeting these needs are organized are an important part of the gaming experience. ... [B]oth the machinic rhythm of play itself, and the wider rhythms of everyday life also have significant impacts on the experience of gaming" (2010, 38, 48, 41). Although I am indeed concerned primarily with that focal circuit of the player's body incorporated with the videogame hardware and audiovisual representation in the act of play "itself," I believe this concern complements Apperley's own work rather than counters it. Apperley's work remains a significant reminder that this embodied, corporeal circuit is not hermetically sealed but always already situated within particular material and social contexts—not a closed circuit but a subsystem that branches out and is situated in much broader networks and rhythms. The experience of time in videogame play is always already embedded in and mediated by the rhythms of the player's everyday life, not detached from them.

Time in videogame play wraps around on itself even as it "progresses" through rhythms and repetition. With these theoretical accounts of videogame time and rhythms explored, we can now turns to particular phenomena of character death to explore more deeply how a perception of this relationship between progression and repetition is constituted by different videogames.

Die and Try Again

Death and failure have long been central to videogame design. *Spacewar!* (Russell, Samson, Witaenem, et al. 1962), as a competitive videogame played between multiple players, all but demanded that someone be able to fail in order for someone else to be able to win, and that failure arose in the destruction of the losing player's spaceship. Single-player videogames such as *Breakout* (Atari 1976) and *Space Invaders* (Taito 1978) are traditionally framed as player *versus* computer, set up as an unwinnable contest against the computer, reflecting a hacker mythos of self-improvement and machinelike efficiency that is explored in more detail in the next chapter. As videogames became commercialized and made their way to the arcades, where players paid for each play attempt, design decisions around death and failure became central to how profitable a videogame might become, with profit turnover requiring a carefully designed balance between a videogame being accessible and learnable enough that players would put money into it but difficult enough that they would not be able to spend too long playing without either dropping more coins into the slot or stepping aside for the next player to do so.

As videogames left the arcade and became normalized in the home through the 1980s and 1990s, designing around failure and retrying persisted as what was by then conventional videogame design practice. Sudnow discusses this approach in depth in regard to the early Atari ports of arcade games, describing how his constant restarting of *Breakout* the moment he made a mistake conflicted with how the videogame had originally been designed to play: in an arcade, imperfectly, with many mistakes made and many coins dropped:

> To care in the right way you must submit to those stimulations encountered when the full game is played from front to finish [that is, from start to eventual Game Over]. Cut yourself off from these, go for consistency with techniques that work elsewhere, step outside the scheduled front to back way of learning on which the game's program and profit depend, and you'll fail. … Competence is possible only when action is motivated in those ways the game itself motivates it, and the game motivates action in ways proven to be most profitable in a rapid coin turnover scheme. (1983, 162)

Death and failure justify a skill to be learned through repetition, a challenge to be mastered, and a means for a burgeoning creative industry to turn a profit. To die and try again—itself a paradoxical turn of phrase anywhere except concerning videogames—have long been central to videogame play.

Finite Lives

Many arcade videogames capitalized on a model of *inevitable* death, which led to particularly dark and cynical fictions where the player never "won" in an ultimate sense but simply put off losing for as long as possible. Jason Wilson explores how *Missile Command* (Atari 1980) in particular—with its inevitable lose state effected by an off-screen, missile-launching enemy— depicted a dark dystopia that mirrored its own era's anxiety of nuclear holocaust through "an unalterable *condition of war* that held the game's fictional world in a perpetual state of crisis" (2007, 252, original emphasis). The player was trying to "win" against the computer, but this endeavor was ultimately futile; the best the player could achieve was to prevent death for as long as possible, to maintain the perpetual state of crisis. A convergence of progression and repetition appeared: the player had multiple lives to try again and again, but death was also eventually ultimate and permanent to the current play session, concluding in the final Game Over and, often enough, the option to continue at the expense of another coin. Inevitable player death and high-score chasing persist in mobile videogames such as *Ziggurat* (Action Button 2012) (discussed in chapter 2) and *Flappy Bird* (Nguyen 2013): a competent player does not win; a competent player simply prevents failure and death for longer than other players, and then they start again.

As videogames began to be designed natively for home consoles and PCs through the 1980s and 1990s,[2] the design focus, too, moved away from inevitable failure toward alluring narrative closure, yet with many of the coin-drop-influenced features still persisting as conventional video-game design. For instance, into the 1990s it was still common for a console videogame to offer a finite number of character lives, followed by a Game Over screen if those lives were depleted. A videogame such as *Super Star Wars* (LucasArts 1992) might have an ultimate ending, but the player could still get a Game Over and be sent back to the main menu if they died too many times. Much like arcade games, many console videogames offered an opportunity to "continue" after a Game Over, as in *Sonic the Hedgehog* (Sonic Team 1991), which gave the player one extra Continue for each secret Chaos Crystal they found. The ability to obtain an ultimate Game Over increasingly conflicted with both the commitment to obtaining a narrative conclusion (as opposed to simply "beating" the game) and the gradually increasing length of home videogames no longer designed to be finished in a single play session.

In *Spyro the Dragon* (Insomniac Games 1998), for instance, the player still has a finite number of lives, but the videogame's state is saved to the memory card automatically and regularly, meaning a "Game Over" merely adds the arbitrary annoyance of returning to the title screen and reloading the saved file to the beginning of the stage where the player died. Here, ingrained and dominant arcade design norms (a videogame must be challenging, difficult, learnable, and failable, and it must lure more coins out of players' pockets) clashed with the increasing desire of videogames to provide longer experiences that would take multiple play sessions to conclude. Videogames increasingly removed the concept of a finite pool of lives, relegating the Game Over screen to largely a relic of the past. The plat-former *Oddworld: Abe's Oddysee* (Oddworld Inhabitants 1997), for instance, advertised on its cover as a unique feature that the player would have an infinite number of lives; however, rather than a sign that the videogame was easier than other platformers that might only offer three lives, this endless possibility of dying and trying again was used to market boastfully how difficult the game would be: so difficult that you would die a lot, and through regular death you would learn how to advance. Character death (and failure more broadly) thus remained a core and inevitable part of vid-eogame temporal design through the 1980s and 1990s and into the 2000s: not simply as something to be avoided at all cost, but a fundamental and spectacular aspect of progression itself.

Rewind and Overwrite

Some videogames frame character death with time-control mechanics, allowing the player to rewind the videogame as one rewinds a videotape. Such videogames explicitly draw attention to the role of character death as a temporary mistake to be undone through repetition. For instance, *Prince of Persia: Sands of Time* (Ubisoft 2003) is a standard 3D platformer that asks the player to steer a character through various battles and acrobatic feats. The titular Sands of Time item allows the player to hold down a button and rewind time a limited amount to watch their previous actions and encounters unravel in reverse so that they might be reperformed. This ability allows the player to correct mistakes, refight lost battles, and reattempt failed acrobatics. Compounding this ability, the videogame's story is narrated by its playable character, who describes events the player is currently undertaking as though they have already happened. If the player uses up all the Sands of Time and finds their character actually dying in a poorly executed jump, the character narrates, "Oh, that's not how it happened," as the player reloads their game from the previous checkpoint. Whether the character dies or uses the Sands of Time, virtual time is still rewound so that the mistake is rendered inauthentic, an event existing in a temporality from which the player has retreated, but from which they also learned something and progressed past.

Sands of Time draws attention to how the player consciously obscures the inevitability of character death and repetition in their desire for coherent and continuous presence in the virtual world. Although the visual presentation of time rewinding is particular to *Sands of Time* and similar time-manipulating videogames such as *Braid* (Blow 2008) and *Super Time Force* (Capybara 2014), it simply justifies within its diegesis the player's entirely typical unawareness of their own dressage: the player fails at a task and tries the task again with the knowledge (and competency) gained from the previous failure that never happened. In his own analysis of *Sands of Time*, Atkins suggests that videogame play is typically narrativized "post-hoc [sic]," with players downplaying the way videogames are "actually" experienced during play as texts fractured by the multiple and frequent deaths of the playable character in favor of the ideal narrative stitched together from those fragments of successful play (2007, 244). As the playable character dies and is reborn with every fatal mistake the player makes, the player receives "incomplete glimpses of the perfect textual body that give pleasure only in their partiality" (Atkins 2007, 250). Failure is central to videogame play, and in the majority of videogames character death is simultaneously an entertaining and a frustrating experience, both interrupting the continuously experienced videogame but also allowing brief but alluring glimpses of not just what should be but also what *might* be.

Similarly, Janet Murray sees the film *Groundhog Day* (Ramis 1993), in which weatherman Phil Connors is forced to live out the same day of his life again and again, as being "as much like a videogame as a linear film can be" (1997, 36). Perhaps even more relevant to videogames, the film *Edge of Tomorrow* (Liman 2014) uses a similar conceit to have its protagonist William Cage fight in a battle against an alien army again and again until he manages to do so without dying. Whereas *Groundhog Day* allows its protagonist to experiment with his repeated day (to see what he *could* do), *Edge of Tomorrow* has its protagonist repeat a rigid experience in order to learn exact enemy placements and the minute bodily movements needed to stay alive (to see what he *should* do), not unlike the dressage demanded of videogame play and afforded by regular character death. As in Cage's case, the videogame player's emergent superpower is remembering what is yet to happen. It is only after play that the "felicitous" (Jayemanne 2017, 34) play fragments are stitched together into one coherent and continuous narrative of what "actually" happened, much like the best clippings of a film shoot are stitched together to obscure an actor's many bloopers.

The implication "is that we should consider videogame play as a matter of live performance in the moment of play, rather than a matter of straightforward reception or decoding where meaning is only revealed when the text is decoded in full" (Atkins 2007, 248). This idea of the videogame text as a "live performance" coheres with an embodied textuality emerging as the player-and-videogame in the moment of play and echoes analogies by other theorists, such as Graeme Kirkpatrick's comparison of videogame play to dance and David Sudnow's comparison of videogame play to jazz piano. The key difference, however, is that the professional dancer or pianist does not, one hopes, spend their performance stopping and starting and learning as they perform. The "live performance" of videogame play is not a continuous, virtuosic performance but a stumbling connection of repeated attempts that strive to mimic the virtuosic but that in reality are cut and edited together across character deaths, checkpoints, and play sessions. Just as earlier chapters argued for how a videogame's virtual world is perceptually constructed as a tangible space, how a videogame perceptually depicts and deals with the passage of time through death and progression is central to how the videogame is performed and experienced—that is, how it functions textually.

Even if after the fact the player suppresses those failed temporal strands as inauthentic, those strands remain part of the live performance, influencing future plays of the videogame: a boss's weak point learned too late in one battle can be exploited right from the start of the next attempt; the enemy who ambushed me is now ambushed by me in turn; *Tomb Raider* (2013) and *Dead Space* provide graphic, morbidly animated death scenes of my characters, who in their respective stories never die, providing a rewarding and graphic but noncanonical spectacle for my failure before returning me to a canonical timeline; a high score in *Space Invaders* comes only with the practice that requires dozens or perhaps hundreds of deaths and restarts (and a score from a past play session to compete against). The character dies and is resurrected, but the player persists, taking the previous attempts and inauthentic strands with them into the next life. More than the ideal imagining of how a videogame might be progressed continuously, death, failure, and repetition are core to the temporal pleasures (and frustrations) of videogame texts.

Repeating Character, Progressing Player

If the character's mortality is central to most videogames, it is overcome through the player's immortality through the "saved game." Either automatically or manually, the overwhelming majority of contemporary videogames save the player's progress on the videogame hardware, freezing a moment in time to return to it later. Jayemanne discusses the significance of "saving the game" as "establish[ing] a point at which the performances conducted thus far are synchronized—marking a game state from which further performances can be undertaken (each of which will be diachronic with respect to one another)" (2017, 271). Atkins, too, draws attention to saving the game as drawing together selected performances into an "ideal" performance while leaving others aside (2007, 247). The ability to save the game is central to the player's immortality in the videogame circuit, assuring the player that there will always be another chance.[3]

This centrality is perhaps seen most clearly in those videogames that explicitly threaten the sanctity of the saved game. In *Metal Gear Solid* (Konami 1998), for instance, when my protagonist is being tortured, he is explicitly threatened that unless I, the player, choose to submit, my saved game will be deleted upon death, thus raising the stakes in a way that simply threatening character death never can. Similarly, horror videogame *Eternal Darkness* (Silicon Knights 2002) sometimes pretends to corrupt the player's saved data, extending toward the player the terror and sense of vulnerability that horror videogames typically reserve for the playable character. When virtual worlds are depicted in works of fiction such as *The Matrix* (Wachowski and Wachowski 1999), the stakes are raised so that "when you die in the Matrix, you die in real life"; removing the ability to "try again" by putting the actual, corporeal body at risk adds weight to what is perceived as an otherwise trivial endeavor. The "permanent-death" videogames discussed in the next section perform in a similar manner: suddenly it is no longer just the character at risk of death; the player is now at risk of having their connection to the videogame severed, at risk of losing all the time invested to reach the synchronized events of their playing of the videogame up to this point.

The persistence of the player in the face of character death points to a paradox around failure, repetition, and progression: character death is a punishment insofar as it dismisses the time the player invested in that instance of play from the previous save point to the character's demise. But the death of the playable character is also a significant element *of* progression, of learning how to play the videogame, and it is often a spectacle in its own right. How videogames depict the temporal and spatial disruptions brought about by character death and resurrection is a core aspect of how the embodied rhythms of videogame play are constituted. The treatment of death and repetition by a videogame might imbue the player with a sense of trepidation; it might alternatively prompt a gung-ho attitude wherein the player decides to leap into every situation without fear.

In 2001, when conventional videogame design still treated character death with dramatic music, overwrought animations, and long loading screens before returning the player to some long-past checkpoint, *Halo* (Bungie) offered a save system that updated automatically after every few minutes of progress. Death can come sudden and swift in *Halo*, with a single well-placed grenade or poorly planned assault. Upon the character's death, the camera switches to a third-person point of view to watch the character's body flop from the fatal blow, but then the game returns to the previous checkpoint within seconds—sometimes before the character's body has even landed. Here, the setbacks of character death are at their most insignificant: little time has to be repeated, and less time has to be spent waiting for play to recommence. This feature gives *Halo* a particular pacing in which character death is but the faintest hiccup in the ongoing performance and affords a gung-ho play style wherein the player can jump into the fray and take risks, confident they will lose little if they fail because death won't be much of an interruption.

Other videogames embrace this paradox of repetition and progression explicitly, depicting character death as a process of learning and progression in itself by presenting it as a *forward* progression of time, not a rewinding to some previous state. *Super Meat Boy* (Team Meat 2010), for instance, is a difficult platforming videogame that commonly requires dozens of deaths to complete a short stage. This feature isn't frustrating, however, because resurrection is near instantaneous, and, significantly, the nondiegetic music played over the stage does not stop and restart with each death but continues uninterrupted, stitching each failure together as rhythmic beats toward eventual completion. Visual flourishes, too, reinforce the notion of progress in *Super Meat Boy* as splats of blood left on the surface of the stage from previous deaths persist through each reattempt, suggesting that the previous deaths were not undone but rather progressed beyond. This progression has a particularly spectacular payoff when the level is finally completed, and the player is rewarded with a replay of every diachronic iteration of all their past failed attempts playing simultaneously in a flow of Meat Boys that literalize Jayemanne's idea of videogame play as "performative multiplicities" (2017, 134), splatting themselves against blades and into salt piles until the single survivor—the successful "authentic" run—reaches the goal (see figure 5.1). Here, every single "failure" provides a contribution to the spectacle of the replay because each provided an important step in configuring the player through dressage to the particular challenges of that stage.

Figure 5.1
The player's multiple attempts in a single level shown together in replay mode in *Super Meat Boy* (Team Meat 2010).

Other videogames also depict character death as a moving forward of time in a variety of ways. The infamously difficult *Demon's Souls* (From Software 2009) and *Dark Souls* (From Software 2011) are action-oriented, role-playing videogames with a large cult following. The vicious monsters that the player must face and the intricate controls the player must comprehend mean that character death is inevitable for novice and expert player alike—"Prepare to die!" taunts the back cover of the retail release of *Dark Souls*. Upon death in *Dark Souls*, I return to the previous bonfire checkpoint, keeping all items I obtained before death but losing all the valuable souls—the game's currency—I had gathered; I then have the opportunity to venture forward again and find my own corpse to reclaim those souls. Here the forward progression of time after death is diegetically explicit as the player-character traverses to and stands over the character's own corpse. This sequence dampens the possible frustration produced by the game's steep learning curve in that time spent before a death rarely feels "wasted" as time instead constantly progresses forward. To die in *Dark Souls* or *Demon's Souls* is to learn how to progress.

Grand Theft Auto III, too, suggests that character death sends me forward in time, not backward, and I appear at the in-game hospital six in-game hours after the "death" occurred. I lose my weapons, some money, and my progress if I am halfway through a mission, but time is shown to have moved "forward" in the world on both the in-game clock and through the world's day–night cycle, and any hidden items I obtained before death remain obtained. Whereas *Demon's Souls* and *Dark Souls* depict time in this way to soften the blow of multiple deaths, which can be considered cruel and frustrating, *Grand Theft Auto III* does it to *trivialize* the impact of those deaths in the first place: a juvenile playground world where the player is meant to cause chaos would be less alluring if death were a significant setback.

Most commonly, in multiplayer videogames the presence of multiple players in the system means time can only ever move forward upon character death and resurrection. The dead character is instead "respawned" while other players continue to play. This ability communicates to the player that death here is not a setback or failure to be forgotten but that repetition of attempts and death are part of what it means to progress in these videogames, all part of the ebb and flow of the videogame's rhythms.

Different videogames use fictional depictions of death or failure to afford particular dressage of the player. The linear repetitions brought about by the interruptions in the character's life make the player perceive failure in a certain way and constitute the embodiment of time during play in a certain way: some videogames imbue caution through potential punishment, whereas others encourage experimentation and determination. If the videogame text is produced in the live, present, warts-and-all performance of player-and-videogame, then that text is constituted by past failures and future potentials as well as by various authentic and inauthentic temporalities that both frustrate and entertain the player, sending them both back and forward in time.

Permanent Death

A single run of Derek Yu's videogame *Spelunky* (2008) does not take long. I must navigate my little explorer down a series of procedurally generated levels viewed from a side-on perspective, past different challenges and beasts. A single mistake can lead to my death very quickly, and when it does, not only do I have to start the whole adventure again, but the adventure itself also changes. The shapes of the level changes; different items and enemies will be in different places. Although with each death I learn to play the videogame better, with each death I also lose a particular instance of the videogame forever. There is a sense in *Spelunky* that each death is to some extent permanent.

If character death typically converges failure and progression, pasts and futures, authenticity and inauthenticity, and cyclical and linear processes, then videogames such as *Spelunky* that depict character death as being in some way permanent insightfully contrast this embodied constitution of time in videogame play. As opposed to the relative frivolities of the examples of conventional character death given earlier, "permanent death" terminates a videogame if the character dies even once, forcing the player all the way back to the beginning of the videogame. If the videogame is one that procedurally generates levels, such as *Spelunky* or *Minecraft*, that instance of the videogame is lost forever. Although most videogames allow—or even encourage—the reckless sacrificing of the character's body in the name of experimentation and practice, permanent death shifts the flow of videogame time toward continuous synchrony. Instead of making small mistakes and trying again, every decision I make in a play of *Spelunky* is in the authentic temporality of my character's march forward; there is no going back and trying again because death feels absolute. Here, my superpower of knowing what is going to happen is subdued by my being anchored, in tandem with the character, to the temporal flow of videogame play.

Whereas the insignificance of character death typically calls the player to *play with* the playable character as much as they might identify with the character (Atkins 2007, 247), permanent death demands that the player tread carefully, thinking before they act and treating the character's corporeal fragility as significant as their own. As a consequence, the tone of the player's performance in a permanent-death videogame is less one of experimentation and more one of caution and consideration, constant progression rather than repetition.

Although a sense of permanency certainly exists in those arcade videogames discussed in the previous section that inevitably end in Game Over, those videogames commonly give the player a finite but plural number of lives that still give the player an immortality over individual instances of character mortality. Videogames that deliberately strive to imbue a sense of permanency in death, however, commonly give the character only one life, and one death will terminate this particular instantiation of the player-and-videogame. Traditionally, permanent death belongs to the niche roguelike genre, spawned by the game *Rogue* (Toy and Wichman 1980) and exemplified in the genre's contemporary interpretation in *Spelunky*. Death in such videogames is "permanent" in the sense that the videogame procedurally generates the world each time the player enters it. Items, monsters, and room layouts are different each time; if the player dies, their one chance of completing that particular instance of the videogame is lost. The knowledge gained by the player between lives is less one of knowing what precise arrangement of challenges await them and more one of the poker player knowing what cards exist in a shuffled deck.

Other videogames beyond the roguelike genre have experimented with providing permanent-death modes. An update to *Minecraft*, for instance, provided the opportunity to start a new world as a permanent-death world. Upon the character's death, the videogame automatically deletes the world and any progress the player has made within it. In the mech-themed videogame *Steel Battalion* (Capcom 2002), there are two layers of character death: once the player's giant robot (ostensibly the player's avatar as they steer it through the world) is destroyed, the player has a set amount of time to eject the pilot from the cockpit before the mech explodes; if the player fails, the pilot dies, and the player's progress in the videogame is deleted. In videogames with multiple playable characters, too, some characters die permanently, but the videogame is still able to progress by means of the bodies of other characters. In story-driven videogame drama *Heavy Rain* (Quantic Dream 2010), for instance, the player's perspective swaps between four different characters connected by a shared story. If the player makes poor choices or fails as one character, that character may die, but the story will progress with the other characters. The constant march forward of

Heavy Rain's temporality (and its aggressive automatic saving of the game to ensure the player does not try to undo past mistakes) gives a sense of permanency to the player's narrative-based choices, establishing consequences that will persist rather than be undone.

In other videogames, permanency through death is more implied than explicit. *DayZ* (Hall 2012) is a multiplayer survival videogame in which the player's character wakes up on the shore of a zombie-infected country. The character must try to survive by scavenging in towns and forests for food, water, and weapons. Other player-characters can be encountered, but whether they can be trusted is never clear. When the player's character dies, they respawn back at the beach on the edge of the map. Technically, this is no different than the character respawning in any other multiplayer videogame; however, the loss of all resources and the unravelling of days or weeks of progress give the death a sense of permanency. That attempt to survive has been entirely obliterated. The death feels "permanent" insofar as all the labor invested since the start of the previous life is lost, even as the world and its other players persist. As such, when I play *DayZ*, every moment is stressful and anxious; every sound is startling. Whereas in a different videogame I might just rush into a dangerous town and hope for the best, in *DayZ* I often spend up to ten minutes on a hilltop, not moving, watching the town for movement before I sneak in. Because a single mistake will be permanent, I do not experiment with failure and repetition the way I would in most videogames. So lying on a hill for ten minutes doing "nothing" feels like a powerful, meaningful aspect of my ongoing engagement with *DayZ*. It is part of my authentic temporality of survival.[4]

Permanent death does not have to be programmed into the videogame. In the remainder of this section, I look at two projects in which the player voluntarily opted into permanent death: Benjamin Abraham's Permanent Death project (see Abraham 2009) undertaken with the first-person shooter *Far Cry 2* (Ubisoft 2008), and my own Toward Dawn project undertaken with *Minecraft* (before permanent death was added to this game as a formal feature) between 2010 and 2012 (see Keogh 2010–2012).[5] In each of these projects, the player made a pact to voluntarily delete their saved game if they died. Permanent-death plays of videogames that do not include a designed option for permanent death supersede the stop–start "what if" of traditional experimentation with a close coupling of the player's concerns with the character's bodily existence and a real-time, uninterrupted narrativization of play—what is happening right now is what happens, and that is it. Looking at how Abraham's and my own play behaviors and priorities were altered by the looming threat of permanent death and at the invest-ment garnered from readers of the blogs we wrote on our projects shows how these projects demonstrate that permanent death, like all character death, is most significant in how it influences the player's lived experience of the player-and-videogame assemblage and constitution of played time.

Permanent Death in *Far Cry 2*

Since its release in 2008, *Far Cry 2* has developed a cult following for its bru-tal difficulty and unpredictable systems. A first-person shooter that sees the player travel as a self-serving mercenary across a fictional African country in the middle of a civil war, the videogame first asks the player to carefully plan for each encounter before it throws curveballs that dash those plans. A gun might jam in the middle of a skirmish; the wind might change direc-tion and surround the playable character with the flames the player hoped to use to ambush opponents; at any point, the character's malaria might render the character momentarily useless. The entire game is peppered with a cynicism that suggests that no matter how hard the player tries, things will fall apart.

Yet *Far Cry 2*'s intended harshness is dampened in the face of the player's immortality. Following a discussion with the game's lead designer Clint Hocking about the "impermanence of player decisions in the face of prevalent saving and reloading," critic Benjamin Abraham decided to con-duct an experiment in which he made the promise that when he started a new game of *Far Cry 2*, he would delete his saved file if his character died (Abraham 2013, 1). Abraham kept an online diary of his journey with his blog series "Permanent Death," and attracted a wide readership within the then-nascent games criticism and blogging community. After the project was over, Abraham compiled the blog posts into an ebook by the same title. At the beginning of his first post, Abraham discussed why he opted to con-duct the permanent-death play of the game: "Death in games is often very … temporary. I want to find out what happens to me as a player if I make my videogame death much more permanent" (2009).

Journalist Kieron Gillen, writing of Abraham's project, argues that what was special about Abraham's experiment was not simply that Abraham tried to create a more difficult experience for himself but that he created an experience that he could use as a source of writing. That is, through the pressures of permanent death, the tone of playing *Far Cry 2* changed for Abraham so that every action he performed (or reconsidered) carried its own narrative weight: "When game over *means* game over, everything changes" (Gillen 2009, original emphasis). As opposed to the "post-hoc" narrativization observed by Atkins, when the character's death is permanent, there is no opportunity to revisit the past and fix mistakes. The permanent-death videogame is not experienced as a series of textual and temporal fragments aiming for an ideal or felicitous mode of play, as Atkins and Jayemanne observe regarding conventional videogame play; rather, the videogame-as-played *is* the videogame-as-narrativized. Permanent death not only makes the videogame more difficult via harsher consequences but also allows a story to be acted out and narrativized in "real" time due to *persistent* consequences, where a single mistake may be less a blooper and more an ultimate conclusion. The perpetual progression of time that is the player engaging with the videogame is no longer punctuated by the stop–start editing of virtual death and failure but instead emphasized by the virtual's persistence. In Abraham's writing, his preoccupation with not dying permeates every page and every act, and the few mistakes he does make, such as failing to spy a guard standing nearby, create tense moments for the reader caught up in his plight as not just one possible story of playing *Far Cry 2* but rather *the* story of Abraham's playing of *Far Cry 2*.

The pleasure of whimsical experimentation made possible through the player's ultimate immortality across the character's repeated resurrections is by means of permanent death replaced with the pleasure of feeling that every one of Abraham's actions is irreversible. As *Far Cry 2*'s director Clint Hocking puts it in his foreword to Abraham's book, "'Permadeath' ... effectively re-couples player and avatar, an interesting consequence of which is the 'porting over' of the authentic desperation of life's struggle. The permadeath restriction forces a player to adapt to overcome the biggest challenges one will ever confront in a game, or in reality: his or her own fickleness, foolishness, cowardice and frailty" (Hocking 2009, 2). Permanent death limits the experience and constitution of time in videogame play by downplaying those linear processes that stop and restart with the character's death, thus emphasizing the consequential nature of the player's own imperfection. The character's body is no longer a thing to play with or a grotesque spectacle to watch die but a fragile rhythm for the player to get caught up in; the role of the character as the player's umbilical to and as part of the textual experience is highlighted in its vulnerability.

Permanent Death in *Minecraft*

In part influenced by Abraham's project, I undertook my own permanent-death experiment in the aptly named "survival mode" of the videogame *Minecraft*. As in *Grand Theft Auto III*, discussed earlier, death in *Minecraft*'s survival mode is not temporal for the character so much as it is spatial: death means being forced to be somewhere else, not some *when* else. The consequences of a character's death—and the intensity of acting while alive—are constantly in flux, proportional to both the distance traveled from the spawn point and the value of the items in the player's inventory that are dropped upon death. In earlier versions of *Minecraft*, death made the character drop any items they were carrying, and the player and character were teleported back to the position they first entered the world. Later updates to the game added beds that the player could place anywhere in the world and sleep in to alter where they would respawn upon death. The fluctuating consequences of death remain the same: if a zombie kills the player several steps from the spot they would respawn, death might be just a minor inconvenience because the player will spend just a minute running back to the spot of their death to pick up the items they dropped. But if the player has spent the past few hours deep underground, exploring and mining a rich labyrinth of caves, character death might be a harsh and anguishing experience. All that iron, diamond, gold, *and time* lost to a pool of lava or forgotten in a dark recess of the world.

Of course, the harshness of death also depends on what the *Minecraft* player is hoping to achieve. Although more recent updates have added quest and goals, *Minecraft* is known primarily for its open-ended play of simply dropping the player in a procedurally generated world with no guidance. It is not just the player's goals that are highly individualized but also the world the player finds themself in, too. Every new game of *Minecraft* uses algorithms to produce a world with its own unique topography of forests, ocean, and mountains as well as its own subterranean labyrinth of caverns, abandoned mines, and minerals. Although a new world will start at a certain size and is limited to that size on console and mobile versions of the game, on the original PC version more "chunks" of world generate as the player walks around, giving the illusion of an enormous, inexhaustible world spread out in every direction, limited only by the player's commitment and hard-drive capacity. This makes *Minecraft*, like those videogames in the roguelike genre, particularly amenable to the permanent-death rule, with an entire world at risk of being lost upon the character's death.

In previous sessions of *Minecraft* play, motivated by *Minecraft*'s perpetual world generation, I occasionally would take my avatar on long walks into the unknown. I would spend hours lost in a forest or on a foreign continent. This interest in exploring the unknown eventually became my primary way of engaging with *Minecraft*, and in 2010 I commenced a publicly documented project where I would play as a nomad, walking east toward the dawn. I called the project Toward Dawn; the plan was simply to see what was "out there" in one particular world. As beds had not yet been implemented in *Minecraft* when I started the project, the farther I walked from my initial spawn point, the more progression would be lost on my eventual death. Whereas Abraham created a permanent-death style of playing *Far Cry 2* through the promise to himself and his readers that he would delete his file after death, the constraints built into *Minecraft* meant I did not have to make such an oath—the farther I walked, the less likely I would be to repeat this journey if I were to die.

The risk of permanent death changed the way I engaged with *Minecraft* in significant ways. Most importantly, my relationship with the landscape around me altered dramatically. Just as Abraham's every action became a conscious consideration of how to remain alive in *Far Cry 2*, my every step farther into this world became fraught with anxiety. I would track the safe route down a mountain without falling farther than two blocks, whereas before I might have leapt recklessly from the top of the mountain into a pool of water below. I would never dare to head outside at night or too deep underground, scared as I was of the monsters lurking in each. Instead, I would spend the ten minutes of nighttime sitting in my hastily constructed shelter, gripping my sword, and spying for monsters I would have to deal with come morning. The ominous threat of character death bringing an

Figure 5.2
My journey east in *Minecraft* (Mojang 2011).

end to the adventure focused my attention to a heightened level of vigi-
lance, watching with the greatest care every step my character took. The
numerous threats focused my attention on the corporeality of my character, which was now caught up with my own. Activities that would previously have typically felt mundane, such as sitting in a boat in the middle of
the ocean for ten minutes waiting for night to pass, were rendered meaningful in their own right.

As the game continued and I journeyed farther, I had more to lose, and
death became an ever more devastating proposition. Instead of a post hoc
narrativization that had me mentally stitch together the successful fragments of play into a canonical memory that obscured those fragments
where I made mistakes, the permanency of my character's potential death
meant I was living the narrative of my character's life continuously in present tense as I played. Sitting idly at my computer for ten minutes as my
character floated in the middle of the ocean was not an interruption of play
but an active and playful engagement where my concerns for character
death and game termination were at the fore of my mind.

Just as with Abraham's Permanent Death project, with my experiment
permanent death was not just a consequence that would affect me eventually but an omnipresent consideration that permeated my every action
leading up to that eventual death. It weighed on every act. If my character
died, my journey east would be over, and I would never see this world
again. It was the *potential* of character death—and what actual investment
would be lost with that death—that influenced every moment of play. In
any previous world, I would not have thought twice about exploring an
ocean, potentially drowning, losing my equipment, and returning to my
base. But now there was so much more at stake. The player of a permanent-
death game no longer throws the character's body around in experimental
whims; the stakes are much too high for that. "What if" is no longer a reason to play *with* and be taught by the videogame but a reason to play the
videogame with more caution. The world is no longer full of possibilities;
it is now full of dangers that may short-circuit the player-and-videogame
assemblage at a moment's notice.

On the player's desire to stitch the fragments of felicitous videogame
play together into the "ideal" text, Atkins observes that "the moments of
bliss in the videogame text are generated through reference to an imagined perfect text, the platonic absolute or ideal which is always absent from
actual play—not the intermittent fragmentary text we have on screen, but
a text that exists in potential only in our imagination" (2007, 251). Permanent death cuts through the stop–start fragments of typical videogame play

to reach for that desired ideal and continuous text, the videogame played from start to finish as one continuous and authentic performance. Such permanent-death projects and the emotional commitment they foster are not an argument for permanent death as more "meaningful" than typical character death. Rather, they demonstrate how actual rhythms of video-game play are always mediated by the way character death (or repetition more broadly) are both depicted and imagined through the videogame's temporality and what impact on progression they bring with them. In con-trast, the mobile videogame *Ziggurat* (detailed in chapter 2) also restarts after only one death, but the brevity of a single play session (rarely lon-ger than a few minutes) ensures this one death is not imbued with the same sense of permanency as a death in *DayZ*, which is not actually perma-nent at all. What the various depictions of character death as permanent or impermanent across the videogames and projects detailed in this chap-ter suggest is rather that how players perceive time through any particular videogame is tied up with the labor of failure in a synergy of progression and repetition.

The *Minecraft* anecdote that began this chapter, in which I fell into lava and lost two hours' worth of valuable resources, was not about a permanent-death experience per se. My character respawned back at my base, and the diegetic time of the virtual world moved forward. The sun was in the mid-dle of the sky when I first went underground, and now, many in-game days later, it was just rising on a new one. The crops I had planted when I ventured out had since grown into maturity, and the ore I had placed in my furnace before leaving was now smelted. While alive, I was not playing "as if" my death would be permanent; I knew that it wasn't. Yet the sense I felt of a tangible, permanent loss upon death was undeniable—both of my own labor invested in the game over the past two hours and of the rare resources that had been removed from this world forever.

A complex ensemble of processes constitute videogame temporality, some of which I perceive as cyclical and ongoing and others I perceive as linear and repetitious. Repetition and progression, retries and conclusions, diachronic alternatives and synchronic experiences are caught up in the embodied rhythm of videogame play, where the diegetic experience of tem-porality is perceived through multiple diegetic and nondiegetic strategies such as music that does not halt on the character's death in *Super Meat Boy* or a world that will never be seen again in *Minecraft*.

Videogames use the permanency or impermanency of failure (or the lack of possible failure) to forge a particular coupling between the player's actual labor over time and the authentic and inauthentic performances of the playable character within the videogame's world. If videogames are experienced in the present tense—a performed text actively constructed between player and videogame in the moment of play—then they are also caught up in broader corporeal rhythms and contexts where pasts and futures make themselves present through failure and repetition or through the threat thereof. To properly account for the embodied textuality of videogame play is to account not just for how temporal events in a particular videogame are remembered post hoc but also for how they are dynamically and continuously constructed through bodily performances perceived as both authentic and inauthentic, through cyclical progression and linear repetition.

6 From Hackers to Cyborgs

If my nightmare is a culture inhabited by posthumans who regard their bodies as fashion accessories rather than the ground of being, my dream is a version of the posthuman that embraces the possibilities of information technologies without being seduced by fantasies of unlimited power and disembodied immortality, that recognizes and celebrates finitude as a condition of human being, and that understands human life as embedded in a material work of great complexity, on which we depend for our continued survival.

—N. Katherine Hayles, *How We Became Posthuman* (1999)

Anna Anthropy's *Dys4ia* (2012, figure 6.1) is a short, autobiographical videogame. I use the arrow keys on my computer's keyboard to play through a variety of brief minigames, each only a few seconds long, while the on-screen text describes Anthropy's experience undergoing hormone-replacement therapy. Each of the minigames mechanically reinforces the message of the on-screen text. "I feel weird about my body," says one of the opening screens as I try to navigate an oddly shaped block through a gap in a wall that it simply won't fit through. Later in the videogame, my character is in a doctor's waiting room. I can move my character around, but I cannot figure out what exactly I am meant to do. Eventually I get it: I'm meant to do nothing. All I can do is wait for the number in the corner to slowly tick down. After a rapid succession of minigames that require me to figure out how to progress through them, this sudden, slow *waiting* is jarring and anxiety inducing. There is nothing for me as a player to do except wait and feel the restlessness one feels while in a waiting room.

Moments when I cannot do anything as a player exist in all sorts of videogames. A very different example: as the opening credits of the blockbuster military shooter *Call of Duty 4: Modern Warfare* (Infinity Ward 2007) commence, my perspective plunges from the god's-eye view of a military satellite down to the surface of the planet and into the body of a fictional

Figure 6.1
The waiting room in Anna Anthropy's *Dys4ia* (2012).

country's president being dragged out of his palace during a military coup. I, as this character, am thrown into the back of a car and driven across the city (see figure 6.2). I have no control over the captive leader's navigation, but I can choose where to look by rotating the gamepad's right thumbstick. Through the windows of the car, the military coup plays out before me in a series of vignettes: people running into their homes and locking their doors; a tank rolling down the street; government supporters lined up against the wall; a man spraying graffiti in an alleyway. All the while, the car radio blasts the speech of the usurper who is responsible for my capture. As the car reaches its destination, I am removed from the car, dragged into an arena, tied to a post. The usurper is before me now, finishing the speech that has been broadcast throughout my car journey. He is handed a gun by a character just at the edge of my character's vision (my television screen) and executes me with a point-blank shot to the head, setting up the plot for the rest of the game.

Both *Dys4ia*'s waiting room and *Modern Warfare*'s opening credits are powerful and evocative scenes, but they are scenes where I ostensibly cannot "do" anything. I cannot leave the waiting room; I cannot escape the car; I cannot determine when the waiting-room scene will end; I cannot determine where the car will go. I can only look around, listen, and wait until each videogame allows me to progress. Yet I am undeniably still engaged with each videogame. Despite a lack of what some would call "gameplay"

Figure 6.2
The player-character being driven to their execution in "The Coup," *Call of Duty 4: Modern Warfare* (2007).

in either of these sequences, I am still actively experiencing them. Through my inability to do anything but look and listen at the scenes around me, I am incorporated into the experience of the anxious or despondent characters. What I am capable of "doing" in each scene is less important than how that scene incorporates me as a situated being capable of looking, listening, and touching.

Throughout this book, I have advanced a phenomenology of videogame experience that accounts for the player's engagement of the videogame as seen, heard, and touched—that is, as perceived. In the introduction, I said that the reason for doing this was to interrogate the certain ground of what we think we know about videogames. It was videogames such as *Dys4ia* and *Modern Warfare* that motivated me to take on this project because the ways we traditionally understand videogames struggle to account for their pleasures at all. In this final chapter, I demonstrate how accounting for the embodied textuality of videogame play renders legible those videogames that privilege engagements and pleasures beyond the strictly configurative ones of goal-based challenge and mastery. In the introduction to this book, I contested mechanistic notions of videogame play that tacitly narrow the embodied and material engagements one has with a videogame to those that are explicitly configurative while downplaying our parallel and no less fundamental engagements with audiovisuals and tangible input devices. A focus on intentional and configurative action reduces to a peripheral concern our appreciation of the fully embodied experience of engaging with a videogame, rendering moments such as *Modern Warfare*'s transit scene into secondary "nonplay" engagements to be put aside before we try to understand the videogame's pleasures rather than to be understood as videogame pleasures in their own right.

The past two decades have seen the rise not only of moments in videogames like this scene in *Modern Warfare* but also of entire videogames like *Dys4ia* built around minimal, experiential engagements. Videogames such as *Dear Esther* (The Chinese Room 2012), *Proteus* (Key and Kanaga 2013), *Journey* (Thatgamecompany 2012), *Gone Home* (Fullbright 2013), *Lim* (k 2012), and *Mainichi* (Brice 2012) focus primarily on the player's navigation and sensorial perception of a virtual space while minimizing mechanical or configurative challenges. If videogames are considered as emerging from and subservient to nondigital forms of games that privilege a foundation of mechanical systems, then such experiential videogames struggle to be comprehended at all. Indeed, popular videogame discourses commonly downplay or dismiss each of these experiential videogames as either poor-quality games where the player does not do anything or, worse, not *really* games at all. The pleasures such videogame experiences provide remain opaque if we evaluate videogames primarily "as games." They reveal their pleasures only when we evaluate videogames as corporeal, embodied, audiovisual-haptic experiences. That is, *as videogames*.

Comprehending these experiences is a cultural and political imperative. As the tools both to create and to distribute videogames have become easier to access in recent years, different kinds of people have begun more visibly to make and distribute different kinds of videogames. Most notably, an explosion of nonmale, queer, and transgender videogame creators have emerged, and, unsurprisingly, the videogames they are making are nothing at all like those that have been produced by the historically male-dominated commercial "videogame industry." Although many of the videogames fashioned by these new creators have found critical acclaim (not least of all Anthropy's *Dys4ia*), core videogame demographics cultivated by the videogame industry have struggled to grasp how such works can be considered "games" at all because these works forgo the traditionally valued qualities of challenge, choice, and mastery.

Anger from male videogame fans that one such creator, Zoë Quinn, would put an interactive fiction videogame *Depression Quest* (2013) on popular videogame-distribution platform Steam led directly to the ongoing misogynistic harassment campaign referred to as "Gamergate." Although a full account of the history and repercussions of this complex campaign is not possible here (see Shaw and Chess 2015 for one account), Gamergate came about directly because a core hegemony of videogame culture could not comprehend how *Depression Quest* could be considered a videogame and thus could explain its critical success only in terms of unethical and conspiratorial journalism practices. If we think of videogames exclusively through the lens of the term *game*, then we remain incapable of accounting for those experiential videogames produced by those on the margins of videogame culture. Worse, we doom them to stay marginal.

For Alexander Galloway, videogame moments that depend primarily on an audiovisual engagement (as opposed to the player's ability to exert change) do so because of their reluctance to embrace "the pure uniqueness of video gaming" (2006, 11). I, however, reject the notion that a "pure uniqueness" of the videogame form ever truly existed beyond the rhetorical strategies of a new media industry (and subsequent scholarly discipline) trying to demarcate a discursive space for itself. I have already shown how videogames are fundamentally and formally audiovisual-haptic. At the "core" of videogames is not "rules" or "mechanics" to be intellectually engaged with but lights and sounds and buttons to be carnally incorporated. From this perspective, a videogame such as *Dys4ia* or the opening sequence of *Modern Warfare* is no less exemplary of videogame form than more mechanically configurative videogames, even as they jar with traditional understandings of "game" forms more generally.

Traditional modes of appreciating videogames "as games" are not capable of accounting for what videogames have become. This chapter makes the case for how an appreciation of videogames that accounts for both their textual and experiential properties—that is, their embodied textuality—can allow us to comprehend those experiential videogame performances where the player is "doing nothing." Like all videogames and, indeed, all texts, such experiences demand particular integrations of flesh, sensorial perception, hardware, and audiovisual signs that are no more or less experiential than those demanded by the most complex, mechanistic videogame works. A phenomenology of videogame experience allows a more nuanced appreciation of the diverse spectrum of embodied pleasures and meanings of individual videogame works beyond the narrow, normative, and market-driven standards against which videogames have historically been predominately measured.

What is at stake here are two different modes of identifying with and evaluating videogame forms—one hegemonic and the other marginal: two different *technicities*. I draw on David Tomas's coining of the term *technicity* in his exploration of William Gibson's *Sprawl* novels to account for the "different systems of identity composition" that emerges in computer-dominated culture (1989, 123), and I rely on the work of Jon Dovey and Helen Kennedy (2006) productively building on Tomas's outline to bring a discussion of technicity directly to videogame culture. Concerns of technicity intersect with concerns of gender, ethnicity, and class to account for how particular social and cultural relationships and power dynamics are formed through technological competency, access, and literacy. Technicity provides a way to explore how certain modes of identifying with technology become dominant and hegemonic in order to obscure myriad other "marginal, subaltern or oppositional identities which define themselves in reference to the dominant group" (Dovey and Kennedy 2006, 64).

I propose two technicities through which the narrow "core" values of videogame experience might be decentered to allow for a broader appreciation of a multiplicity of videogame embodiments: the hacker and the cyborg. Videogames are historically entrenched in hacker paradigms of empowerment and control that cultivate a normative, dominant, technofetishist, and ultimately masculinist player identity that solidifies the values of certain modes of videogame experience. However, if videogames are dominantly understood as empowering a player to make choices and perform meaningful actions on a world, then what oppositional play styles and design ideologies are marginalized by this dominant understanding? Reconceptualizing the player as an integrated cyborg allows a transition from considerations of videogame play as primarily an exertion of power to primarily an experience of embodied intercorporeality (of which an exertion of power is but one potential expression). It allows us to ask: what *else* can videogames be? Videogame experience lost its corporeality through the mythos of the hacker, but that corporeality can be reclaimed through the figure of the cyborg.

In this chapter, I echo the concerns of those scholars who have long strived to elucidate embodied experiences beyond the dominant and hegemonic. N. Katherine Hayles proposes:

[If] there is a relation among the desire for mastery, an objectivist account of science, and the imperialist project of subduing nature, then the posthuman offers resources for the construction of another kind of account. In this account, emergence replaces teleology; reflexive epistemology replaces objectivism; distributed cognition replaces autonomous will; embodiment replaces a body seen as a support system for the mind; and a dynamic partnership between humans and intelligent machines replaces the liberal humanist subject's manifest destiny to dominate and control nature. (2005, 288)

Videogames are enthusiastically and dominantly imagined and marketed as "more interactive" than film or literature, so they have long naturalized the ideals of a liberal rational subject (mastery, autonomy, meritocracy, individualist agency, viewing from nowhere)—itself a dominant conceptualization of the "human" that, as we saw in chapter 1, "may have applied, at best, to the fraction of humanity who had the wealth, power, and leisure to conceptualize themselves as autonomous beings exercising their will through individual agency and choice" (Hayles 2005, 286).

A dedication to the cyborgian or posthuman amalgamation of player and videogame, however, challenges these notions and demands a reconsideration of the player as other than an intentional, autonomous agent. The player, as this book has situated them, is not "in charge" of the videogame's systems but assimilated into them so that the system *is* the player-and-videogame across bodies and worlds. I play from somewhere. I make choices as to how to hold my body during videogame play, but I do so always against the affordances and constraints provided by the videogame. The videogame is mediated by the player, and the player is mediated by the videogame.

The first section in this chapter traces how dominant videogame values emerged from the masculinized history of the computer hacker and solidified in the figure of the "gamer" in the 1980s and 1990s, which we have only started to interrogate in recent years. The second section sets up the cyborg-player as a contrast to the hacker-gamer through the historical deployment of the cyborg as an explicitly feminist conceptualization of embodied being. The cyborg, in contrast to the hacker, challenges dominant values and understandings of videogame play to expose a much broader spectrum of pleasures. The third section complicates this potentially too simple hacker/cyborg binary by demonstrating how the cyborg-player is not the antagonist to the hacker-gamer but rather the broader spectrum of identities that the hacker-gamer often stands in for—not dissimilarly to how white, Western Man often discursively stands in for the much broader spectrum of human identities. Just as the gamer is but a (dominant) subset of the diverse range of videogame players who exist, the hacker is but a (dominant) subset of the diverse, cyborgian range of ways that flesh and machine come together. The figures of the hacker and the cyborg intersect and influence each other as dominant and oppositional technicities. They are lenses through which to examine and comprehend how players are culturally habitualized to perceive their own incorporation with the videogame and how they evaluate the videogame through that perception.

Gamers as Dominant Hackers

That both the dominant videogame industry and its cultivated fan culture continue to be significantly gendered is neither a new nor a controversial claim (see, for example, Wajcman 1991; de Peuter and Dyer-Witheford 2005; Dovey and Kennedy 2006; Kennedy 2007; Hjorth and Richardson 2009; Lister, Dovey, Giddings, et al. [2003] 2009; Juul 2010; Shaw 2011; Taylor 2012; Kocurek 2015). The videogame industry is disproportionately and historically male (especially at the upper levels of creative leads and producers); mainstream videogame journalism predominately employs male editors and writers and addresses a readership of "gamers" who are commonly presumed to be male (de Peuter and Dyer-Witheford 2005; Kirkpatrick 2012; Nicoll 2017a; Cote 2015). As videogame culture became normatively masculine, certain tastes were cultivated as dominant (in no small part through the formation of a gamer habitus, as chapter 3 explores), and others were dismissed as marginal.

By the time a critical mass of academics began paying serious critical attention to videogames in the early 2000s, this normalization was already well under way, which could not help but influence the values that game studies adopted. For example, Dovey and Kennedy point to the way Juul's "classic game model" definition of games sees more open-ended videogames such as *SimCity* (Maxis 1989), which attract more gender-balanced audiences than most "core" game experiences, as "deviations" from the model rather than core videogame experiences in their own right. This view, they argue, "implicitly works to reinforce the notion that these are not *really* games and their players are not *really* gamers. ... The heavily gendered culture of the computer game therefore produces a privileged (but naturalized or normalized) set of play preferences and practices" (2006, 37). A dominant culture normalizes itself by ensuring that other values remain peripheral. It is important, then, to understand where and how this normatively masculine videogame culture emerged so that its presumptive values can be interrogated.

Computing as Masculine Culture

The history of videogames is enmeshed with the history of computing. Although rich commonalities can be traced from videogames back to the new media artworks of the 1960s, such as those by Fluxus artist Nam June Paik (J. Wilson 2004, 88); to the penny arcades, nickelodeon cinemas, panoramas, and theme-park attractions of the nineteenth century (Huhtamo 2005; Lister, Dovey, Giddings, et al. [2003] 2009, 115–123; Golding 2014);

and back further to the visual logics of the baroque era (Ndalianis 2004; Jayemanne 2017), the institutions and people formative to the early years of electronic computing created the first videogames and shaped the social contexts through which the medium would be popularly understood. Videogames had and continue to have a dominant epistemology as computer programs, and computer programming has a dominant epistemology as a masculinist practice.

Yet in the late 1940s, as Alan Turing was working on an algorithm that would allow a hypothetical "computing machine" to play chess against a human player, most computers were literally women. The title *computer* once belonged to those human clerks hired to punch out calculations that would be passed on to gunner officers to aim artillery or other weaponry during World War II. These human computers were commonly women because the work required of them was often seen as clerical and was thus easily gendered as "women's work" (Abbate 2012, 20). As the work of human computers was transferred to computing machines such as the Colossus (used at Bletchley Park in the United Kingdom) and the Electronic Numerical Integrator and Computer (ENIAC, designed at the University of Pennsylvania and funded by the US Army), it was primarily women who were tasked with the new job of figuring out how to program such machines. As the role of digital computing shifted perceptually from a menial number-crunching task to one of significant mathematical importance, however, it shifted from feminized labor to masculinized labor, and those early women programmers working during World War II largely lost their positions as computers and programmers with the end of hostilities (Abbate 2012, 34). For decades, the founding contribution made by women to computer programming was lost to history and hidden in classified documents until several projects, including Kathy Kleiman's ENIAC Programmers Project, rediscovered their stories.[1]

When the ENIAC and Colossus women programmers were physically excluded from the explicitly masculinized space of the military base and mathematics faculty, women in general were nominally excluded from decades of computing. Through the dressage of everyday life, computers became a habitus that men were "naturally" attuned to, despite the administrative and feminized origin of computers, which made it clear this relationship between men and computers was never "natural" at all. By 1962, when a group of male student hackers (Steve Russell, Peter Samson, Wayne Witaenem, and Martin Graetz) at a military-funded lab at MIT repurposed the PDP-1 computer to create the first videogame, *Spacewar!* (Crogan 2011, 38), computers were almost exclusively the realm of wealthy, military-affiliated university institutes, situated in spaces that had already been long inscribed as masculine.

Such an anecdotal etymology of "the computer" transitioning from the organic (nature) to the mechanical (culture) and from the clerical (feminine, banal) to the militaristic (masculine, meaningful) provides a compelling origin myth for the digital computer through which Dovey and Kennedy understand the videogame as "both the prodigal son of the military/industrial/capitalist complex and its illegitimate unruly child" (2006, 36). Dovey and Kennedy's gendering in this analogy is deliberate. As computers became increasingly significant devices through the latter half of the twentieth century, they became entrenched in broader patriarchal structures already inscribed as masculine and embedded in those parts of society already inscribed as masculine: the science lab, the math classroom, and, in the home, the son's bedroom rather than the daughter's (Wajcman 1991, 154; Lister, Dovey, Giddings, et al. [2003] 2009, 246).

The Hacker Mythos

It is telling to take seriously the notion that the hacker of the 1960s and 1970s functions not just as an origin story for the contemporary videogame but as a precursor of the modern, consumerist identity of the gamer. The culture of hackers holds a position in the history of computers that is at once central and marginal, with hackers being not only responsible for many advances in computer science but also in tension with the engineering mindset of their professors' generation, which saw computers as simply tools aimed at certain goals. Sherry Turkle ([1984] 2005) conducted ethnographic research on the hacker student culture of MIT's campus through the 1980s. She shows how for the hacker of this period the point often was not to use the computer to master some task but to master the computer itself:

> Their culture supports them as holders of an esoteric knowledge and defenders of the purity of computation seen not as a means to an end but as an artist's material whose internal aesthetic must be protected. ... They are caught up in an intense need to master their medium. In this they are like the virtuoso pianist or the sculptor possessed by his or her materials. ... They give themselves over to [their medium] and see it as the most complex, the most plastic, the most elusive and challenging of all. To win over computation is to win. Period. (191)

Through a desire to appreciate and master computers for their own sake, hackers gave birth to the videogame form. What better way to appreciate computers' innate aesthetics than to play with them?

However, hackers also imbued in videogames an ethos, attitude, and culture "that [was] produced by the conjunction of particular kinds of young men, technology and the mathematical systems of coding that are the language of computing" (Dovey and Kennedy 2006, 38). The mythos of hackers building up technology in campus dorm rooms and garages reinscribes a dominant masculinity that feminist scholars of technology have traced. In particular, work by Turkle and Judy Wajcman (1991) is significant here. Turkle's ethnographic research revealed a culture that is masculinist and hostile to women, that appreciates formal complexity for its own sake, and that views complex systems as something that must be defeated in contest ([1984] 2005, 194–197). Tellingly, when Turkle expresses to one of her interviewees that she wants to understand the "feel" of hacking, the hacker suggests she play the currently popular videogame *Adventure* (Atari 1979). *Adventure*, Turkle found, captured the hacker experience of "living with his [*sic*] code" much better than a typical computer programming course: "It is the introductory computer course that fails to give its students a sense of what programming is to its virtuosi. When systems get complex they become worlds that you can live in" ([1984] 2005, 206). Although videogames do not require the same programming literacy as hacking complex computer systems or hardware, they typically value similar experiences of comprehending complex systems and similarly celebrate the user-player's virtuosity at mastering those systems. The hacker prioritizes the pleasure of bringing complex, untamed systems under control, of bringing a digital Culture to a digital Nature.

Wajcman, writing in the late 1980s and early 1990s, was wary of Turkle's hermetic account of hacker culture, which verges on gender essentialism. She instead contextualizes the hacker mythos within broader cultural factors such as race, class, sexuality, gender, and age. In her book *Feminism Confronts Technology*, Wajcman notes that although the individuals that make up hacker collectives commonly self-identify as losers or loners, these "mainly white middle-class men [draw] on the culturally dominant form of masculinity for their notions of risk, danger and virility in their work" (1991, 144). She highlights the "complex relationship between knowledge, power and technology" (144) that is pointed to through how the men in these hacker collectives both lack and possess power through their technical expertise: many hackers are marginalized from dominant understandings of masculinity built on physical prowess, but they also possess particular cultural and societal privileges through their *technological* prowess.

Importantly, Wajcman situates masculinized computer culture through the genders' historically unequal access to computers. Computers became coded as masculine as they became machines linked with military bases, the sciences, and mathematic faculties of schools and universities. The preexisting gender disparities in educational departments were thus reinscribed through access to computers (Wajcman 1991, 152). Computer practices (and, by extension, discourses around videogame play *as* a computer practice) were naturalized as the realm of the scientific and the mathematic, and thus they inherited those fields' neoliberal and masculine values of control, mastery, and autonomy.

Martin Lister and his colleagues observe that "if computers and video games have made computer technology accessible and popular, they have, in doing so, effectively commodified computer technology, turning the radical hacker ethic into consumerist entertainment" ([2003] 2009, 290). At the same time, Wendy Hui Kyong Chun traces how post–World War II digital computing emerged alongside neoliberalism. The dream for both user-friendly computer interfaces and a neoliberal world was "the resurgence of the *seemingly* sovereign individual, the subject driven to know, driven to map, to zoom in and out, to manipulate, and to act" (2011, 7, 8, original emphasis; see also Burgess 2012). From early on, digital computers assumed a configurative positionality of the user, viewing from above, from nowhere, as opposed to embodied and viewing from somewhere. The configuration of how humans relate to digital computers that the hacker mythos instilled is not natural but very much of its time in the last half of the twentieth century.

Directly influenced by a liberal, rationalist subjectivity (that perceives itself as an objectivity) that is ingrained through an ancestry of the hacker cultures of the previous decades, those contemporary videogame works most valued by videogame critics, enthusiasts, and scholars alike have been those that allow the player to express an individualistic sense of mastery over the computer system (or over other players): players take on powerful roles such as commander, mayor, god, soldier, gangster, and superhero both to save the day and, more often than not, to save the girl. These values were constructed and ritualized through the form's most dominant, replicated works and its sprouting in hacker culture, and critical discourses surrounding videogames embraced these values as seemingly inherent to the videogame form.

From Hacker to Gamer

Whereas Turkle is celebratory of her ability to comprehend the pleasures of hacking through early videogames, Wajcman's explicit linking of videogames, hacker culture, and dominant masculinities is more critical:

Games are the primary attraction of computers for children. Given that it is men (often computer hackers) who design video games and software, it is hardly surprising that their designs typically appeal to male fantasies. ... Many of the most popular games today are simply programmed versions of traditionally male non-computer games, involving shooting, blowing up, speeding, or zapping in some way or another. ... No wonder then that these games often frustrate or bore the non-macho players exposed to them. (1991, 154)

Although videogames today encompass a far broader diversity of genres and forms of attention, Wajcman's observations can still be made of the most commercially visible videogame genres. The legacy of the student hacker of the mid–twentieth century lingers as a normative and formalizing masculinity in the modes of videogame culture and production that began to solidify in the late 1980s. The values of the male hacker (autonomy, configuration, agency, technological virtuosity) became the foundational values of videogames. The videogame "was slotted into a pre-existing male subculture and took on its masculine face" (Wajcman 1991, 155).

The roots of these dominant videogame values in hacker cultures is traced in research conducted by Graeme Kirkpatrick (2012) that highlights the etymologies of the terms *gameplay* and *gamer* as they emerged through the UK enthusiast press through the 1980s and 1990s. The use of *gameplay* to demarcate some sort of unique essence of the videogame form came to indicate "the point at which gaming bid[] for autonomy as a cultural practice," and gameplay is thus deployed deliberately in opposition "to things like graphics, character, plot and so on" (2012). The term *gameplay* is meant to distinguish videogames as a unique cultural practice but instead comes to signify "the tastes and preferences of the authentic gamer" (Kirkpatrick 2012). Indeed, it is common to see those experiential videogames mentioned at the start of this chapter dismissed explicitly for lacking gameplay, as though it were a quantifiable essence that a videogame might possess a certain amount of. A good videogame is not one that possesses gameplay; rather, a videogame is said to possess gameplay if it adequately fits within the normatively masculine values that have been passed down by the hacker.

The hacker mythos of early student and hobbyist computer cultures birthed the videogame industry, and the videogame industry of the late 1980s in turn distilled the hacker into the commodified identity of the gamer. The gamer was crafted and cultivated by a consolidating videogame industry to be a stable, homogenous target audience with narrow tastes defined by "authentic" gameplay. Gameplay as a marker of videogame quality thus became a hegemonic marker: "Successful game designers produce videogames with gameplay and in persuading players this is what they have done they determine what 'gameplay' signifies" (Kirkpatrick 2012). As both Kirkpatrick's (2012) and Amanda Cote's (2015) historical studies show, the gamer who developed the competencies, tastes, and embodied literacies to appreciate gameplay was in turn more assuredly addressed by videogame magazines and marketing into the 1990s as a teenage male who identified *as* a gamer. This gamer was explicitly differentiated from other nongamer identities such as adult, parent, and woman. Through the 1980s and 1990s, the dominant videogames were those produced by and for young men, and it was the success of these videogames that determined what was canonized as a good videogame moving forward.

The lasting effect of the hegemonic and gendered tendencies Kirkpatrick and Cote observe is exemplified in interviews conducted by Adrienne Shaw that explore just who self-identifies as a "gamer." These interviews confirm that "male interviewees were much more likely to identify as gamers than female, transgender or genderqueer interviewees" (2011, 34) and that such self-identification has little to do with how often the interviewees play videogames. In other words, many nonmale videogame players, even if they play videogames frequently, do not consider themselves to be "real" gamers or the videogames that they play to be "real" videogames. Thus, the gamer identity is one not of description but of legitimization and authenticity along predominately gendered lines. All gamers are videogame players, but only a very particular, hegemonic subset of videogame players are gamers.

As a consequence of videogames' historical construction as masculine and their commodified evolution out of a hacker mythos that favors technological competency, formal virtuosity, and systems literacy, discourses around videogames (both scholarly and popular) have produced what Dovey and Kennedy note is "an 'ideal' player subject that is naturalized as 'white,' 'male' and 'heterosexual'" (2006, 63). Dominant understandings of videogame play—taking hacker ideologies as inherent values—obscure what is in fact the heterogeneous spectrum of meaningful and significant experiences players have with videogames. These understandings instead allow a highly gendered and conservatively formalist notion of videogame play to dominate: those videogames that have goals to achieve, complex systems to master, and challenges to overcome are exemplary of *gameplay*—a videogame form perceived as primarily about acting and exerting power. At the same time, those videogames deemed to be too easy (not enough challenge), too cinematic (not enough interactivity), or too linear (not enough opportunity to exert agency) are marginalized as lesser examples of the form.

Just as the hacker is concerned with mastering complicated systems and ultimately beating the form of the computer, so too is the gamer concerned with mastering complicated systems of mechanics and ultimately *beating* the form of the videogame. This configuration-centric evaluation of what a "good" videogame affords the player to do is reinforced through early "ludology" game studies, as Rune Klevjer explicitly notes in his defense of cutscenes when he accuses ludology of being "partly rooted in the dark arcade of the late 70's and early 80's [and] partly rooted in hacker culture" (2002, 193). That the study of videogames in many universities still finds an uneasy home between humanities and computer engineering departments indicates the everydayness of these tensions.

The dominant hacker mythos underpinning videogame evaluation points to the normative, hegemonic, and masculine values underpinning the form's core culture; it points to that core market with the most power and speaks to their values while obscuring a plethora of other audiences and values that persist in marginal videogame cultures but that are delegitimized by a dominant and commodified discourse. Accounting for the embodied experience of videogame play as a coming together of player and videogame can challenge this discourse to provide a space and a method for appreciating those videogame works beyond dominant values of mastery and control and for configuring them not as deviations but as videogame experiences in their own right. To do this requires players who are not dominant hackers but integrated cyborgs.

Players as Integrated Cyborgs

As a response to the masculinizing of science and technology discourses, the cyborg enters critical discourse through Donna Haraway as "an ironic dream of a common language for women in the integrated circuit" (1991b, 149). The cyborg embraces the hybridity, impurity, and ultimate partiality required for flesh to incorporate *with* machine, and this embrace destabilizes the hegemonic dominance of those identifications that seek to transcend and dominate the machine. For Haraway in particular, the cyborg is an explicitly feminist metaphor that contests not just dominant knowledges but also dominant *ways of knowing*: "Perhaps, ironically, we can learn from our fusions with animals and machines how not to be Man, the embodiment of Western logos. From the point of view of pleasure in these potent and taboo fusions, made inevitable by the social relations of science and technology, there might indeed be a feminist science" (1991b, 173). Where the hacker strives for autonomy and dominance over the machine—an all-knowing, god's-eye, viewing-from-above perspective—the cyborg embraces the fact it is always already in part shaped and mediated by the machines with which it integrates: always already partial, always already mediated. Not seeing from above, like God or a configurative and transcendent hacker-gamer, but seeing from *somewhere*, from a situated and partial perspective, through a body that is spliced with its worlds.

Hayles has similarly utopic hopes for her embodied posthuman: "To conceptualize the human in [terms of posthumanism] is not to imperil human survival but is precisely to enhance it, for the more we understand the flexible, adaptive structures that coordinate our environments and the metaphors that we ourselves are, the better we can fashion images of ourselves that accurately reflect the complex interplays that ultimately make the entire world one system" (2005, 290). Here we see why it is urgent that we conceive the player and the videogame as reflexively constructing each other in an intermediating assemblage of flesh and machine: such is the way to accurately reflect the complex interplays of player and videogame that are obscured through dominant teleologies such as the immaterial transcendence of "immersion" and the configurative empowerment of "interactivity." To account for videogame play as it is actually experienced by an embodied being, as opposed to how it is popularly imagined and marketed, requires a move away from the hacker-gamer and toward the cyborg-player.

Beyond "Gameplay"

Against any cultural hegemony that favors a particular, dominant perspective, "we can be sure that there are other stories, identities and creative processes that get written out of the discourse of dominance" (Dovey and Kennedy 2006, 76). Videogames that have not offered pleasures strictly aligned to goal-based ludic play have been marginalized by videogame discourses for some years, as Dovey and Kennedy note regarding Juul's sidelining of *SimCity* in his classic game model. Those videogames that focus less on mastery and control of complex systems and more on participation and integration with audiovisual-haptic sensations are both more accessible and attractive to a broader range of people than just the young *gamers* targeted and trained by the blockbuster videogame industry and simultaneously marginalized as less legitimate by the dominant values that continue to determine the evaluative discourse around videogames.

In *Dear Esther*, for instance, the player wakes up on the shore of an island and makes their way inland to the summit of a mountain. As they walk through the caves and up the paths and along the beaches of the island, various objects and landscapes can be looked at, and a narrator speaks of events surrounding a car crash that occurred in the past. On different plays of the videogame, different artifacts can be found scattered around the world in different locations, and ghostly specters may or may not appear at different moments. *Dear Esther* consciously rejects conventional videogame values of agency, empowerment, choice, and systemic complexity in order to provide a slow, evocative exploratory experience of navigating the space of the island. This minimalism of player ability, however, perplexed many videogame reviewers. Consider this lukewarm review from the Australian magazine *PC Powerplay*:

Dear Esther is not your traditional concept of a game. ... There's little actual game-play to speak of: you move about with the arrow keys in first-person, and that's pretty much it. There are no enemies, no puzzles, nor any items or objects to interact with. You cannot jump, or sprint, and the game will automatically crouch for you if need be. You have a flashlight, but the game will turn it on and off for you. These automatic actions drive home the feeling that you're not even really in control of your character—you're more of an observer inhabiting their headspace. There is one walking pace, and it's deliberately ponderous so that you might take time to appre-ciate the environment around you because that's really all there is to do. (Hindes 2012, 48)

Instead of comprehending what particular engagements *Dear Esther* offers, the reviewer lists only those formal elements that are not present: objects to interact with, enemy or puzzle challenges, things to "do." The review suggests that *Dear Esther* is a videogame of poor quality because it lacks the typical dexterous challenges to be mastered—you are not even "really in control" of your character. When the reviewer says there is "little actual gameplay," they are taking the narrow (yet dominant) conceptualization of gameplay that reinforces the dominance of the authentic gamer and their authentic videogames and allowing it to stand in for the myriad engage-ments possible for a body entwined with a videogame. Likewise, a demon-strative user review of the similarly experiential videogame *Gone Home* (Fullbright 2013) on review amalgamation site Metacritic complains that "the only semblance of gameplay *Gone Home* has to offer is 90 minutes of pitiful, painfully easy exploration. ... To call this a video game is insulting!" (Account33, 2013). Here, *Gone Home* is not only a videogame of poor value due to its lack of normative qualities but also a threat to the very concept of "videogame."

Dear Esther, Gone Home, Dys4ia, and *Slave of God* (Lavelle 2012) are exemplary of nascent modes of videogame design that do not offer the pleasures of mastery and control that the hacker-gamer identity privileges. Rather, they offer little more than a path to walk down or an environment to explore. There is a distinct lack of anything to "do" in such videogames, a lack of explicit choices to be made beyond the navigational, an inability to affect or alter the world from some position of power. Rather, the pleasures of *Dear Esther, Gone Home, Dys4ia, Slave of God*, and many other videogames produced beyond the confines of the high-budget blockbuster industry are instead phenomenological—explicitly that of situated navigation rather than godlike configuration, a corporeal engagement of the senses rather than an intellectual engagement of systems—and they require an integrated and cooperative relationship between the human and the computer.

Marginalized Videogame Identities

Importantly and not coincidentally, the videogames least capable of being evaluated positively by a hegemonic, hacker-gamer discourse are those that most explicitly react *against* the masculinist dominance of the blockbuster videogame industry. The past decade has seen the rise in casual mobile videogames with popular appeal to demographics beyond the core gamer consumer base (Hjorth and Richardson 2009; Juul 2010; also see chapter 2). Yet the overwhelming commercial and popular success of casual games such as *Candy Crush Saga* (King 2012), *Kim Kardashian: Hollywood* (Glu Games 2014), and *Flappy Bird* (Nguyen 2013) is trivialized by critiques of how simple they are to play and how superficial their content is (see, for example, Schreier 2014)—as though a woman networking in Hollywood is a less-worthy experience to be simulated by videogame play than a hulking space marine saving Earth.

At the same time as the rise in casual mobile videogames, waves of avant-garde developers—many of whom are women, people of color, queer, and/or transgender—have emerged from backgrounds with little investment in preexisting videogame culture and its normative, hacker-influenced values, and the critically acclaimed videogames they have created challenge dominant understandings of the videogame form. These artists (such as Anna Anthropy, Liz Ryerson, Ian McLarty, TheCatamites, Mattie Brice, Soha Kareem, Stephen Lavelle, Arcane Kids, Kitty Horrorshow, Zoë Quinn, and many others) and the platforms that support them (more accessible development tools such as GameMaker and Unity and distribution platforms such as Newgrounds and itch.io) have been forced to confront a dominant understanding of videogames that is incapable of appreciating them. For instance, Robert Yang has created a series of short videogames that explicitly explore issues of male homosexuality. Yet, despite their critical acclaim, Yang's videogames are regularly banned from being played on livestream services such as Twitch due to their explicitly sexual themes (Yang 2016).[2]

Samantha Allen (2013) succinctly highlights how the ideological notions behind a videogame's designed experience either perpetuates or contests hegemonic understandings of videogame play as dependent on mastery and control. In an essay comparing how movement is conceived by the critically acclaimed open-world blockbuster *The Elder Scrolls V: Skyrim* (Bethesda 2011) and how it is conceived by *Dys4ia*, Allen notes that the freedom of movement taken for granted by players in many blockbuster videogames closely parallels the freedom of social movement possessed by the predominately white, straight, and male creators of those videogames. *Skyrim's* "implicitly masculine" open world focuses on allowing the player to determine his individualistic fate with a "supreme motility … [that] functions as an exaggeration of a freedom that [cisgender gamers] already enjoy in the physical spaces of non-game worlds" (2013). Meanwhile, Allen argues, the strictly scripted and sometimes impossible challenges of *Dys4ia*—a videogame explicitly about the experiences of a transgender woman—"allow the player to acutely feel movement constraints, spatial restrictions and the uncertainty, sometimes the impossibility, of success" (2013). Videogames by marginal developers often communicate more explicitly through a *lack* of freedom of movement by means of the various constraints placed on the player in videogames such as *Dys4ia*, *Lim* (see figure 6.3), and *Mainichi*.

In *Mainichi* (the Japanese word for "everyday"), the simple act of walking down the street is complicated by the character's status as transgender because other characters regularly halt the character's progress to whisper near her or outright abuse her. The day repeats, and players can make different choices about how they approach the day and how they present themselves. This option to make new choices initially suggests to the player an ability to improve things through personal choice, but it turns out that regardless of what choices they make, some form of abuse will nevertheless occur. Here, an explicit *lack* of ability to master the videogame's systems through autonomous choice is how *Mainichi* communicates with the player.

Similarly, the player of Yang's videogame *Stick Shift* (2015) has a 48 percent chance of being pulled over by the police and locked out of retrying the

Figure 6.3
merritt k's *Lim* (2012). The player must navigate a simple maze by blending in with other squares. This goal is complicated, however, by the "blend" button, which slows down the player's movement and produces unsettling noises. Sometimes the player's square is pushed beyond the confines of the maze by the other squares, and the game becomes unwinnable.

videogame for a number of hours. This 48 percent probability is equal to, Yang (2015) notes in his artist's statement that accompanies the videogame, the number of lesbian, gay, bisexual, transgender, and intersex survivors of violence in New York who in a survey said they had experienced police misconduct. Here, again, a strict shaping of the player's experience trumps any liberating empowerment the player might feel. Players are incapable of avoiding through either choice or prowess the ending *Stick Shift* has in store for them; they are at the whim of the videogame. Rather than fantasies of empowerment and consequence preferred by the hacker-gamer, these videogames produced by those other than the most empowered members of society—those "who are not allowed to *not* have a body" (Haraway 1988, 575)—are realities of immanence. They destabilize the notion of the player as an idealized liberal subject capable of perceiving themselves as autonomous and empowered. Such videogames can be appreciated only by players who are not hackers determined to understand and control and exert agency over the videogame's systems, but rather cyborgs willing to integrate with, incorporate, and become part of the videogame's systems.

Such videogames do not speak to hegemonic understandings of videogames but react against them. They often find themselves dismissed by both academic and popular discourses as less than legitimate videogames due to a lack of certain virtuosities: the virtuosity of a skilled player to defeat them and the virtuosity of a technologically (and economically) skilled creator to create them. This dismissal is perhaps most relevant of all to the renaissance of interactive-fiction videogames created through the open-access development software Twine (see Hudson 2015; kopas 2015). A free tool that allows the production and distribution of interactive-fiction works through basic HTML, Twine has become a hotbed for alternative and amateur videogame works. merritt kopas observes that "in the context of a medium that historically hasn't made any space for explorations of weakness, hurt, or struggle," Twine videogames "explore complex issues around embodiment and affect in wildly divergent ways" (2015, 4).[3] Unsurprisingly, these works have also met strong opposition from established videogame discourses, which claim they are not "real" games despite the long and intermingled history of videogames and hypertext fiction. Because Twine opens up the possibilities of videogame creation to a broader audience, it risks destabilizing the dominant values sedimented in core videogame culture and is thus seen as a threat.

A narrow focus on videogame play that privileges autonomous action and the mastery of complex systems through individualist agency obscures this broader spectrum of embodied textualities afforded by videogames that exist beyond the dominant, industrial modes of production and the hacker-gamer identity that such modes of production cultivate for their sustainability. The figure of the cyborg offers an alternative way to consider the player's integration with the videogame as partial, mediated, embodied, and imperfect. Acknowledging the rhetorical and evaluative strategies used both to centralize the hacker-gamer identity and to marginalize the cyborg-player is crucial to allowing a critical comprehension of the videogame form to move beyond and react against its most normative instances.

Domination through Integration, Integration through Domination

In Sega's videogame *Binary Domain* (2012), rebuilding the sunken cities of the near-future, post-climate-change world demands a massive labor force, motivating swift advancements in robotic technologies. However, with new technologies come new anxieties. The United Nations passes the New Geneva Convention, which inscribes into international law the banning of creating robots that can pass as human—a convention for the nonrights of nonhumans. As the videogame begins, the playable character and protagonist, Dan Marshall, joins a UN Security Council–sanctioned task force known as the "Rust Crew" to infiltrate Japan to investigate a suspected breach of the New Geneva Convention by the Amada Corporation. There is reason to believe not only that Amada has created robots that pass as human but also that these robots are themselves unaware of what they are, living their day-to-day lives unaware that they are in fact not "real" humans at all. *Binary Domain* plays as a standard third-person shooter where the player navigates Dan to cover before shooting at advancing robotic armies, but the narrative unfolds more complexly against this mechanically conventional backbone. It becomes increasingly unclear just who is human and who is machine and why it should even matter in the first place. Suspicion turns to each of Dan's allies and enemies before finally turning to the *Binary Domain* player themself. Late in the videogame, after one particularly difficult skirmish, one of Dan's allies mockingly compliments Dan's prowess and asks if he is sure he is not part robot himself. Dan, controlled and augmented by a player wrapped around a videogame controller and facing a television screen, fights so well and is so strong that his squadmate suspects that he may not actually be a "real" human. At the precise moment that *Binary Domain*'s story begins to suggest a more complex relationship between humans and machines, this squadmate ironically suggests that the assemblage of flesh and machine that allows the player to perform so admirably (playable character, virtual camera, and a corporeal player entangled with videogame hardware that enables them to retry the skirmish again and again until they get it right) might be itself a cyborg.

In *Binary Domain*, the anxiety is not of a cyborg that is less than human but of a cyborg that is *more* than human, that is too perfect, that possesses *too much* power through its augmented body, that is a threat to the dominance of the human. This anxiety complicates what this chapter has up to now risked presenting as too straightforwardly an oppositional dichotomy. The hacker and the cyborg, as epistemological metaphors for understanding the formative technicities that mediate videogame culture, do not exist as distinct from one another but as entangled with and constantly reacting against each other.

Dovey and Kennedy point to this intricacy, where the "lone individual genius" hacker is often described as having "[a] machine-like mind[] and inhuman propensities" (2006, 69). In particular, Dovey and Kennedy look at David Kushner's boasting in his book *Masters of Doom* (2003) that videogame developer John Romero could play *Pac-Man* with his eyes closed. Whereas Kushner presents this anecdote as an example of Romero's mastery of the computer, Dovey and Kennedy offer an alternative reading of it wherein the machine has fully trained Romero to respond in the optimal manner (not unlike how all videogames train their players at an input device through repetition). Similarly, players in "speedrunning" communities who work to use exploits and hacks to finish a videogame as quickly as possible are almost computer-like in their split-second inputting of exact-button presses in a strict order. The best hackers, it seems, are cyborgs.

Although *Binary Domain* explicitly, if flippantly, challenges a simple division between autonomous humans "using" technology and subjugated cyborgs who are constituted by technology, this notion is just as present in a range of blockbuster videogames that use the metaphor of cyborgism to explain away the playable character's improbable and exceptional physical strength and dominance over the world, characteristics that are typical of hacker-influenced videogames—where the physical prowess of macho characters in the virtual world becomes directly analogous to the technological prowess of the hacker-gamer in the actual world. Master Chief, the playable character of *Halo* (Bungie 2001), is a biologically engineered super-soldier, augmented further with alien-technology armor and recharging shields; *Assassin's Creed* (Ubisoft Montreal 2007) uses the framing device of a character connected to a machine enacting another character to explain the first character's powerful abilities; the playable character of *Bioshock* (2K Boston 2007) augments their body with powerful potions; Solid Snake of *Metal Gear Solid* (Konami 1998) is an engineered supersoldier augmented by nanomachines; in *Deus Ex: Human Revolution* (Eidos 2011), a videogame explicitly concerned with technological augmentation of the human body, the hardest difficulty setting the player can choose is explained as being for players who are "one with the machine." Such cyborgism is not limited to science-fiction worlds. The playable characters of contemporary military shooters such as *Call of Duty: Modern Warfare 3* (Infinity Ward 2011) are augmented with unmanned drones, night-vision goggles, and laser sights; the undead ranger of Tolkien fantasy game *Middle-Earth: Shadow of Mordor* (Monolith 2014) is augmented by an Elven wraith that affords all sorts of superpowers. Across all these videogames is the implicit or explicit suggestion that humans' *dominance* over their world—be that world virtual or actual—has always depended on their *integration* with nonhuman technologies, that a transcendence over machines relies on an immanence with machines.

The point is not that some videogames demand hackers and that others demand cyborgs, but that *all* videogame play augments and restricts the player's corporeal experience in particular, cyborgian ways through sights, sounds, and interfaces. The dominant values of the hacker-gamer are but a subset of a much broader spectrum of potential values afforded by the embodied textuality of videogame play. Those values that have long dominated understandings of videogame play (mastery, agency, autonomy) have been instilled by those who, to echo Hayles, "[have] the wealth, power, and leisure to conceptualize themselves as autonomous beings exercising their will through individual agency and choice" (2005, 286). Videogames by marginal developers such as those described earlier in this chapter, in contrast, contest the dominance of these hegemonic and narrow ways of appreciating videogame experience. They demonstrate and embrace a broader spectrum of experiences afforded by the embodied textuality of videogame play.

In *Modern Warfare*, my kidnapping and execution during the opening scenes is not the only time I am forcibly and unavoidably killed. In a later level, I take on the role of an American marine invading the same fictional Middle Eastern country in the hopes of toppling the same military leader who executed me (as the president) during the coup. After fighting through the skies and through the streets in a series of impressive and violent set pieces, the American forces become aware of an armed nuclear warhead in the city and are forced to retreat. They are too late, however, and I watch from the rear of a transport helicopter as the expanding mushroom cloud catches up to and devours me, my character, the helicopter, everything. Moments later, my character wakes among the bodies and ruin of the crashed helicopter. Whereas movement in *Modern Warfare* is typically fluid and swift, here my player-character can only crawl at a slow pace as I drag their broken body out onto the street. After a while, I try pressing the button that toggles crouching, and my character (slowly, painfully) stands themself up. But they are still clearly injured; the camera lurches forward with each step to suggest an exaggerated limp as I walk down the destroyed street. In this short stage, there are no enemies, no weapons, no challenges. I simply limp my character's broken body forward for a short while before they inevitably collapse and die.

Here in the blockbuster *Call of Duty* franchise, which is exemplary of the hypermasculine, militaristic empowerment at the core of dominant commercial videogame production, I am subservient to the will of the videogame and the fragile corporeality of the character's virtual body. Neither of these inevitable deaths of my playable characters can be adequately accounted for by an analysis that privileges mechanical action, empowerment, and individual choice. The pleasures of these scenes are not the mechanical mastery of a technological object but, first and foremost, complex and shifting embodied experiences that incorporate hands and controllers; eyes and images; ears and sounds; and dynamic bodies, worlds, and temporalities. Such scenes highlight the urgency of Seth Giddings and Helen Kennedy's claim that videogames demand "a new conceptual language [that attends] to both the operations of nonhuman agency and the human pleasures of lack of agency, of being controlled, of being *acted upon*" (2008, 30, original emphasis). It is at this ontological intersection of both controlling and being controlled by technology that Haraway's cyborg enters the critical discourse. It is through the cyborg-player that the embodied textuality of videogame experience is rendered legible.

This chapter has traced how videogame play lost its corporeality through the mythos of the hacker and how that corporeality might be reclaimed through the figure of the cyborg. The important point is not that posthumanist cyborgs are a hybrid of machine and organism, whereas rationalist hackers are not, but that the dualisms that allow the hacker to be seen as distinct from the machine—Nature distinct from Culture, Man distinct from Machine, mind distinct from body, gamer distinct from nongamer—are themselves constructed mythologies at the services of dominant and hegemonic values. Focusing on the inherent cyborgism of videogame play—where human players are integrated with, embodied through, and constituted by the videogame—instead provides fruitful ground to explore broader capabilities of the videogame form, along with more nuanced ways of comprehending the experiences players are capable of having with such a form.

Cyborgism puts back into play the corporeality of videogame engagement, the play of bodies, that is commonly displaced by calls to "gameplay" and "immersion" and "interactivity" as pregiven qualities. It allows an appreciation for those videogames and manifestos from recent years that work explicitly to decenter the concerns of a preexisting, autonomous, hermetic player in videogame design and to understand the player more as one element in a much larger circuit than as looming over and comprehending a system (see Brice 2014; Polansky 2014; k 2015). It allows a reconsideration of the videogames of the past, which are often dismissed as technologically "primitive" in comparison to present or future videogames rather than viewed as embodied experiences with sights, sounds, and interfaces in their own right. It allows for understandings such as Daniel Golding's (2013c) that see the player as navigating from within rather than configuring from above, not unlike Haraway's feminist subjectivity that insists we *always* see from somewhere (1988, 882). It allows us to account for the materialities of those videogames that can *only* be videogames, for which the audiovisual skin and the mechanical skeleton are utterly inseparable. It allows an opportunity to understand what is actually happening in those moments of videogame play when the player is "doing nothing." It allows a space for the myriad players who would rather be cyborgs than goddesses. It renders legible, as this entire book has strived to render legible, a more nuanced understanding of videogame experience as an embodied textuality that flickers across actual and virtual worlds as a play of bodies.

Conclusion

We count and count and count until we invent a numbering system, based on ten digits, and some years later, having long since lost sight of how that system originally related to our anatomy's way of seizing hold of the world, we use ten digits to type instructions directing electricity to outline our body's mathematics back at itself. And we're thus now incarnated in the coolest digital version of ourselves to ever come along, a self-actuating, glistening little creature under glass that we now and then poke at through wires.

—David Sudnow, *Pilgrim in the Microworld* (1983)

Nintendo's *Game & Wario* (2013) is a collection of small videogames that take advantage of the WiiU's tablet GamePad controller. In one of these games, "Fruit" (see figure 7.1), one player chooses a character on the remote screen of the GamePad controller and walks around a city block crowded by similar-looking albeit computer-controlled characters to collect several pieces of floating fruit within the allotted time. At the same time, up to four other players are looking at the same game space on the television screen. These players hold no input devices, nor are their motions being detected in any way. They are simply looking at the television, trying to determine which of the many on-screen characters is the thief-player. It is up to the first GamePad player to ensure while playing that their character fits in with those controlled by the computer, matching their behaviors so as not to be too conspicuous. At the end of the round, the GamePad is passed around the players, and each guesses who the thief-player was from a lineup of suspects.

"Fruit" provides a fitting analogy on which to conclude this book. Those players who are not the thief are very much still *players* of the videogame, as "Fruit" itself identifies them in its on-screen prompts. Yet they are not playing a videogame in any conventionally understood way. They are not inputting; they are not "interacting"; they are merely looking, listening,

Figure 7.1
The player-character hidden amid nonplayable characters in the minigame "Fruit" in
Nintendo's *Game & Wario* (2013).

and paying attention (also possibly talking and collaborating). Without
any form of input device, they are still playing a videogame; they are playing "Fruit" through an embodied, perceptual engagement that encompasses more than an intentional pushing of buttons to configure on-screen
imagery—they are playing "Fruit" through the act of looking at lights and
the act of listening to sounds. At the same time, the very challenge these
players face in trying to distinguish the thief from the computer-controlled
characters—trying to pinpoint a "player" distinct from the "videogame"—
echoes the difficulty faced by videogame scholars in trying to distinguish
between the player and the videogame as discrete objects of study, while the
player gripping the controller is doing all they can to fuse the two together
and ensure such a distinction remains impossible.

This book has forwarded a phenomenology of videogame experience
that understands and appreciates videogame play as at once experiential
and textual, as perceived through an amalgam embodiment *of* the videogame that is dynamic, emergent, and situated. It has done this by deliberately resisting any urge to essentialize or purify the videogame form as
somehow distinct from other media while at the same time showing a
close commitment to the particular engagements demanded of the videogame form. It has called into doubt the presumption that qualities such as
agency, choice, interactivity, and immersion are foundational aspects of the

videogame form and instead interrogates videogames as emergent perceptual experiences constituted by the player's embodied, situated, intercorporeal engagement with them as seen, heard, and touched. The chapters of this book have been concerned not with what players do with videogames but with how players come to be embodied through a videogame so as to feel a sense of copresence across worlds and bodies. Videogame play is not easily distilled into discrete "actual" and "virtual" elements. To comprehend the experience of videogame play is instead to focus on the *splice*. To appreciate videogame experience, we must embrace the irreducible, contradictory, and embodied entanglement of bodies and worlds, not try to resolve it. It is here, in the dynamic play of bodies that is the perceptual assemblage player-and-videogame, that the pleasures and meanings of videogame play can be comprehended.

In the introduction, I confessed that I harbor a suspicion that the scholarly study of videogames presupposes too much regarding how the experience of videogames is constituted. A focus on player "actions" (what the player chooses to do) is ultimately *dis*embodying, a historically constructed mythos coming at the expense of the fully embodied, sensorial experience of engaging with a videogame as sights, sounds, and haptics. A phenomenology of videogame experience instead starts counterintuitively not with the player's organic body or conscious intentions but with the emergence of the player's embodiment through the videogame—the player-and-videogame as experienced by the player-and-videogame. At the same time, the essentialist tendencies toward understanding videogames as digitalized nondigital games at the expense of appreciating the conduits between a broader spectrum of media and forms with which videogames materially intersect are no longer sufficient if we are to appreciate videogames *as videogames*—the particular, messy, intricate coming-togethers of media and forms that videogames are. To understand the experience of videogame play, we must embrace (without resolving) the splices actual/virtual, player/character, embodied/textual, active/passive, acting/interpreting. A phenomenology of videogame experience must account for the player-and-videogame as a reflexive, dynamic, irreducible whole.

This is what I hope this book contributes to the fields of cultural and media studies broadly and videogame studies specifically: a more nuanced vocabulary to problematize and account for those engagements with the videogame often taken for granted as either the background against which videogame action happens or as peripheral to that action. As Merleau-Ponty problematizes the taken-for-granted-ness of the effect of our embodied perception on our conscious perception and sense of being-in-the-world, so we must challenge and interrogate the often taken-for-granted experience of playing a videogame. Two mechanically similar videogames might *feel* substantially different, and so videogames require tools of textual analysis that can account for this distributed corporeality. We cannot remove the "non-play" components of a videogame and hope to arrive at a pure, essential "gameness" that in any way represents the experiences players have with that videogame. We must instead accept and account for the videogame in all its embodied and material messiness. We must comprehend how videogames are perceived.

I started this project with the goal of understanding how videogames mean, how they function in and as popular and creative culture. In the introduction, I suggested that what game studies has come to conceptualize "games" to be is no longer sufficient to account for what videogames have become. It is not sufficient to differentiate videogames from other screen media because of some unique possession of "interactivity" or ability to "immerse" a player. It is not sufficient to say that a videogame allows a player to choose what to do when a film does not. It is not sufficient to say that the player enters the world of a videogame in a way that the reader of a novel does not. Likewise, it is no longer sufficient to evaluate videogames on purely technological terms that render individual works invisible within a couple of years even as film studies and popular-music studies are capable of talking about the same works decades later. Nor is it sufficient to make claim to what technology might allow videogames to become "one day." When once it was perhaps strategic to highlight the uniqueness or potential of videogames with respect to other media by calling attention to an inherent "gameness" or "digitality" in order to validate studying them at all or to dismiss the immaturity of contemporary videogame works with a call to what videogames might "one day" become, both videogames and their study are now mature fields—too mature for us to be self-consciously concerned about either their uniqueness or their untapped potential. If the true significance of videogames is to be accounted for, their uniqueness must no longer be exaggerated. That uniqueness was too successful in cordoning off the study of videogames from the broader critical push of media studies because videogames were considered an odd outlier of digital culture rather than the rich, diverse, and significant cultural form that they have become. Now, what is important is that we understand the *context* of videogames in the broader media ecology—how they are similar to other media forms, how they deviate, and how like all media they fundamentally shape the culture that produces them. A media studies that does not account for videogames as a form already as robust and vital as cinema or music—and as deserving of critical attention—does damage to our comprehension of contemporary media.

What is required—what is perhaps inevitable—is what Barry Atkins predicted a decade ago: a more formalized school of *videogame studies* that is bifurcated from game studies and that "must also attend to the specificity of the image and the game if they are to adequately account for the object of their attention" (2006, 133). Videogame studies, just like film studies, television studies, and popular music studies, would comprehend the form's particular cultural significance without having to speak for all forms of game or play. Doing so would provide an opportunity to evaluate a videogame work without reducing it to a digitalized nondigital game. It would provide a path forward where both blockbuster videogames produced by a consumerist industry and personal works produced by individual artists can be understood as competent works of the videogame form that demand particular embodied engagements through eyes-on-screens, ears-at-speakers, and muscles-at-input-devices. It would provide a way not only for videogames to be differentiated from both earlier audiovisual media and nondigital games but also for the rich commonalities and overlaps with each to be recognized, investigated, and embraced.

At this point in time, the consequences of not more formally distinguishing videogames from traditional understandings of "games" would be both theoretically stifling and formally unsustainable. With the rise of easier-to-use videogame-development tools and free platforms for digital distribution, the past decade has seen a surge of new demographics creating videogames more visibly: women, queer folk, nonwhite folk, and transgender folk are making themselves increasingly visible as videogame developers and critics, and, not surprisingly, the videogames they are creating are dramatically different from the videogames that have been produced by a traditionally white and male industry for the past several decades. The videogames they are creating, such as those highlighted in chapter 6, simply *don't fit* within the conceptualizations of videogames that predate their visibility. The very nature of the videogames this avant-garde of developers is creating has been answered by violences from a hegemonic videogame culture defending an outdated comprehension of what videogames are. Although Gamergate was at its core a jaded and abusive man mobilizing an online mob to harass a developer because of their gender, the anger that gave that mob momentum was one centrally concerned with who gets to decide what videogames are. If we are to comprehend the contemporary videogame in the myriad contemporary forms shaped by these newly visibly demographics of developers, then its presumed formal qualities must be interrogated and, in some cases, done away with. We must fundamentally reconsider how videogames are perceived and experienced. They do not necessarily provide goals, challenges, or even choices, but they do always provide an audiovisually projected playspace juxtaposed with an actual playspace that the player plays *from*—poking at and peering into the virtual world. There is always an embodied experience across worlds—an embodied textuality—to be appreciated. If this book accomplishes anything, I hope it opens up new theoretical space for videogame forms to be appreciated in all their heterogeneity, pigeon-holed no longer into narrow definitions of "game" and equally narrow dreams of the possibilities of tomorrow's technology.

More can always be done, and this exploration opens various potential avenues for future research. Both online and local-multiplayer videogames provide crucial opportunities to challenge and further complicate my observations, not by negating the primary player-and-videogame assemblage identified in this book but by asking what happens in the assemblage of multiple player-and-videogame assemblages? Similarly, the rising trend of spectated videogame play through Let's Play videos and livestreaming provides exciting challenges for a phenomenology of videogame experience when many people experience videogames primarily as viewed rather than played media.

What is perhaps most lacking in my study is a more materialist concern for the videogames "themselves" in relation to the player—the technological, economic, political, social, and cultural affordances and constraints that underlie the player's engagements. It is one thing to understand how a certain combination of animation and music is perceived by players, but another to understand why they were combined in such a way in the first place. Greig de Peuter and Nick Dyer-Witheford's book *Games of Empire* (2009) is the exemplar of such an approach, but more recent inquiries from a speculative realism perspective hold much promise, such as James Ash's book *The Interface Envelope* (2015) and Benjamin Abraham's (2015, 2016) nascent research on videogames and climate change. Stephanie Boluk and Patrick LeMieux's (2017) *Metagaming*, meanwhile, provides an extensive critical account of the broader culture that the player-and-videogame explored here resides in and emerges from. I do not believe leaving these trajectories unexplored here to be a flaw in the phenomenology of videogame experience I have forwarded but rather as an opening to other avenues down which a grounded, material, and embodied approach to videogames as part of the media ecology can be expanded and built on to ensure the intricate web of player-and-videogame is never considered too neat, unified, generalized, or sealed.

Through looking at images on screens, listening to sounds through speakers, and moving fingers and limbs across and against tactile input devices, videogame play augments embodied perception in such a way that the player can perceive a tangible sense of presence across words and across bodies. The player does not simply step into a new body, nor do they simply step into a new world. Instead, videogames are peered into, poked around. Videogame play is a partial becoming. It is *a play of bodies* that alters, distributes, enhances, restricts, and skews embodied perception to partially and imperfectly embody other presences and contexts. To perceive through a videogame is to incorporate it into a distributed, immanent, and partial lived experience; to experience videogame play is to take on an imperfect and unstable cyborgian embodiment of flesh, hardware, and audiovisuals across worlds and bodies. Before and as the foundation for any conscious engagement with a videogame as text is a bodily engagement with the videogame as experienced form. The creative works that belong to the videogame corpus possess an *embodied textuality* that produces meaning across their experiential and textual qualities as spliced and irreducible. What a videogame is about is inseparable from what that videogame feels like to play. To play a videogame is to play across worlds and to play with bodies.

Notes

Introduction

1. See Jill Walker (2001) for a discussion of the use of second-person address and identification in videogame vernaculars.

2. It is worth noting that it is not only videogames that suffer from an ontological conflation of videogames and nondigital games. The contemporary study of non-digital games also suffers when the discipline of "game studies" is dominated by theorists working exclusively in the realm of videogames. For examples of signifi-cant scholarly work on nondigital games in the nascent field of "analogue game studies," see the scholarly journals *Analog Game Studies*, *Game & Puzzle Design*, and *Board Game Studies* as well as the research on eurogames by Stewart Woods (2012). As part of my effort not to conflate videogames and analogue games, in this book I have committed to the one-word spelling *videogame* (as opposed to *video game*), which sees videogames as a hybrid of audiovisuality and game aspects, and I have worked to avoid using the term *game* as a shorthand for *videogame* wherever reading clarity allows.

Chapter 1

1. "Manifesto for Cyborgs" was first published in *Socialist Review* in 1985, but throughout this book I reference Haraway's revised essay, "A Cyborg Manifesto" (1991b), collected in her book *Simians, Cyborgs, and Women* (1991c).

2. Such dualisms echo the liberal humanist separation of Man (Culture) from World (Nature) that Bruno Latour critiques in *We Have Never Been Modern* (1991) as the "purification" practices of modern thought that create "two entirely distinct onto-logical zones: that of human beings on the one hand; that of nonhumans on the other" (10–11). See Giddings 2007 for a Latourian approach to the player-and-video-game assemblage.

3. There are significant echoes here of Latour's work on "actor-networks" (1991, 1992, 2005), which calls for all objects in the world to be understood as possessing an agency distinct from conscious intentionality in the way they mediate the existence of other objects. His work on "quasi-objects" shows that every object or subject is in fact an object-subject hybrid in its mediating of other object-subjects.

4. Although it should be noted that more recent scholarship has produced nuanced understandings of the experience of immersion (see, e.g., Calleja 2011; Cairns, Cox, and Nordin 2014) by distancing conceptualizations of immersion away from a discrete presence in a virtual world, it remains significant for my project to interrogate earlier but nonetheless persistent understandings of videogames as desirably immersive in order to account for the full embodied experience of engaging with a videogame across worlds.

5. See Ndalianis 2004, Golding 2014, Jayemanne 2017, and Nicoll 2017b for significant transhistorical accounts that situate the visual strategies of the videogame form within a broader art history discourse.

6. There is a clear parallel here with the visual strategies of theater, where the wall that would exist between the audience and an interior setting depicted on the stage is omitted so that the dramatic action can be viewed. See Brenda Laurel's foundational work *Computers as Theaters* ([1991] 2014) for a more extensive consideration of the relationship between videogames and theater.

7. Other developers have also discussed how videogames come to feel particular ways. See Jan Willem Nijman's (2013) discussion of "screenshake" (discussed in chapter 4) and Kyle Gabler and his colleagues' (2005) discussion of "juice," which is in turned furthered by both Jesper Juul's discussion of "juiciness" (2010, 45; see chapter 2) and Lisa Brown's (2016) discussion of the nuances of juice (see chapter 4).

8. David Kanaga's observations on the phenomenological similarities between engaging with music and engaging with videogames is explored in chapter 4 as part of a broader conversation on audiovisuality.

Chapter 2

1. In this chapter, I use the term *mobile videogames* to refer to videogames played on mobile phones. I consider it different from the term *portable videogames*, which refers to those videogames created for dedicated portable gaming devices, such as the Nintendo 3DS or the PlayStation Vita. For an exploration of both the differences and similarities between mobile and portable videogames, see McCrea 2011.

2. Although Apple's iPhone remains connected to the concept of the smartphone, just as Microsoft is connected to the concept of the personal computer, in recent years many more people use smartphones that run Google's less-regulated Android operating system. Most of what is said about iPhones in this chapter is also applica-

ble to smartphones produced by other corporations and running different operating systems, but here my focus is solely on the iPhone to avoid unnecessary generalizations across similar (but in no way identical) mobile platforms.

3. At the time of writing, virtual-reality headsets are once again in vogue with the recent release of Rift from Oculus VR, Vive from HTC, and PlayStation VR from Sony. Although these new technologies certainly offer more convincing virtual-reality experiences than their forebears of the 1990s, echoes remain of the same technofetishist rhetoric that marks the virtual world as something we will "one day" be able to just step into. The potential (though in no way assured) future success of virtual-reality technology does not negate the observations made in this section. Rather, it exemplifies the desire to experience the virtual *as* perceptually tangible through strategically suppressing attention away from the physical and embodied framing of videogame play on which the virtual depends.

4. See Dale Leorke's dissertation "Location-Based Gaming and the Politics of Play in the City" (2015) for an extensive history of both location-based and augmented-reality games as well as for a critique of the surrounding literature.

5. The observer factor is complicated by larger-screen devices, such as Apple's iPad, for which various videogames have been created that allow multiple players to engage on a single screen, such as *Fingle* (Game Oven 2011), *Toca Tea Party* (Toca Boca 2011), and *Glitch Tank* (Brough 2012).

6. Although there is much enthusiasm around the seemingly naturalness of mimetic interfaces, it is important to emphasize that neither mimetic nor traditional interfaces are inherently "better," but simply that mimetic interfaces afford videogames that are more immediately accessible for those players who have not committed the time needed to learn—to incorporate—more complex input devices (Juul 2010, 119). This tension between accessibility and competency is discussed further in the next chapter.

7. Such committed modes of engaging with *Angry Birds* are also exemplified by the proliferation of both written and video player guides providing detailed instructions on how to receive a three-star rating. See, for example, the walkthroughs available on the fan sites Angry Birds Wiki (http://angrybirds.wikia.com/wiki/Angry_Birds _Wiki:Level_Walkthroughs) and Angry Birds Nest (http://www.angrybirdsnest.com/ category/walkthroughs/angry-birds/).

8. Significantly, from an economic perspective, increasing each game's difficulty has also allowed Rovio to better implement "in-app purchases," offering frustrated players the opportunity to spend actual money to get out of a tight situation.

9. *Ziggurat* also has an option to change the control input to "slingshot mode," allowing the player to imitate *Angry Birds*.

Chapter 3

1. Videogame vernaculars are complicated by trademarked brand names and a diversity of vocabularies, so in general I use the term *gamepad* to refer to the broad category of videogame input devices that consist of a range of buttons and triggers on a padlike device held in the hands as opposed to the tabletop devices such as the keyboard or the joystick. Nintendo has more recently used the name "GamePad" to refer explicitly to the input device for its WiiU console, which incorporates a large touchscreen with traditional gamepad design, but the word *gamepad* remains used in common parlance to refer to this general family of input devices. Gamepads are also commonly referred to by the more general term *controller*, which I have decided is too broad a term for this chapter's analysis because many input devices can be considered controllers but not gamepads, such as dance-mat controllers. Likewise, the term *input device* is rarely used in common videogame vernaculars, but no other term encompasses both those devices created exclusively for video-game play and those that videogames adapted to, such as the keyboard, mouse, and touchscreen.

2. Many scholars and designers are beginning to critique the "systems of control" that dominant controller design perpetuates, as controllers are thought of solely as devices of *input* rather than pleasurable, tactile engagements in their own right. See Sicart 2017 for an overview of this discussion.

3. As with the term *gamepad* itself, there is no consensus in popular vernacular around videogames as to what to call each of these components of the gamepad, and various corporations have chosen to use different, trademarked names, which speaks to just how intricately commodified embodied literacies are. Here I have chosen the terms *action buttons* (sometimes also known as *face buttons*), *triggers*, and *thumbsticks* (also known as *analog sticks*) because they are commonly used, but I do not wish to imply that these components must be known by these names. I am more interested in the function of each of these input modes than in what they are called.

4. See Golding 2014 for a more thorough discussion of the synthesis of vision and movement in first-person videogames. See Black 2017 for a detailed description of the different haptic relationships among player, viewpoint, and character in both first- and third-person videogames.

5. Interestingly, more than a decade before vibration became standard in gamepad games, Sudnow hints at its potential contribution as he complains about the lack of "heft" in the *Breakout* paddle: "my hand goes through its movements without any sense of an impact on things" (1983, 206).

Chapter 4

1. This is not to say that one cannot play a videogame with the sound turned down. Indeed, as discussed in chapter 2, many players of mobile videogames play either with the sound turned off or while listening to their own music. Many hearing-impaired people, too, play a wide range of videogames. You *can* remove the audio of a videogame, just as you can mute a film. The point, rather, is that the audiovisual presentation—or lack thereof—is fundamental to how the videogame phenomenon is perceived.

2. In a more recent talk, designer Lisa Brown (2016) discusses the "nuance of juice." Brown constructively moves past the prescriptive and quantitative approaches of the designers who focus primarily on adding *more* juice or game feel to focus instead on *how* a particular videogame should feel for its player.

3. Kanaga uses a range of grammatical stylings in his train-of-thought essays, including inconsistent use of capitalization, ellipses, and italics. Where I quote his work, I have reproduced these marks in full. All emphases are Kanaga's own unless otherwise stated.

4. Such a shared ontology of course only makes sense in languages, such as English, in which the verb *play* is the same for both music and games.

5. Larissa Hjorth and Ingrid Richardson similarly use the musical notion of "ambience" as one that "discloses a game's texture, affect and the embodied modality of the player" (2015, 106).

6. For instance, the abrupt and silent appearance and disappearance of "Sony Computer Entertainment Europe presents" and "Naughty Dog presents" at the beginning of *The Last of Us* (Naughty Dog 2013) serve to communicate a certain restrained tone that permeates the whole videogame. Indeed, in this chapter's primary focus on music and noise, it is just as important to consider the meaningful use of silence in moments of videogame play.

Chapter 5

1. I have written extensively elsewhere on *Final Fantasy VII* and memory (Keogh 2014).

2. See Donovan 2010 and Nicoll 2017a for detailed accounts of this transitional history.

3. Although I say the player is "immortal" in the play circuit to suggest that the virtual events that regularly slaughter the character are of no harm to the persisting player, the player remains anchored in the corporeal fragilities of their own body. A sobering example of this anchoring is the various highly publicized reports of

players dying from exhaustion or malnutrition after playing videogames for a prolonged period of time (see Apperley 2010, 43; Parkin 2015).

4. See Carter, Gibbs, and Wadley 2013 for a thorough analysis of death in *DayZ*.

5. Although *Minecraft* was ostensibly released in 2011, it has been publicly available since 2009, with regular updates adding new features to the unfinished videogame. The Toward Dawn project thus took place in an ever-changing game.

Chapter 6

1. For Kathy Kleiman's ENIAC Programmers Project, see http://eniacprogrammers .org/eniac-programmers-project/. See also Janet Abbate's book *Recoding Gender: Women's Changing Participation in Computing* (2012) for a more detailed history of women's role in the ENIAC and Colossus computers and for a more extensive tracing of the history of how computing work shifted from feminized labor to masculinized labor.

2. It is important to stress that such videogame creators cannot simply be characterized as "indie." They commonly exist outside of both blockbuster and indie videogame discourses and more commonly rally under banners such as "zinester games" (following Anthropy 2012); "art games" (Parker 2013); "do-it-yourself games"; and, most recently, "altgames" (Kareem 2015; Quinn 2015). I explore elsewhere (Keogh 2015) the tensions between blockbuster, indie, casual, and do-it-yourself videogame design cultures.

3. Compellingly, many Twine works deal explicitly with corporeality and viscera and cyborgism. Eva Problems's *SABBAT* (2013) has the player perform rituals with animal viscera to morph their body into a powerful demon; Tom McHenry's *Horse Master* (2013) has the player take care of both a monstrous creature and a drug addiction; and Porpentine's *CYBERQUEEN* (2012) has the player meticulously tortured and dissected in gruesome detail by a sentient computer system. A history exists here, too, in Shelley Jackson's literary hypertext *Patchwork Girl* (1995), which explores the distributed and monstrous subjectivities of both corporeal beings and digital texts (see Hayles 2005).

References

Aarseth, Espen. 1997. *Cybertext: Perspectives on Ergodic Literature*. Baltimore: John Hopkins University Press.

Aarseth, Espen. 2004. Genre Trouble: Narrativism and the Art of Simulation. In *First Person: New Media as Story, Performance, and Game*, ed. Noah Wardrip-Fruin and Pat Harrigan, 45–55. Cambridge, MA: MIT Press.

Abbate, Janet. 2012. *Recoding Gender: Women's Changing Participation in Computing*. Cambridge, MA: MIT Press.

Account33. 2013. *Gone Home* User Review. *Metacritic*, August 19. http://www .metacritic.com/game/pc/gone-home/user-reviews?dist=negative.

Abraham, Benjamin. 2009. Permanent Death—the Complete Saga. *Subterranean Loner Rendered Comatose*, December 4. http://drgamelove.blogspot.com.au/2009/12/ permanent-death-complete-saga.html.

Abraham, Benjamin. 2013. Imposed Rules and "Expansive Gameplay": A Close Reading of the *Far Cry 2* Permadeath Experiment. In *Digra '13: Proceedings of the 2013 DiGRA International Conference: DeFragging Game Studies*. Atlanta: Georgia University of Technology.

Abraham, Benjamin. 2015. *Video Game Visions of Climate Futures: ARMA3 and Implications for Games and Persuasion. Games and Culture*. OnlineFirst. http://journals.sagepub .com/doi/abs/10.1177/1555412015603844#articleCitationDownloadContainer

Abraham, Benjamin. 2016. Digital Gaming in a Time of Climate Change. Paper presented at the Digital Games Research Association Australia National Conference, Melbourne, November 18.

Ahmed, Sara. 2006. *Queer Phenomenology: Orientations, Objects, Others*. Durham, NC: Duke University Press.

Allen, Samantha. 2013. TransMovement: Freedom and Constraint in Queer and Open World Games. *The Border House*, February. https://web.archive.org/web/ 20150421090035/http://borderhouseblog.com/?p=10113.

Anthropy, Anna. 2012. *Rise of the Videogame Zinesters: How Freaks, Normals, Amateurs, Artists, Dreamers, Dropouts, Queers, Housewives, and People Like You Are Taking Back an Art Form.* New York: Seven Stories Press.

Apperley, Thomas H. 2010. *Gaming Rhythms: Play and Counterplay from the Situated to the Global.* Amsterdam: Institute of Network Cultures.

Apperley, Thomas H., and Darshana Jayemanne. 2012. Game Studies' Material Turn. *Westminister Papers in Communication and Culture* 9 (1): 5–26.

Arnold, Michael. 2003. On the Phenomenology of Technology: The "Janus-Faces" of Mobile Phones. *Information and Organization* 13:231–256.

Ash, James. 2013. Technologies of Captivation: Videogames and the Attunement of Affect. *Body & Society* 19 (1): 27–51.

Ash, James. 2015. *The Interface Envelope: Gaming, Technology, Power.* London: Bloomsbury.

Atkins, Barry. 2006. What Are We Really Looking At? The Future-Orientation of Video Game Play. *Games and Culture* 1 (2): 127–140.

Atkins, Barry. 2007. Killing Time: Time Past, Time Present, and Time Future in *Prince of Persia: The Sands of Time.* In *Videogame, Player, Text*, ed. Barry Atkins and Tanya Krzywinska, 237–253. Manchester, UK: Manchester University Press.

Bardini, Thierry. 2000. *Bootstrapping: Douglas Engelbart, Coevolution, and the Origins of Personal Computing.* Stanford: Stanford University Press.

Barthes, Roland. 1977. *Image, Music, Text.* London: Fontana Press.

Bateson, Gregory. 1972. *Steps to an Ecology of Mind: Collected Essays in Anthropology, Psychiatry, Evolution, and Epistemology.* San Francisco: Chandler.

Bennett, Jane. 2009. *Vibrant Matter: A Political Ecology of Things.* Chapel Hill, NC: Duke University Press.

Black, Daniel. 2017. Why Can I See My Avatar? Embodied Visual Engagement in the Third-Person Video Game. *Games and Culture* 12 (2): 179–199.

Bogost, Ian. 2006. *Unit Operations: An Approach to Videogame Criticism.* Cambridge, MA: MIT Press.

Bogost, Ian. 2008. The Phenomenology of Videogames. In *Conference Proceedings of the Philosophy of Computer Games 2008*, ed. Stephan Günzel, Michael Liebe, and Dieter Mersch, 22–43. Potsdam: Potsdam University Press.

Bogost, Ian. 2012. *Alien Phenomenology, or What It's Like to Be a Thing.* Minneapolis: University of Minnesota Press.

Boluk, Stephanie, and Patrick LeMieux. 2017. *Metagaming: Playing, Competing, Spectating, Cheating, Trading, Making, and Breaking Videogames*. Minneapolis: University of Minnesota Press.

Bourdieu, Pierre. 1984. *Distinction: A Social Critique of the Judgement of Taste*. Cambridge, MA: Harvard University Press.

Brice, Mattie. 2014. Queer as in Fuck Me—a Design Manifesto. *Alternate Ending*, November 18. http://www.mattiebrice.com/queer-as-in-fuck-me-a-design-manifesto/.

Brown, Lisa. 2016. Vector 2016—the Nuance of Juice Talk. YouTube, September 9. https://www.youtube.com/watch?v=qtgWBUIOjK4.

Burgess, Jean. 2012. The iPhone Moment, the Apple Brand, and the Creative Consumer: From Hackability and Usability to Cultural Generativity. In *Studying Mobile Media: Cultural Technologies, Mobile Communication, and the iPhone*, ed. Larissa Hjorth, Jean Burgess, and Ingrid Richardson, 28–42. New York: Routledge.

Butler, Judith. 1988. Performative Acts and Gender Constitution: An Essay in Phenomenology and Feminist Theory. *Theatre Journal* 40 (4): 519–531.

Cairns, Paul, Anna Cox, and A. Imran Nordin. 2014. Immersion in Digital Games: Review of Gaming Experience Research. In *Handbook of Digital Games*, ed. Marios C. Angelides and Harry Agius, 339–361. Piscataway, NJ: IEEE Press.

Calleja, Gordon. 2011. *In-Game: From Immersion to Incorporation*. Cambridge, MA: MIT Press.

Carter, Marcus, and Staffan Björk. 2015. Cheating at *Candy Crush Saga*. In *Social, Casual, and Mobile: Changing Games*, ed. Tama Leaver and Michele Wilson, 261–274. London: Bloomsbury.

Carter, Marcus, Martin Gibbs, and Greg Wadley. 2013. Death and Dying in *DayZ*. In *Proceedings of the 9th Australasian Conference on Interactive Entertainment: Matters of Life and Death*. New York: ACM Digital Library. DOI:10.1145/2513002.2513013.

Chan, Dean. 2008. Convergence, Connectivity, and the Case of Japanese Mobile Gaming. *Games and Culture* 3 (1): 13–25.

Chesher, Chris. 2004. Neither Gaze nor Glance, but Glaze: Relating to Console Game Screens. *Scan: Journal of Media, Arts, Culture* 1 (1).

Chion, Michel. 1994. *Audio-Vision: Sound on Screen*. New York: Columbia University Press.

Chun, Wendy Hui Kyong. 2011. *Programmed Visions: Software and Memory*. Cambridge, MA: MIT Press.

Consalvo, Mia. 2012. Slingshot to Victory: Games, Play, and the iPhone. In *Moving Data: The iPhone and the Future of Media*, ed. Pelle Snickars and Patrick Vonderau, 184–194. New York: Columbia University Press.

Cote, Amanda C. 2015. *Writing "Games": The Gendered Construction of Gamer Identity in Nintendo Power (1994–1999)*. Games and Culture. N.p.: OnlineFirst.

Crick, Timothy. 2011. The Game Body: Toward a Phenomenology of Contemporary Video Gaming. *Games and Culture* 6 (3): 259–269.

Crogan, Patrick. 2011. *Gameplay Mode: War, Simulation, and Technoculture*. Minnesota: University of Minnesota Press.

Csikszentmihalyi, Mihaly. 1990. *Flow: The Psychology of Optimal Experience*. New York: Harper and Row.

De Peuter, Greig, and Nick Dyer-Witheford. 2005. A Playful Multitude? Mobilising and Counter-mobilising Immaterial Game Labour. *Fibreculture* 5.

De Souza e Silva, Adriana. 2006. From Cyber to Hybrid: Mobile Technologies as Interfaces of Hybrid Spaces. *Space and Culture* 9:261–278.

Donovan, Tristan. 2010. *Replay: The History of Video Games*. East Sussex, UK: Yellow Ant.

Dovey, Jon, and Helen Kennedy. 2006. *Game Cultures: Computer Games as New Media*. Berkshire, UK: Open University Press.

Du Gay, Paul, Stuart Hall, Linda Janes, Hugh Mackay, and Keith Negus. 1997. *Doing Cultural Studies: The Story of the Sony Walkman*. London: Sage.

Dyer-Witheford, Nick, and Greig de Peuter. 2009. *Games of Empire: Global Capitalism and Video Games*. Minneapolis: University of Minnesota Press.

Edge. 2012. An Accidental Empire: How Apple Became the Hottest Property in Portable Videogaming. 236 (January): 76–84.

Ellison, Cara. 2013. Wot I Think: *Slave of God. Rock Paper Shotgun*, January 4. http://www.rockpapershotgun.com/2013/01/04/slave-of-god-review/.

Farman, Jason. 2009. Locative Life: Geocaching, Mobile Gaming, and Embodiment. In *Proceedings of the Digital Arts and Culture Conference*. Irvine: University of California.

Gabler, Kyle, Kyle Gray, Shalin Shodan, and Matt Kucic. 2005. How to Prototype a Game in under 7 Days. *Gamasutra*, October 26. http://www.gamasutra.com/view/feature/130848/how_to_prototype_a_game_in_under_7_.php.

Galloway, Alexander R. 2006. *Gaming: Essays on Algorithmic Culture*. Minneapolis: University of Minnesota Press.

Giddings, Seth. 2007. Playing with Nonhumans: Digital Games as Technocultural Form. In *Worlds in Play: International Perspectives on Digital Games Research*, ed. Suzanne De Castell and Jennifer Jenson, 115–128. New York: Peter Lang.

Giddings, Seth. 2009. Events and Collusions: A Glossary for the Microethnography of Video Game Play. *Games and Culture* 4 (2): 144–157.

Giddings, Seth, and Helen Kennedy. 2008. Little Jesuses and Fuck-off Robots: On Aesthetics, Cybernetics, and Not Being Very Good at *Lego Star Wars*. In *The Pleasures of Computer Gaming: Essays on Cultural History, Theory, and Aesthetics*, ed. Melanie Swalwell and Jason Wilson, 13–32. Jefferson, NC: McFarland.

Gifford, Kevin. 2010. All about the PlayStation 1's Design. *1UP*, August 25. https://web.archive.org/web/20110705174449/http://www.1up.com/news/playstation-1-design.

Gillen, Kieron. 2009. The Sunday Papers. *Rock Paper Shotgun*, July 5. http://www.rockpapershotgun.com/2009/07/05/the-sunday-papers-75/.

Golding, Daniel. 2013a. Listening to *Proteus*. *Meanjin* 72 (2): 108–115.

Golding, Daniel. 2013b. *Thirty Flights of Loving* and the Invention of Videogame Space. *Crickey*, September 4. http://blogs.crikey.com.au/game-on/2012/09/04/thirty-flights-of-loving-and-the-invention-of-videogame-space/.

Golding, Daniel. 2013c. To Configure or to Navigate? On Textual Frames. In *Terms of Play: Essays on Words That Matter in Videogame Theory*, ed. Zach Waggoner, 28–46. Jefferson, NC: McFarland.

Golding, Daniel. 2014. Moving through Space and Time: A Genealogy of Videogame Space. PhD diss., University of Melbourne.

Edge. 2008. *Grand Theft Auto 4*. 189 (June): 82–85.

Greenland, Colin. 1986. A Nod to the Apocalypse: An Interview with William Gibson. *Foundation* 36 (Summer): 5–9.

Grodal, Torben. 2003. Stories for Eye, Ear, and Muscles: Video Games, Media, and Embodied Experiences. In *The Video Game Theory Reader*, ed. Mark J. P. Wolf and Bernard Perron, 129–155. New York: Routledge.

Grosz, Elizabeth. 1994. *Volatile Bodies: Toward a Corporeal Feminism*. Bloomington: Indiana University Press.

Haraway, Donna. 1985. Manifesto for Cyborgs: Science, Technology, and Socialist Feminism in the 1980s. *Socialist Review* 80:65–108.

Haraway, Donna. 1988. Situated Knowledges: The Science Question in Feminism and the Privilege of Partial Perspective. *Feminist Studies* 14 (3): 575–599.

Haraway, Donna. 1991a. The Biological Enterprise: Sex, Mind, and Profit from Human Engineering to Sociobiology. In *Simians, Cyborgs, and Women: The Reinvention of Nature*, 43–68. New York: Routledge.

Haraway, Donna. 1991b. A Cyborg Manifesto: Science, Technology, and Socialist Feminism in the 1980s. In *Simians, Cyborgs, and Women: The Reinvention of Nature*, 149–182. New York: Routledge.

Haraway, Donna. 1991c. *Simians, Cyborgs, and Women: The Reinvention of Nature*. New York: Routledge.

Harper, Todd. 2013. *The Culture of Digital Fighting Games: Performance and Practice*. New York: Routledge.

Hayles, N. Katherine. 1999. *How We Became Posthuman: Virtual Bodies in Cybernetics, Literature, and Informatics*. Chicago: University of Chicago Press.

Hayles, N. Katherine. 2004. Print Is Flat, Code Is Deep: The Importance of Media-Specific Analysis. *Poetics Today* 25 (1): 67–90.

Hayles, N. Katherine. 2005. *My Mother Was a Computer: Digital Subjects and Literary Texts*. Chicago: University of Chicago Press.

Heck, Ben. 2006. Single-Handed Wireless Xbox 360 Controller. Ben Heck.com. http://benheck.com/Games/Xbox360/controls/1hand/singlehandcontroller.htm.

Hindes, Daniel. 2012. *Dear Esther*. PC Powerplay 201 (March): 48–49.

Hjorth, Larissa. 2003. Kawaii@keitai. In *Japanese Cybercultures*, ed. Nanette Gottlieb and Mark McLelland, 50–59. New York: Routledge.

Hjorth, Larissa. 2007. The Game of Being Mobile: One Media History of Gaming and Mobile Technologies in Asia-Pacific. *Convergence* 13:369–381.

Hjorth, Larissa, Jean Burgess, and Ingrid Richardson. 2012. Studying the Mobile: Locating the Field. In *Studying Mobile Media: Cultural Technologies, Mobile Communication, and the iPhone*, ed. Larissa Hjorth, Jean Burgess, and Ingrid Richardson, 1–10. New York: Routledge.

Hjorth, Larissa, and David Chan, eds. 2009. *Gaming Cultures and Place in the Asia-Pacific Region*. London: Routledge.

Hjorth, Larissa, and Ingrid Richardson. 2009. The Waiting Game: Complicating Notions of (Tele)presence and Gendered Distraction in Casual Mobile Gaming. *Australian Journal of Communication* 36 (1): 23–35.

Hjorth, Larissa, and Ingrid Richardson. 2015. Mobile Videogames and Ambient Play. In *Social, Casual, and Mobile: Changing Games*, ed. Tama Leaver and Michele Wilson, 105–116. London: Bloomsbury.

Hocking, Clint. 2009. Foreword to Benjamin Abraham, *Permanent Death—the Complete Saga*. Subterranean Loner Rendered Comatose, December 4. http://drgamelove .blogspot.com.au/2009/12/permanent-death-complete-saga.html.

Hudson, Laura. 2015. Twine, the Video-Game Technology for All. *New York Times Magazine*, November 19. http://www.nytimes.com/2014/11/23/magazine/twine-the -video-game-technology-for-all.html.

Huhtamo, Erkki. 2005. Slots of Fun, Slots of Trouble: An Archeology of Arcade Gaming. In *Handbook of Computer Game Studies*, ed. Joost Raessens and Jeffrey Goldstein, 3–22. Cambridge, MA: MIT Press.

Ihde, Don. 1993. *Postphenomenology: Essays in the Postmodern Context*. Evanston, IL: Northwestern University Press.

Ihde, Don. 2009. *Postphenomenology and Technoscience*. New York: State University of New York Press.

Ito, Mizuko, Daisuke Okabe, and Misa Matsuda. 2005. *Personal, Portable, Pedestrian: Mobile Phones in Japanese Life*. Cambridge, MA: MIT Press.

Jackson, Shelley. 1998. Stitch Bitch: The Patchwork Girl. *Paradoxa* 4:526–538.

Jayemanne, Darshana. 2005. The Nip and the Bite. In *Proceedings of the DiGRA 2005 International Conference: Changing Views: Worlds in Play*. Vancouver, Canada.

Jayemanne, Darshana. 2017. *Performativity in Art, Literature, and Videogames*. London: Palgrave Macmillan.

Juul, Jesper. 2005. *Half-Real: Video Games between Real Rules and Fictional Worlds*. Cambridge, MA: MIT Press.

Juul, Jesper. 2010. *A Casual Revolution: Reinventing Video Games and Their Players*. Cambridge, MA: MIT Press.

Juul, Jesper. 2013. *The Art of Failure: An Essay on the Pain of Playing Video Games*. Cambridge, MA: MIT Press.

k, merritt. 2014. Interrupting Play: Queer Games & Futurity. NYU Game Center, February. http://mkopas.net/files/talks/InterruptingPlayQueerGamesFuturity.pdf.

k, merritt. 2015. *Dreaming Digital Play*. Accessed November 26, 2016. http:// dreamingdigitalplay.tumblr.com/.

Kanaga, David. 2011. Elements of Music as Elements of Games. *Wombflash Forest*, June 13. http://wombflashforest.blogspot.com.au/2011/06/elements-of-music -as-elements-of-games.html.

Kanaga, David. 2012. Played Meaning (Concerning the Spiritual in Games). *Wombflash Forest*, June 16. http://wombflashforest.blogspot.com.au/2012/06/played -meaning-concerning-spiritual-in.html.

Kanaga, David. 2013. Music & Games as Shifting Possibility Spaces. *Wombflash Forest*, November 19. http://wombflashforest.blogspot.com.au/2013/11/music-games-as -shifting-possibility.html.

Kanaga, David. 2014. Music Object, Substance, Organism. *Vimeo*, n.d. https:// vimeo.com/90271157.

Kareem, Soha. 2015. The Games That Are Too Underground to Be Indie. *Vice*, April 23. http://motherboard.vice.com/read/the-games-that-are-too-underground-to-be -indie.

Kennedy, Helen. 2007. Female *Quake* Players and the Politics of Identity. In *Videogame, Player, Text*, ed. Barry Atkins and Tanya Krzywinska, 120–138. Manchester, UK: Manchester United Press.

Keogh, Brendan. 2010–2012. *Towards Dawn: Leaving The Miner's Life Behind*. http:// towardsdawns.blogspot.com.au/.

Keogh, Brendan. 2014. Cybernetic Memory and the Construction of the Posthuman Self in Videogame Play. In *Design, Mediation, and the Posthuman*, ed. Dennis M. Weiss, Amy D. Propen, and Colbey Emmerson Reid, 233–248. London: Lexington Books.

Keogh, Brendan. 2015. Between Triple-A, Indie, Casual, and DIY: Sites of Tension in the Videogames Cultural Industries. In *The Routledge Companion to the Cultural Industries*, ed. Kate Oakley and Justin O'Connor, 152–162. New York: Routledge.

Kirkpatrick, Graeme. 2009. Controller, Hand, Screen: Aesthetic Form in the Computer Game. *Games and Culture* 4 (2): 127–143.

Kirkpatrick, Graeme. 2011. *Aesthetic Theory and the Video Game*. Manchester, UK: Manchester University Press.

Kirkpatrick, Graeme. 2012. Constitutive Tensions of Gaming's Field: UK Gaming Magazines and the Formation of Gaming Culture 1981–1995. *Game Studies* 12 (1).

Kirkpatrick, Graeme. 2013. *Computer Games and the Social Imaginary*. Cambridge: Polity Press.

Klevjer, Rune. 2002. In Defense of Cutscenes. In *Computer Game and Digital Cultures Conference Proceedings*, ed. Frans Mayra, 191–202. Tampere, Finland: Tampere University Press.

Klevjer, Rune. 2012. Enter the Avatar: The Phenomenology of Prosthetic Telepresence in Computer Games. In *The Philosophy of Computer Games*, ed. John Richard Sageng, Hallvard Fossheim, and Tarjei Mandt Larsen, 17–38. New York: Springer.

Kocurek, Carly A. 2015. *Coin-Operated Americans: Rebooting Boyhood at the Video Game Arcade*. Minneapolis: University of Minnesota Press.

kopas, merritt. 2015. *Videogames for Humans: Twine Authors in Conversation.* New York: Instar Books.

Kushner, David. 2003. *Masters of Doom.* New York: Random House.

Latour, Bruno. 1991. *We Have Never Been Modern.* Cambridge, MA: Harvard University Press.

Latour, Bruno. 1992. Where Are the Missing Masses? The Sociology of a Few Mundane Objects. In *Shaping Technology/Building Societies: Studies in Sociotechnical Change,* ed. Wiebe E. Bijker and John Law, 225–258. Cambridge, MA: MIT Press.

Latour, Bruno. 2005. *Reassembling the Social: An Introduction to Actor–Network Theory.* New York: Oxford University Press.

Laurel, Brenda. [1991] 2014. *Computers as Theatre.* 2nd ed. New York: Addison-Wesley.

Lefebvre, Henri. 2004. *Rhythmanalysis: Space, Time, and Everyday Life.* Translated by Stewart Elden and Gerald Moore. London: Continuum.

Leorke, Dale. 2015. Location-Based Gaming and the Politics of Play in the City. PhD diss., University of Melbourne.

Lister, Martin, Jon Dovey, Seth Giddings, Iain Grant, and Kieran Kelly. [2003] 2009. *New Media: A Critical Introduction.* 2nd ed. New York: Routledge.

Lucas, Kenneth J. 2013. The Musical Art of UN EP. *Unwinnable,* October 8. http://www.unwinnable.com/2013/10/08/the-musical-art-of-un-ep/#.VEbb-IuUfKg.

MacCallum-Stewart, Esther. 2014. "Take That, Bitches!" Refiguring Lara Croft in Feminist Game Narratives. *Game Studies* 14(2).

Marks, Laura U. 2002. *Touch: Sensuous Theory and Multisensory Media.* Minneapolis: University of Minnesota Press.

Mauss, Marcel. 1973. Techniques of the Body. *Economy and Society* 2 (1): 70–88.

McCrea, Christian. 2009. Watching *Starcraft*: Strategy and South Korea. In *Gaming Cultures and Place in Asia-Pacific,* ed. Larissa Hjorth and Dean Chan, 179–193. New York: Routledge.

McCrea, Christian. 2011. We Play in Public: The Nature and Context of Portable Gaming Systems. *Convergence* 17 (4): 389–403.

Merleau-Ponty, Maurice. 1964. *Sense and Non-sense.* Evanston, IL: Northwestern University Press.

Merleau-Ponty, Maurice. 2012. *Phenomenology of Perception.* Translated by Donald A. Landes. New York: Routledge.

Montfort, Nick, and Ian Bogost. 2009. *Racing the Beam: The Atari Video Computer System*. Cambridge, MA: MIT Press.

Murray, Janet H. 1997. *Hamlet on the Holodeck: The Future of Narrative in Cyberspace*. Cambridge, MA: MIT Press.

Ndalianis, Angela. 2004. *Neo-baroque Aesthetics and Contemporary Entertainment*. Cambridge, MA: MIT Press.

Newman, James. 2002. The Myth of the Ergodic Videogame: Some Thoughts on Player–Character Relationships in Videogames. *Game Studies* 2 (1).

Nicoll, Benjamin. 2017a. Bridging the Gap: The Neo Geo, the Media Imaginary, and the Domestication of Arcade Games. *Games and Culture* 12 (2): 200–221.

Nicoll, Benjamin. 2017b. Videogame Anarcheology: A Cultural Study of Minor Game Systems. PhD diss., University of Melbourne.

Nijman, Jan Willem. 2013. The Art of Screenshake. YouTube, December 16. https://www.youtube.com/watch?v=AJdEqssNZ-U.

Parisi, David. 2015. A Counterrevolution in the Hands: The Console Controller as an Ergonomic Branding Mechanism. *Journal of Games Criticism* 2 (1): 1–23.

Parker, Felan. 2013. An Art World for Artgames. *Loading* 7 (11): 41–60.

Parkin, Simon. *Death by Video Game*. London: Serpents Tail.

Pias, Claus. 2011. The Game Player's Duty: The User as Gestalt of the Ports. In *Media Archeology: Approaches, Applications, and Implications*, ed. Erkki Huhtamo and Jussi Parikka, 164–183. Berkeley: University of California Press.

Polansky, Lana. 2014. The Customer Is Often Wrong (Fuck the Player). *Sufficiently Human*, December 30. http://sufficientlyhuman.com/archives/599.

Quinn, Zoë. 2015. Punk Games. *Offworld*, March 16. http://boingboing.net/2015/03/16/punk-games.html.

Retro Gamer. 2016. 30 Years of Entertainment. 155:18–27.

Rhodes, L. 2012. The Critic. *Culture Ramp*, September. http://cultureramp.com/new-games-critic.

Richardson, Ingrid. 2005. Mobile Technosoma: Some Phenomenological Reflections on Itinerant Media Devices. *Fibreculture* 6.

Richardson, Ingrid. 2007. Pocket Technospaces: The Bodily Incorporation of Mobile Media. *Continuum* 21 (2): 205–215.

Richardson, Ingrid. 2009. Sticky Games and Hybrid Worlds: A Post-phenomenology of Mobile Phones, Mobile Gaming, and the iPhone. In *Gaming Cultures and Place in Asia-Pacific*, ed. Larissa Hjorth and Dean Chan, 213–232. New York: Routledge.

Richardson, Ingrid. 2011. The Hybrid Ontology of Mobile Gaming. *Convergence* 17 (4): 419–430.

Richardson, Ingrid. 2012. Touching the Screen: A Phenomenology of Mobile Gaming and the iPhone. In *Studying Mobile Media: Cultural Technologies, Mobile Communication, and the iPhone*, ed. Larissa Hjorth, Jean Burgess, and Ingrid Richardson, 133–151. New York: Routledge.

Rogers, Tim. 2004. The Literature of the Moment: A Critique of *Mother 2*. *Large Prime Numbers*, August 27. http://archive.is/fMD7F.

Rogers, Tim. 2010. In Praise of Sticky Friction. *Kotaku*, June 8. http://kotaku.com/5558166/in-praise-of-sticky-friction.

Rogers, Tim. 2012. Introducing *ZiGGURAT*. *Kotaku*, February 22. http://kotaku.com/5887445/introducing-ziggurat.

Ryan, Marie-Laure. 2001. *Narrative as Virtual Reality: Immersion and Interactivity in Literature and Electronic Media*. Baltimore: John Hopkins University Press.

Schreier, Jason. 2014. Flappy Bird Is Making $50,000 a Day with *Mario*-Like Art [UPDATE 3]. *Kotaku*, February 6. http://kotaku.com/flappy-bird-is-making-50-000-a-day-off-ripped-art-1517498140.

Shaw, Adrienne. 2011. Do You Identify as a Gamer? Gender, Race, Sexuality, and Gamer Identity. *New Media & Society* 14 (1): 28–44.

Shaw, Adrienne, and Shira Chess. 2015. Reflections on the Casual Games Market in a Post-GamerGate World. In *Social, Casual, and Mobile Videogames: The Changing Gaming Landscape*, ed. Tama Leaver and Michele Wilson, 277–289. New York: Bloomsbury.

Sicart, Miguel. 2017. Queering the Controller. *Analog Game Studies* 4 (4).

Simon, Bart. 2009. Wii Are out of Control: Bodies, Game Screens, and the Production of Gestural Excess. *Loading* 3 (4): 1–17.

Sobchack, Vivian. 1992. *The Address of the Eye: A Phenomenology of Film Experience*. Princeton, NJ: Princeton University Press.

Sontag, Susan. [1964] 2009a. Against Interpretation. In *Against Interpretation and Other Essays*, 3–14. London: Penguin.

Sontag, Susan. [1965] 2009b. On Style. In *Against Interpretation and Other Essays*, 15–36. London: Penguin.

Stein, Abe. 2013. Indie Sports Games: Performance and Performativity. *Loading* 7 (11): 61–77.

Sudnow, David. 1983. *Pilgrim in the Microworld*. New York: Warner Books.

Sudnow, David. [1978] 2001. *Ways of the Hand: A Rewritten Account*. Cambridge, MA: MIT Press.

Surman, David. 2007. Pleasure, Spectacle, and Reward in Capcom's *Street Fighter* Series. In *Videogame, Player, Text*, ed. Barry Atkins and Tanya Krzywinska, 204–221. Manchester, UK: Manchester University Press.

Surman, David. 2008. Notes on Superflat and Its Expression in Videogames. *Refractory* 13.

Surman, David. 2009. Pokémon 151: Complicating Kawaii. In *Gaming Cultures and Place in Asia-Pacific*, ed. Larissa Hjorth and Dean Chan, 158–178. New York: Routledge.

Swalwell, Melanie. 2008. Movement and Kinaesthetic Responsiveness. In *The Pleasures of Computer Gaming: Essays on Cultural History, Theory, and Aesthetics*, ed. Melanie Swalwell and Jason Wilson, 72–93. Jefferson, NC: McFarland.

Swink, Steve. 2009. *Game Feel: A Game Designer's Guide to Virtual Sensation*. Burlington, MA: Morgan Kaufmann.

Taylor, T. L. 2006. *Play between Worlds: Exploring Online Game Culture*. Cambridge, MA: MIT Press.

Taylor, T. L. 2012. *Raising the Stakes: E-Sports and the Professionalization of Computer Gaming*. Cambridge, MA: MIT Press.

Thompson, Tevis. 2013. Fun with Gravity: The Video-Game Arc in *Angry Birds, Star Wars, Time Surfer*, and *ZiGGURAT. Grantland*, February 27. http://www.grantland.com/blog/hollywood-prospectus/post/_/id/68952/fun-with-gravity-the-video-game-arc-in-angry-birds-star-wars-time-surfer-and-ziggurat.

Tomas, David. 1989. The Technophilic Body: On Technicity in William Gibson's Cyborg Culture. *New Formations* 8 (Summer): 113–129.

Turkle, Sherry. 1995. *Life on the Screen: Identity in the Age of the Internet*. London: Phoenix Books.

Turkle, Sherry. [1984] 2005. *The Second Self: Computers and the Human Spirit. 20th Anniversary Edition*. Cambridge, MA: MIT Press.

Wajcman, Judy. 1991. *Feminism Confronts Technology*. University Park: Pennsylvania State University Press.

Walker, Jill. 2001. Do You Think You're Part of This? Digital Texts and the Second Person Address. In *Cybertext Yearbook 2000*, ed. Markku Eskelinen and Raine Koskimaa, 24–51. Jyväskylä, Finland: Publications of the Research Centre for Contemporary Culture.

Weiss, Gail. 1999. *Body Images: Embodiment as Intercorporeality.* New York: Routledge.

Wilburn, Thomas. 2008. Catching Waveforms: *Audiosurf* Creator Dylan Fitterer Speaks. *Ars Technica,* March 12. http://arstechnica.com/gaming/2008/03/catching -waveforms-audiosurf-creator-dylan-speaks/.

Wilson, Douglas. 2011. *Brutally Unfair Tactics Totally OK Now*: On Self-Effacing Games and Unachievements. *Game Studies* 11 (1).

Wilson, Jason. 2004. "Participation TV": Early Games, Video Art, Abstraction, and the Problem of Attention. *Convergence* 10:83–100.

Wilson, Jason. 2007. Gameplay and the Aesthetics of Intimacy. PhD diss., Griffith University.

Woods, Stewart. 2012. *Eurogames: The Design, Culture, and Play of Modern European Board Games.* Jefferson, NC: McFarland.

Yang, Robert. 2014. "Get Better" dev diary 1, ideas and notes. *Radiator Design Blog,* February 1. http://www.blog.radiator.debacle.us/2014/02/get-better-dev-diary-1-idea -and-notes.html.

Yang, Robert. 2015. "Stick Shift" as Activist Autoerotica. *Radiator Design Blog,* April 3. http://www.blog.radiator.debacle.us/2015/04/stick-shift-as-activist-autoerotica.html.

Yang, Robert. 2016. Why I Am One of the Most-Banned Developers on Twitch. *Polygon,* July 14. http://www.polygon.com/2016/7/14/12187898/banned-on-twitch.

Young, Iris Marion. 1980. Throwing Like a Girl: A Phenomenology of Feminine Body Comportment, Motility, and Spatiality. *Human Studies* 3:137–156.

Young, Iris Marion. 2005a. Lived Body vs. Gender: Reflections on Social Structure and Subjectivity. In *On Female Body Experience: "Throwing Like a Girl" and Other Essays, 12–26.* Oxford: Oxford University Press.

Young, Iris Marion. 2005b. Throwing Like a Girl: A Phenomenology of Feminine Body Comportment, Motility, and Spatiality. In *On Female Body Experience: "Throwing Like a Girl" and Other Essays, 27–45.* Oxford: Oxford University Press.

Primary Sources

2K Boston. 2007. *Bioshock.* Take Two Interactive.

Action Button Entertainment. 2012. *Ziggurat.* Freshuu.

Anthropy, Anna. 2012. *Dys4ia.* Newgrounds.

Ape and HAL Laboratory. 1994. *Mother 2.* Super Nintendo, Nintendo.

Atari. 1972. *Pong.* Atari.

Atari. 1976. *Breakout.* Atari.

Atari. 1979. *Adventure*. Atari.

Atari. 1980. *Missile Command*. Atari.

Backflip Studios. 2009. *Paper Toss*. Backflip Studios.

Bethesda Game Studios. 2011. *The Elder Scrolls V: Skyrim*. Bethesda Softworks.

Blendo Games. 2012. *Thirty Flights of Loving*. Blendo Games.

Blow, Jonathan. 2008. *Braid*. Microsoft Live Arcade.

Bon Iver. 2007. Skinny Love. On *For Emma, Forever Ago*. Jagjaguwar.

Brice, Mattie. 2012. *Mainichi*. Mattie Brice.

Brough, Michael. 2012. *Glitch Tank*. Michael Brough.

Brough, Michael. 2016. *Imbroglio*. Michael Brough.

Bungie. 2001. *Halo: Combat Evolved*. Microsoft.

Capcom. 1991. *Street Fighter II: The World Warrior*. Capcom.

Capcom. 2002. *Steel Battalion*. Capcom.

Capybara Games. 2014. *Super Time Force*. Microsoft.

Cardboard Computer. 2013. *Kentucky Route Zero*. Cardboard Computer.

Core Design. 1996. *Tomb Raider*. Eidos Interactive.

Creative Assembly. 2014. *Alien: Isolation*. Sega.

Crystal Dynamics. 2013. *Tomb Raider*. Square Enix.

Dennaton Games. 2012. *Hotline Miami*. Devolver Digital.

DMA Design. 2001. *Grand Theft Auto III*. Rockstar Games.

Die Gute Fabrik. 2013. *Johann Sebastian Joust*. Die Gute Fabrik.

Douglas, Alexander. 1952. *OXO*. Alexander Douglas.

EA Canada. 2014. *FIFA '15*. EA Sports.

Eidos Montreal. 2011. *Deus Ex: Human Revolution*. Square Enix.

Fatboy Slim. 1998. Right Here, Right Now. On *You've Come a Long Way Baby*. Skint Records.

Firemint. 2009. *Real Racing*. Firemint.

Fittèrer, Dylan. 2008. *Audiosurf*. Steam.

From Software. 2009. *Demon's Souls*. Atlus.

From Software. 2011. *Dark Souls*. Namco Bandai Games.

Fullbright. 2013. *Gone Home*. Fullbright.

Game Oven Studios. 2011. *Fingle*. Game Oven Studios.

Gearbox Software. 1999. *Half-Life: Opposing Force*. Sierra Studios.

Gearbox Software. 2001. *Half-Life: Blue Shift*. Sierra Studios.

Gibson, William. 1984. *Neuromancer*. New York: Ace Books.

Glu Games. 2014. *Kim Kardashian: Hollywood*. Glu Mobile.

Halfbrick Studios. 2010. *Fruit Ninja*. Halfbrick Studios.

Hall, Dean. 2012. *DayZ*. Dean Hall.

Harmonix. 2003. *Amplitude*. Sony.

Harmonix. 2005. *Guitar Hero*. RedOctane.

Harmonix. 2007. *Rock Band*. EA.

Higinbotham, William. 1958. *Tennis for Two*. William Higinbotham.

Id Software. 1993. *Doom*. GT Interactive.

Infinity Ward. 2007. *Call of Duty 4: Modern Warfare*. Activision.

Infinity Ward. 2011. *Call of Duty: Modern Warfare 3*. Activision.

Insomniac Games. 1998. *Spyro the Dragon*. Sony.

Ion Storm. 2000. *Deus Ex*. Eidos Interactive.

Jackson, Shelley. 1995. *Patchwork Girl*. Eastgate Systems.

Key, Ed, and David Kanaga. 2013. *Proteus*. Ed Key and David Kanaga.

King. 2012. *Candy Crush Saga*. King.

Konami. 1998. *Metal Gear Solid*. Konami.

Konami. 2004. *Metal Gear Solid 3: Snake Eater*. Konami.

k, merritt. 2012. *Lim*. merrit k.

Lavelle, Stephen. 2012. *Slave of God*. Increpare.

Lima Sky. 2009. *Doodle Jump*. Lima Sky.

Liman, Doug. 2014. *Edge of Tomorrow*. Village Roadshow.

LucasArts. 1992. *Super Star Wars*. Nintendo.

Maxis. 1989. *SimCity*. Electronic Arts.

McHenry, Tom. 2013. *Horse Master*. Tom McHenry.

MediaMolecule. 2013. *Tearaway*. Sony.

MicroProse. 1991. *Civilisation*. Microprose.

Mojang. 2011. *Minecraft*. Mojang.

Monolith Productions. 2014. *Middle-Earth: Shadow of Mordor*. Warner Bros. Interactive Entertainment.

Namco. 1980. *Pac-Man*. Namco.

Namco. 2005. *We Love Katamari*. Namco.

Naughty Dog. 1996. *Crash Bandicoot*. Sony.

Naughty Dog. 2013. *The Last of Us*. Sony Computer Entertainment Europe.

Nguyen, Dong. 2013. *Flappy Bird*. GEARS Studio.

NimbleBit. 2011. *Tiny Tower*. NimbleBit.

Niantic. 2016. *Pokémon Go*. Google.

Nintendo. 1981. *Donkey Kong*. Nintendo.

Nintendo. 1985. *Super Mario Bros*. Nintendo.

Nintendo. 1986. *The Legend of Zelda*. Nintendo.

Nintendo. 1993. *Star Fox*. Nintendo.

Nintendo. 1994. *Super Metroid*. Nintendo.

Nintendo. 1996. *Super Mario 64*. Nintendo.

Nintendo. 2000. *The Legend of Zelda: Majora's Mask*. Nintendo.

Nintendo. 2006. *Wii Sports*. Nintendo.

Nintendo. 2013. *Game & Wario*. Nintendo.

Nintendo. 2014. *Mario Kart 8*. Nintendo.

Oddworld Inhabitants. 1997. *Oddworld: Abe's Oddysee*. GT Interactive.

Pajitnov, Alexey. 1984. *Tetris*.

PopCap Games. 2001. *Bejeweled*. PopCap Games.

PopCap Games. 2007. *Peggle*. Popcap Games.

Porpentine. 2012. *CYBERQUEEN*. Porpentine.

Problems, Eva. 2013. *SABBAT*. Eva Problems.

Quantic Dream. 2010. *Heavy Rain*. Sony Computer Entertainment.

Quinn, Zoë. 2013. *Depression Quest*. Zoë Quinn.

Ramallo, Fernando, and David Kanaga. 2015. *Panoramical*. Polytron.

Ramis, Harold, dir. 1993. *Groundhog Day*. Columbia Pictures.

Right Square Bracket Left Square Bracket. 2012. *Dyad*. Right Square Bracket
    Left Square Bracket.

Rockstar North. 2002. *Grand Theft Auto: Vice City*. Rockstar Games.

Rockstar North. 2004. *Grand Theft Auto: San Andreas*. Rockstar Games.

Rockstar North. 2008. *Grand Theft Auto IV*. Rockstar Games.

Rovio Entertainment. 2009. *Angry Birds*. Chillingo.

Rovio Entertainment. 2012. *Angry Birds: Star Wars*. Rovio Entertainment.

Russell, Steve, Peter Samson, Wayne Witaenem, and Martin Graetz. 1962.
    Spacewar!

Sega. 2012. *Binary Domain*. Sega.

Sega AM2. 1999. *Shenmue*. Dreamcast: Sega.

Silicon Knights. 2002. *Eternal Darkness*. Nintendo.

Snyder, Iain. 2013. *UN EP*. Unwinnable.

Sonic Team. 1991. *Sonic the Hedgehog*. Sega.

Sony Computer Entertainment. 1997. *Gran Turismo*. Sony Computer
    Entertainment.

Squaresoft. 1997. *Final Fantasy VII*. Sony Computer Entertainment Europe.

Supergiant Games. 2011. *Bastion*. Warner Bros. Interactive Entertainment.

Taito. 1978. *Space Invaders*. Taito.

Team Ico. 2005. *Shadow of the Colossus*. Sony Computer Entertainment.

Team Meat. 2010. *Super Meat Boy*. Microsoft Game Studios.

Team Soho. 2002. *The Getaway*. Sony Computer Entertainment Europe.

Thatgamecompany. 2009. *Flower*. Sony Computer Entertainment.

Thatgamecompany. 2012. *Journey*. Sony Computer Entertainment.

The Chinese Room. 2012. *Dear Esther*. The Chinese Room.

Toca Boca. 2011. *Toca Tea Party*. Toca Boca.

Toy, Michael, and Glenn Wichman. 1980. *Rogue*. Michael Toy and Glenn
    Wichman.

Traveler's Tales. 2005. *Lego Star Wars: The Video Game*. Eidos Interactive.

Ubisoft. 2008. *Far Cry 2*. Ubisoft.

Ubisoft Montreal. 2003. *Prince of Persia: Sands of Time*. Ubisoft.

Ubisoft Montreal. 2007. *Assassin's Creed*. Ubisoft.

United Game Artists. 2001. *Rez*. Sega.

Valve Corporation. 1998. *Half-Life*. Sierra Entertainment.

Visceral Games. 2008. *Dead Space*. Electronic Arts.

Wachowski, Lana, and Lilly Wachowski, dirs. 1999 *The Matrix*. Village Roadshow Pictures.

Yang, Robert. 2015. *Stick Shift*. Robert Yang.

Yu, Derek. 2008. *Spelunky*. Mossmouth.

Zeng, Hu Wen. 2014. *Piano Tiles*. Hu Wen Zeng.

ZeptoLab. 2010. *Cut the Rope*. Chillingo.

Index